Travel + places

GREAT WESTERN RAILWAY

MAP OF THE COMPANY'S SYSTEM

D1492449

Lines over which ....
Railways with which the G.W.R. runs in connec....
Other Railways ....
Coach Routes .... Steamer Routes ....
Company's Docks and Waterside premises ....
Company's Hotels ....
Cathedral City or the more important ancient ecclesiastical buildings ✚

Sea distances are given in Nautical Miles

GWR

HANDBOOK

1923-47

GWR

HANDBOOK

THE GREAT WESTERN RAILWAY 1923-47

DAVID WRAGG

First published in 2006 by Sutton Publishing, Thrupp, Stroud, Gloucestershire
Re-issued in December 2010 by Haynes Publishing

A catalogue record for this book is available from the British Library

ISBN 978 08573 3005 5

Library of Congress catalog card no 2010927384

Published by Haynes Publishing,
Sparkford, Yeovil, Somerset BA22 7JJ, UK
Tel: 01963 442030 Fax: 01963 440001
Int.tel: +44 1963 442030 Int.fax: +44 1963 440001
E-mail: sales@haynes.co.uk
Website: www.haynes.co.uk

Haynes North America Inc.,
861 Lawrence Drive, Newbury Park, California 91320, USA

Design and typeset by Dominic Stickland

Printed and bound in the USA

Contents

Unknown today is the concept of a farm removal by a special train, as in the case of this one headed by 4–6–0 class 40XX No. 4044 near Bletchington. The locomotive is followed by two horse-boxes and a number of cattle wagons. *(HMRS/J. Tatchell ADC500)*

Acknowledgements

In writing any book such as this an author is always indebted to those who help with such important matters as, for example, the quest for photographs. In this case I am especially grateful to the late Mr A.E.W 'Bert' Colbourn of the Historical Model Railway Society for the use of their considerable archive of material on the Great Western Railway and its predecessors. Thanks are also due to the staff of the National Railway Museum, especially Mr Phillip Atkins, Reading Room Manager, and his colleagues, and to Kevin Robertson for photographs from his books.

David Wragg
Edinburgh

Automatic train control was perhaps the Great Western's 'great idea', enhancing railway safety and no doubt playing its part in giving the company an excellent safety record. This is No. 5063 *Earl Baldwin*, with the ATC ramp, which when raised sounded a warning, and if not cancelled could stop the train. *(Kevin Robertson)*

Introduction

Railways in the West and Wales

There are two ways of running a railway; the Great Western Way and the Wrong Way.

Revd W. Awdry

'If God had been a railwayman,' the Brigadier said to me, with a gleam in his eye, 'he would have been a Great Western Railwayman!' Gleam in the eye or not, one couldn't doubt that he meant it and that it was said not completely in jest. No railway has become so ingrained in the public consciousness as the Great Western. This remains true even though some six decades have passed since the Great Western was taken over by the state, along with the other three of the so-called 'Big Four' railway companies that were created by the grouping that came into being on 1 January 1923. Of course, the Great Western was different. For a start, there was a Great Western Railway on 31 December 1922 and there was still a Great Western Railway on 1 January 1923. Legally and politically, it was a different company, or was it? After all, grouping added less than a further 25 per cent of route mileage to the Great Western, so it dominated the other companies completely. It was the only one of the so-called 'Western Group' of companies that ran to London, as well as being more than four times larger than the rest combined. By celebrating its centenary in 1935, the Great Western really drove the point home, for as far as its management was concerned, it really was still the same railway. A cartoon in the first post-grouping issue of *The Great Western Railway Magazine* was entitled 'A Survival of Title'.

By contrast, the London, Midland & Scottish had to suffer years of rivalry between those who supported the London & North Western way of doing things and those who supported the Midland Railway way of doing things, and even a few who took the Lancashire & Yorkshire approach. The Southern at times still seemed to be three different railways, something emphasised by its divisional structure. The London & North Eastern also seemed to regionalise itself, perhaps because life at King's Cross was so different from that at Liverpool Street, and indeed the Great Northern and the Great Eastern do seem to have been two self-contained railways that should never have been merged.

But there was more to it than that. A quick glance at the titles of some of the books on the Great Western will give you more than a clue. They shout out how people felt about the company, playing on the initials 'GWR' with titles such as *Gone With Regret*, while many will say that it stood for 'God's Wonderful Railway' or 'Great Way Round'. The latter was not always a compliment, as until it started its programme of building more direct routes in the early years of the twentieth century, many did suggest that GWR meant taking the great way round, and even the rival London & South Western's route between London and Plymouth was competitive.

Those who had worked for one of the other railways that had been ordered to become part of the Great Western must have found it difficult at first. Those from the Cambrian must have felt that they were looked down upon as coming from a markedly inferior railway. At the Taff Vale and the Cardiff, the desire of the politicians to merge railway companies after the First World War must have had more than a hint of irony as both had planned their own merger in about 1908, and been refused permission by the very same politicians.

Perhaps the truth is that the Great Western was the one grouping that worked and made sense. One could argue over the Southern, and really the Great Northern and Great Eastern should and could have been kept separate, while the same could be said about the Midland and the London & North Western. Nowhere was the creation of the post-grouping GWR more necessary and more beneficial than in South Wales, where an integrated railway network materialised for the first time.

It would be grossly unfair to say that the great times began with grouping. Rather, it had all started earlier. The GWR's greatest years were those that followed the abandonment of the broad gauge and effectively ended with the outbreak of the Second World War, despite the difficulties caused by recession. Great Western railwaymen did their best to ensure that they got through the even more difficult war years that followed, despite the threat of state ownership.

The irony was that it was the Great Western and the derailment at Sonning on Christmas Eve 1841 that forced Parliament to take an interest in the railways. Parliament found that third-class passengers were being conveyed on flat trucks without sides, those with sides being reserved for second-class passengers, while only first-class travellers had a roof over their heads. Parliament took a hand, insisting on cheap 'Parliamentary trains' with covered rolling stock, but the rolling stock was bleak and the trains slow, as they had to call at every station.

It was not legislation that really improved the lot of the third-class passenger, but an ambitious and daring railway management with a strong competitive instinct. Yet that was not the Great Western. The big step forward came when the Midland Railway abolished second-class fares and scrapped its, admittedly small, stock of third-class carriages. Gradually, other railway companies were forced to fall in line because of competitive pressures. They couldn't abolish third-class travel as that was effectively protected by the 'Parliamentary train' legislation, but they could, and did, start to treat the third-class passenger as an increasingly valuable and valued customer during the fourth quarter of the nineteenth century.

Like the Southern Railway, the Great Western Railway worked hard at improving services on its branch lines between the wars, and showed the way towards a more efficient railway with its espousal of diesel railcars not just for the branches but also for what might today be described as 'secondary main lines'. Both railway companies were quick to see the potential of air transport, but this postwar opportunity was denied them, with air transport being nationalised even earlier than the railways themselves.

Work on improving speeds during the 1930s helped to ensure that railway travel remained not merely competitive, but also became fashionable. All the time the GWR was looking ahead, and its management was always abreast of developments elsewhere. It created strong integrated bus companies by merging its own extensive bus network into the emerging local bus companies, creating Western National and Western Welsh and laying the foundations for Crosville, for example. It also started what would today be known as 'bustitution', with bus services replacing the less viable and less attractive branch lines.

Passenger comfort was enhanced by new rolling stock, but even the Great Western could only move forward as quickly as passengers would allow it, and corridor coaches with end doors had to wait some time as there was customer resistance at first. Nevertheless, the extra width of the 1935 rolling stock for the 'Cornish Riviera' definitely put the passenger first, while the experiments with buffet cars brought refreshment aboard trains within reach of many more passengers.

This is the story of a railway for which the highest standards were the only standard. It had self-belief and confidence, and while conservative on some issues, was open-minded and interested in change when it could be convinced that this was the way forward. It had a clear identity that went beyond colour schemes, typefaces and branding and extended into the very style of its stations, locomotives and carriages. No wonder it was missed by so many.

> Alas! The curtain falls, the lights are low:
> Pride of Brunel, now it is time to go;
> But when old days are dim, when we have gone.
> May all thy grand traditions still live on.

Final verse of a poem by N. Ross Murray in the final edition of *The Great Western Railway Magazine*, December, 1947.

A SURVIVAL OF TITLE.

THE GREAT WESTERN: "Hooray! Never even blew me cap off!"

"None of the companies which survive the amalgamation upheaval have come out of it with so much enhanced prestige as the Great Western. It is the only one to retain its old and familiar title."—"South Wales News" leading article.)

Reproduced from the "South Wales News," Monday, November 27, 1922.

There was an inevitable sense of triumph in this cartoon in the first post-grouping issue of *The Great Western Railway Magazine* in January 1923, reproduced from the *South Wales News*. The 'old' GWR accounted for more than 80 per cent of the new company's route mileage, and more than three-quarters of its personnel.

That this was no ordinary railway company can be judged from this souvenir menu cover for a dinner given to GWR employees at Weston-super-Mare by the local season ticket holders in March 1924. Clearly the season ticket holders arrived home just as the day-trippers were thinking of leaving! *(Great Western Railway Magazine)*

Chapter One

The Ancestors and the Neighbours

Although the Great Western has been widely acclaimed as the railway company with the longest history and the only one to survive the grouping of 1923, the railway company that emerged on 1 January 1923 was a different company from that which had been formed in the 1830s. The famous grouping imposed by the Railways Act 1921 did not create new railway companies by name, but instead described them as 'groups', of which the Great Western re-emerged from the 'Western Group'. In each case, the new groups consisted of larger companies, known as constituent companies, and smaller companies that were described simply as subsidiary companies, as indeed some already were. It is important to bear in mind that the original Great Western Railway was just one of the constituent companies, but through being by far the largest and the only one with a true main-line network and access to London, it was the one that prevailed.

Under the terms of the Act, the Western Group constituent companies numbered seven. These were the original Great Western Railway; Barry Railway; Cambrian Railway; Cardiff Railway; Rhymney Railway; Taff Vale Railway; and the Alexandra (Newport & South Wales) Docks & Railway. One important difference between these and the subsidiary companies was that all were entitled to have a representative on the board of the merged entity. This stipulation was not always well received by the Great Western Railway directors. The Taff Vale they could accept, as there had been close links between the two companies, but the Cambrian, with the largest route mileage, was something of a disaster financially and operationally, while the Cardiff was a financial liability.

Subsidiary companies within the Western Group, of which there were twenty-seven, included the Brecon & Merthyr Tydfil Junction Railway; Burry Port & Gwendraeth Valley Railway; Cleobury Mortimer & Ditton Priors Light Railway; Didcot, Newbury & Southampton Railway; Exeter Railway; Forest of Dean Central Railway; Gwendraeth Valleys Railway; Lampeter, Aberaeron & New Quay Light Railway; Liskeard & Looe Railway; Llanelly & Mynydd Mawr Railway; Mawddwy Railway; Midland & South Western Junction Railway; Neath & Brecon Railway; Penarth Extension Railway; Penarth Harbour Dock & Railway; Port Talbot Railway & Docks; Princetown Railway; Rhondda & Swansea Bay Railway; Ross & Monmouth Railway; South Wales Mineral Railway; Teign Valley Railway; Vale of Glamorgan Railway; Van Railway; Welshpool & Llanfair Light Railway; West Somerset Railway; and Wrexham & Ellesmere Railway. Of these, all but one were absorbed on 1 January 1923, with the sole exception being the Midland & South Western Junction Railway because of prolonged negotiations over the terms of its transfer to the GWR. Eventually, agreement was reached and the MSWJ was taken into GWR ownership in September 1923. Some of these companies were effectively within the Great Western fold already, being operated by it, while others were part of other railways, with the Van Railway being operated by the Cambrian.

Most of the constituent subsidiary companies had their own history but the Great Western dominated the group, and therefore managed to avoid the infighting between the London & North Western and the Midland Railway that so afflicted the London, Midland & Scottish, or what became almost effectively a continuance of the pre-grouping situation on the Southern. However, each company deserves some consideration here, starting with the constituent companies and then the subsidiary companies.

The 'old' GWR was to be represented for many years after the grouping by its locomotives and carriages, with the former including this 0–6–0 Dean goods locomotive, seen in Swindon shed in 1930. *(HMRS AAC029)*

Apart from prolonged negotiations ensuring that the Midland & South Western Junction Railway did not become part of the 'new' Great Western until September 1923, other companies not mentioned in the legislation later passed to the Great Western Railway. These included the Weston, Clevedon & Portishead Light Railway and the Corris Railway, while the Hammersmith & City Railway, the underground line that was the joint property of the Great Western Railway and the Metropolitan Railway, did not need to be covered in the legislation.

In this chapter the constituent companies of the grouped Great Western Railway are all covered along with the significant subsidiaries, while to give a complete picture the Hammersmith & City Railway and the many independent railways that survived alongside the Great Western are also covered.

Constituent Companies

The Great Western Railway

By the early nineteenth century Bristol had long been one of the most important cities in the United Kingdom, and it was not surprising that a number of proposals for a railway between London and Bristol were promoted from 1824 onwards. The first of these to have any impact was that of the Great Western Railway in 1832, which originated in a desire among the merchants and financiers of Bristol for a fast railway line to London. Their first attempt to gain parliamentary sanction in 1834 failed, but in 1835 authorisation was obtained and the GWR was able to raise capital of £2.5 million, equal to about £140 million today, and a further £830,000 (£45 million today) in loans. The new company had as its engineer the young Isambard Kingdom Brunel, who convinced the directors of the merits of his scheme for a broad gauge railway, which he judged, rightly, to offer the prospect of higher speeds. To the objection that this would result in difficulties in through operation with other companies, he suggested that in areas where company boundaries met, the issue could be resolved through laying mixed gauge track, something that did not work easily or effectively in practice.

Managed by the company secretary, Charles Saunders, the GWR and Brunel wasted little time, and in 1838 operations began between London and a station close to Maidenhead in Berkshire. Brunel ordered locomotives true to his vision of a high-speed railway, but the first locomotives had, of course, to operate what was in effect an outer-suburban service, although it would not have been recognised as such at the time. The locomotives became the responsibility of the first locomotive superintendent, Daniel Gooch.

The entire 116-mile line from London to Bristol via Bath was opened in 1841, but costs had risen from a projected £3.3 million to more than £6 million. Many shareholders blamed Brunel for the slow completion and the high price, regarding his broad gauge as a mistake, and had even tried to get rid of him in 1839. Undoubtedly, broad gauge was more expensive to build than standard gauge, but given the fact that civil engineering technology was in its infancy, the trustworthiness of any estimate of completion costs at the time would seem to have been doubtful.

From what might be regarded as its trunk route, the GWR soon expanded, with branches to Basingstoke, Gloucester, Hungerford, Oxford and Windsor opened by 1849, while other companies supported by the GWR had also extended the line from Bristol to Plymouth using the same broad gauge. Gloucester had been reached in 1845, and the worst nightmares of the sceptics came true as the GWR met the standard gauge Birmingham & Gloucester Railway. The confusion only became worse when the Midland Railway leased the broad gauge Bristol & Gloucester, intending to link it into the standard gauge, so that in 1854 standard gauge trains were able to reach Bristol using mixed gauge track.

The considerable amount of space at track level that was the legacy of the broad gauge can be seen clearly in this splendid photograph of 4-6-0 60XX No. 6003 *King Henry IV* heading an express while still in 'as new' condition. *(HMRS/J. Tatchell ADG035)*

Meanwhile, the GWR was racing ahead of its competitors, almost literally, with the introduction of express trains between London and Exeter in 1845 that covered the 194 miles of the route via Bristol at 43mph, including three stops, making these the world's fastest expresses at the time. Expansion included the opening of a mixed gauge line from London to Birmingham in 1852, bringing the GWR into direct competition with the London & North Western Railway. Two years later, the GWR purchased the Shrewsbury & Birmingham and Shrewsbury & Chester companies, and with running powers to Birkenhead found itself with a route network that extended as far north as Merseyside. When the Cornwall Railway opened in 1859, this proved to be a satellite of the GWR and its allies, who had subscribed a fifth of its capital, and by 1867 through trains were running from London to Penzance.

Not content with the West, the Great Western had already ventured into Wales well before this time. In 1845 the GWR's satellite South Wales Railway obtained parliamentary approval for a broad gauge line from the GWR near Gloucester through to the coast at Fishguard. It opened to Carmarthen in 1852, but never reached Fishguard, being diverted instead to Milford Haven, which it reached in 1856, and from which steamers plied to Waterford in Ireland. The broad gauge of the SWR meant that through trains could run from South Wales to London and the Midlands, but all of the valley lines bringing coal to the SWR were built to standard gauge, and so costly transshipment was necessary. The SWR and the West Midland Railway were both absorbed into the Great Western in 1865, giving it a total route mileage of 1,105 miles. By this time the mixed gauge had been extended from Oxford to London, the work being carried out between 1856 and 1861.

The broad gauge was especially unpopular in South Wales, as it inhibited efficient movement of coal and iron ore. It took strong pressure from industrialists and mine owners to persuade the GWR to convert the SWR to standard gauge, but when the argument was won and the decision taken, the entire 300 miles was switched, with completion taking just one weekend in 1872. By 1876, the only substantial remaining broad-gauge operation was that from Penzance to London.

The railway insolvency crisis of 1866 had forced considerable economies on the company, by this time under the chairmanship of its one-time locomotive superintendent Daniel Gooch. Nevertheless, investors had great confidence in the GWR, which was just as well since the average dividend between 1841 and 1879 amounted to just 3.8 per cent. There were also heavy investments still to be made, of which the most significant by far was the Severn Tunnel, built between 1873 and 1886, at which time it was the longest underwater tunnel in the world. The need for economy and the demands of the Severn Tunnel may have been behind the lack of further significant route extensions during the years up to 1900, although the system did in fact grow owing to the absorption of other companies, so that by 1900 the GWR had 2,526 route miles, the longest of any of Britain's railways. Financial difficulty certainly lay behind the limitations on investment in rolling stock, although innovation was not completely lacking, with the first insulated vans for frozen meat being introduced during the 1870s. To its credit, the company also operated safely, having just one fatal accident between 1874 and 1936.

Daniel Gooch died in office in 1889 at the age of seventy-three, being given the credit for saving the company, but blamed by many for economies that were excessive and in the end counter-productive. His successors returned to developing the company, with successive superintendents of the line reshaping the passenger services, while first William Dean and then later, after 1902, George Churchward, started to produce a line of worthy locomotives.

Progress was aided by the abolition of the broad gauge by 1892, so that through carriages could be offered between Liverpool, Manchester and Leeds to the fast-growing resort of Torquay. Restaurant cars were introduced in 1896, the company having freed itself of the compulsory refreshment stop at Swindon the previous year by offering the owners of the refreshment rooms £100,000 (£8,450,000 at today's prices) in compensation. By 1899 there were quadruple tracks over the entire 53 miles between London and Didcot.

A pre-grouping photograph of the first *King George*, this time 4–6–0 40XX No. 4014, in 1910. It is interesting to note the different forms of putting the company's name on locomotive tenders over the years. *(HMRS/J. Tatchell ADB403)*

The early years of the twentieth century saw a renewed vigour in the GWR. The last three decades of the previous century had seen limited attention paid to development of its own route network, and much traffic had passed to competitors offering more direct services – so much so that many wags described the GWR as the 'Great Way Round'. Competition alone did not inspire all of the 'cut-off' routes built in the period between 1903 and 1910, however, as the most significant was the new direct route from London to Cardiff, on which the company had a monopoly, bypassing Bath and Bristol, and at a distance of 145 miles saving 10 miles over the route via Bath and 35 miles compared with that via Gloucester. London to Exeter received a new direct route of 174 miles, instead of the previous 194 miles that had compared so badly with the London & South Western's 172 miles. In conjunction with the Great Central, a more direct route was opened between London and Birmingham, cutting the distance from 129 miles to 111 miles, making it more competitive with the London & North Western's 113 miles. These routes required considerable new construction, with 30 miles of new track for the Cardiff line, 33 for Exeter and no fewer than 58 for the Birmingham route.

The new routes were accompanied by new carriages hauled by Churchward's excellent new locomotives, so that journey times started to fall considerably, while from 1906 onwards the company became pioneer of automatic train protection. That same year the company built a large new harbour at Fishguard and introduced three turbine-powered packet steamers for the Irish market, while between 1909 and 1914 it provided boat trains for passengers off Cunard transatlantic liners, taking them to London from Fishguard (261 miles) in $4\frac{1}{2}$ hours, after building a line into the harbour.

The GWR had a relatively quiet First World War, but afterwards tried first to fight off the proposed grouping, and then fought to have the six other constituent companies regarded as subsidiary companies so as not to have to provide a seat for a representative of each on the parent board. In both confrontations it was unsuccessful.

Alexandra (Newport & South Wales) Docks & Railway

As the name implies, this was originally a dock company, formed in 1865 to build a new dock at Newport. It took ten years to complete the work because of the company's financial weakness, but once it was finished local business interests argued that a railway connection with the Rhondda would enable it to attract a share of the booming South Wales coal traffic. In 1878 the Pontypridd, Caerphilly & Newport Railway was established, with running powers over the lines of five other railways to bring coal to Newport docks, and this opened in 1884. In preparation for the opening of the new railways, the Alexandra changed from being a 'docks' company to a 'docks and railway' in 1882, and in 1887 it purchased the Pontypridd, Caerphilly & Newport Railway. While freight, and especially coal, was the predominant traffic, a passenger service between Pontypridd and Newport was introduced, but this passed to the Great Western in 1899, leaving the Alexandra's passenger services confined to a service between Pontypridd and Caerphilly. Meanwhile, the docks prospered and grew, with further expansion in the years leading up to the outbreak of the First World War, when the company managed to pay a dividend of 5 per cent. The actual railway route mileage owned by the company amounted to just 9.5 miles, making it the smallest of any of the constituent companies covered by the Railways Act 1921.

Barry Railway

As demand for coal grew during the second half of the nineteenth century the docks at Cardiff soon proved to be completely inadequate to meet the demand, and the pressure increased to use other ports for the export of the coal. A group of mine owners pressed to build a new dock at Barry, to the west of Cardiff, in 1883, but faced opposition from the Taff Vale and Rhymney railway companies. However, in 1884 they were successful and obtained parliamentary approval. The company was allowed to build a 19-mile-long line from Trehafod, to the north of Pontypridd, where it had a junction with the Taff Vale, and three short branches. The line opened in February 1889, followed in July by the new port, with a dock area of 73 acres, which was increased to 120 acres in 1898. Later, there were also connections with the Great Western at Bridgend, established in 1900, and with the Brecon & Merthyr Railway near Caerphilly in 1905.

The new port was an immediate success, so that by 1892 its traffic equalled a third of that of Cardiff, and by the outbreak of the First World War it handled as much coal as Cardiff and Penarth combined. It was the only truly railway-owned port, but depended on its connection with other railways for most of its traffic. The commercial success was reflected in the dividends paid, which during the period 1894–1920 averaged 9.5–10 per cent. On the debit side, much of this economic success was the result of overzealous cost-cutting, with as many as a third of its locomotives out of service awaiting repairs.

Cambrian Railway

The Cambrian Railway was by far the largest of the constituent companies absorbed into the Great Western in 1923. Despite its title, a significant part of its overall route mileage of 295 miles lay over the border in England, including Oswestry, its headquarters and main works. Home territory for the Cambrian was the unlikely and sparsely populated area of mid-Wales, so underdeveloped that the first locomotives for one of its predecessors, the Llanidloes & Newtown Railway opened in 1859, were delivered by horse teams

The Cambrian Railway was formed in 1864 from four small companies, the Llanidloes & Newtown Railway, Oswestry & Newtown Railway, Newtown & Machynlleth Railway and

In terms of route miles, but not numbers of locomotives, the Cambrian Railway was the largest company absorbed at the grouping, but relatively few of its locomotives were retained by the Great Western post-grouping. This is one ex-Cambrian locomotive, 0–6–0 CAM15, renumbered 844, still in pre-grouping condition as this was still only 1923, believed to be in the station at Harlech. *(HMRS/J.P. Richards ACC507)*

the Oswestry, Ellesmere and Whitchurch Railway, as a defensive measure to keep the English railway companies away from mid-Wales. The new company was joined the following year by the Aberystwyth & Welsh Coast Railway, almost doubling its track mileage. A further major expansion came in 1888, when it took over the working of the Mid Wales Railway, which operated between Moat Lane and Talyllyn Junction, but had running powers through to Brecon. The largest town on the Cambrian network was Wrexham, served by the Wrexham & Ellesmere Railway which became part of the Cambrian in 1895. The Cambrian also absorbed or worked several other railways, including the 6½-mile Van Railway, completed in 1871, the Mawddwy Railway, also of around 6½ miles, running through the Upper Dovey Valley, and the 19½-mile Tanat Valley Light Railway, dating from 1904. There were also two narrow gauge lines, the 1ft 11½in Vale of Rheidol Railway, opened in 1902, and the 2ft 6in-gauge Welshpool & Llanfair Light Railway opened the following year.

Serving such a difficult area, the Cambrian, despite the nationalist leanings of its founders, soon became heavily dependent upon several of the major English companies for through traffic, and inevitably these included the Great Western at Oswestry as well as the Midland at Three Cocks Junction and, its closest associate, the London & North Western at Whitchurch and Welshpool. The two main lines for the Cambrian, both of which handled considerable holiday traffic, were the 96 miles between Whitchurch and Aberystwyth and the 54 miles from Dovey Junction to Pwllheli.

Given the unpromising traffic of its territory, the Cambrian remained impoverished for its entire existence, with much single track. It went bankrupt twice, and was often accused of being badly run. Nevertheless, in 1913 it carried 3 million passengers and a million tons

The longest route and track mileage inherited at grouping by the Great Western was that of the Cambrian Railway, an impoverished company mainly serving rural mid-Wales and the borders, so that no doubt the arrival of a curved-frame 'Duke' class locomotive on its main line was seen as an improvement. *(Kevin Robertson)*

of goods traffic. It suffered a major accident at Abermule in January 1921, when an express hit a stopping train head-on, killing seventeen people and injuring many more, giving rise to much debate over the safety of single-line railways.

The GWR was disappointed that the Cambrian became a constituent company, no doubt to the delight of the latter railway's shareholders who received a guaranteed income for the first time.

Cardiff Railway

The Cardiff Railway had its origins in the Cardiff Docks. The growing port had originally depended on a canal to bring coal to the docks for transshipment, but this proved inadequate as the demand for coal rose, and the situation was not resolved until the Taff Vale Railway opened from Merthyr Tydfil in 1841. The TVR was later joined by the Rhymney Railway in 1858, while the docks at Cardiff continued to expand. Additional port facilities were opened 2 miles away at Penarth from 1859 to 1865, with a railway connection leased to the TVR. While the Great Western Railway had reached Cardiff as early as 1850, its broad gauge was ill-suited to the conditions in the valleys, where standard gauge ruled completely, and so it carried little coal traffic until after the coal and iron masters succeeded in securing a conversion to standard gauge in 1872.

Nevertheless, the docks and the TVR and Rhymney lines to Cardiff had themselves become so congested by 1882 that the mine owners secured powers to build the Rhondda & Swansea Bay Railway, determined to move their traffic away from Cardiff. In 1884 other coal-mining interests obtained authority to build a new port at Barry, 8 miles from Cardiff, with its own Barry Railway operating down the Rhondda. The new port and railway opened in 1889, and with the support of the mine owners started to take traffic away from

Cardiff, although the port survived as coal output doubled between 1889 and 1913, so that there was sufficient business to keep all of the port facilities busy. It was not until 1897 that the Cardiff Docks obtained parliamentary approval to change its name to the Cardiff Railway and build new lines northwards to connect with the Taff Vale at Treforest and at Pontypridd, creating a further 11½ route miles in addition to the existing 120 track miles within the Bute Docks (named after the local landowner, the Marquis of Bute). The Cardiff Railway had its own locomotives and two steam railcars for passenger traffic. Yet even so, given the heavy concentration of competing and connecting lines and inter-port rivalry, the company soon found itself in protracted disputes with other railways and costly litigation. This must have been a factor in the poor financial performance of the Cardiff Railway, with its shareholders getting a dividend of just 1 per cent in 1921 compared with 9 per cent at the Rhymney.

A proposal to merge with the Taff Vale and the Rhymney in the years before the First World War was vetoed by Parliament, which a little more than a decade later was to force these two companies and others to combine into the new GWR. Nevertheless, even before the grouping the three companies came under a single general manager.

Rhymney Railway

The Rhymney Railway was preceded by an old tramway connecting the Rhymney Ironworks with Newport, known locally as the 'Old Rumney Railway'. In 1851 the Marquis of Bute encouraged the company to replace the tramway with a railway to serve the new dock being built at Cardiff. The Rhymney Railway obtained the necessary consent in 1854/5, running down the right bank of the Rhymney Valley, and opened in 1858 thanks to running powers over part of the Taff Vale Railway. Finding itself hosting a competitor, the Taff Vale raised its charges, and in one case it took litigation by the Rhymney to force the Taff Vale to reduce its charges by 80 per cent. Seeking a solution by leasing itself to the Bute Trustees, the Rhymney was refused parliamentary consent, a measure that had it been allowed may well have forestalled the creation of the Cardiff Railway. Growing coal traffic solved the problem, with the Rhymney becoming profitable during the 1860s, and in 1864 it obtained approval to build its own line into Cardiff, which opened in 1871. That same year also saw an extension opened between Rhymney and Nantybwch to connect with the London & North Western Railway, and another extension into the Aberdare Valley, largely with the help of running powers over the Great Western Railway. The heavily graded Taff Bargoed line was built jointly with the GWR and reached Dowlais in 1876 and Merthyr Tydfil in 1886. Meanwhile, most of the original lines that had been laid as single track were doubled.

The cost of this expansion was that the company could not afford a dividend as late as 1875, yet tight managerial control saw this rise to 10.5 per cent before the end of the century, despite competition after 1889 from the Barry and Brecon & Merthyr railways. The Rhymney eventually found itself with two major traffic-generating points, Cardiff and Caerphilly, with locomotive repair works opened in the latter town in 1902, while the station was rebuilt in 1913 to cater for the growing passenger traffic. In 1909/10, the Taff Vale also tried to include the Rhymney in its takeover of the Cardiff Railway, but as mentioned above, Parliament refused to authorise this move. Nevertheless, the Rhymney's manager, E.A. Prosser, became manager of the other two companies and worked all three as one, doubtless obtaining many of the benefits of a merger, possibly without some of the short-term costs.

Taff Vale Railway

At first, coal was moved from the valleys in South Wales to the Bute Docks at Cardiff by the Glamorganshire Canal, opened in 1798, which moved coal and iron from Merthyr Tydfil. As production rose, the canal proved inadequate, and in 1836 the Taff Vale Railway received parliamentary approval to build a line over the 24 miles between Merthyr and Cardiff.

Although Brunel was appointed as the engineer, the standard gauge was adopted, doubtless to aid construction in the narrow valleys, although the line presented no significant engineering challenges. In 1839 the new Bute West Dock opened in Cardiff, and the Taff Vale opened in 1841. Two branches were soon added, and a further branch followed in 1845, between Abercynon and Aberdare, which had been the source of much of the coal from South Wales, although this was soon overtaken by the Rhondda.

The TVR was quick to enjoy considerable prosperity, paying an average dividend of 5 per cent during the 1850s, but by the 1880s it achieved a record of 14.9 per cent between 1880 and 1888, the highest dividend paid by any UK company over such a long period. This performance was all the more notable because of growing competition, most significantly from the Rhymney Railway after 1858, while the Bute Trustees, originally supporters of the TVR, soon switched to the Rhymney. The TVR responded by building a new port 2 miles down the River Taff at Penarth, leasing the operating company from 1862. As the congestion in the Cardiff docks continued to worsen, mine owners supported the building of yet another new port at Barry, with its own railway, which was another competitor for the TVR after 1889.

Not everything the TVR built turned to gold, and the 7-mile line built in 1892 to the small port of Aberthaw never succeeded in challenging the operations at Barry. Passenger traffic began to be encouraged during the 1890s, when services were increased by 40 per cent. Incredibly, in 1916 the TVR was able to obtain a court ruling to prevent the Cardiff Railway from opening a competing line near Taff's Well. Earlier, in 1909/10, plans to merge with the Cardiff and Rhymney railways were rejected by Parliament, but the three companies were then run by the same general manager until merged into the GWR in 1923.

The GWR took over some of the passenger services of its constituent companies, such as the Taff Vale Railway, even before the grouping took effect, as this 1922 timetable (upper) for services between Cardiff and Treherbert shows. By 1938 (lower) services had not only become more frequent, but they were also quicker. (Bradshaw)

Subsidiary Companies and Later Acquisitions

Many of the so-called subsidiary companies were small, often worked by larger neighbouring companies, and some simply filled gaps in the network, having been built under separate parliamentary sanction.

Brecon & Merthyr Tydfil Junction Railway

Given the size of some of the companies that became constituents of the new Great Western, and the financial problems besetting the Cambrian, it must have seemed strange that the Brecon & Merthyr Tydfil Junction Railway did not become a constituent company of the so-called 'Western Group' of companies. Nevertheless, the BMTJR was a complex operation, basically being divided into two by a 2½-mile section of the Rhymney Railway between Deri Junction and Bargoed South Junction, and although it possessed running powers, this must have been viewed as a structural weakness.

The northern section of the BMTJR was authorised in 1858 and opened in 1867, running between Brecon and Merthyr Tydfil. South of the Rhymney Railway, the southern section ran to Basseleg and over 3 miles of the Great Western Railway to Newport. This was also achieved by buying the 'Old Rumney Railway' in 1861, and using its route down the left bank of the River Rhymney to build a new railway that opened in 1865. The Old 'Rumney's' upper portion was also pressed into use and in 1905 was linked to the Barry Railway so that coal and ore could be brought down for shipment at Barry. This complicated system led to many problems with its neighbouring lines and made profitability difficult to achieve, while much of the 60 route miles was troublesome to operate.

Burry Port & Gwendraeth Valley Railway

Burry Port, to the west of Llanelli and south of Carmarthen, was one of the ports developed by the owners of the coal mines in response to the growing congestion at the older ports, despite the opening of new port facilities. The Burry Port & Gwendraeth Valley Railway linked the port, which never became sizeable, with the mines in the Gwendraeth Valley, and was very much a minor player. The line was 21 miles long and officially not supposed to carry passengers, who arrived on the line as 'trespassers', but were tolerated so long as they paid 6d for the carriage of their shopping basket!

Cleobury Mortimer & Ditton Priors Light Railway

Built under a light railway order of 1901, this railway retained its independence until taken over by the Great Western Railway in 1922. It ran for 12 miles from Cleobury Mortimer, to the west of Kidderminster in Shropshire, to serve quarries at Ditton Priors, but it also carried agricultural traffic. It opened to goods traffic in July 1908 and to passengers the following November, with halts at Cleobury Town, Stottesdon and Burwarton. Over its short length, there were no fewer than thirteen level crossings and many gradients. In common with many light railways, there were no signals and it was usually worked on the basis of 'a single engine in steam'.

There were only a few four-wheeled passenger carriages, and the GWR withdrew the passenger service on 26 September 1938, although the line remained open for goods traffic.

Liskeard & Looe Railway

This company emerged as an extension of the Liskeard & Caradon Railway opened from Moorswater, where it joined the Liskeard & Looe Union Canal, to South Caradon in November 1844, and extended to Cheesewring Quarries in 1846. Gravity working was used for the loaded wagons carrying tin ore and granite, which were returned to the head of the line using horses. The extension to Looe running alongside the banks of the canal opened at the end of 1860, and from 1862 the line throughout was worked by the Caradon Railway, which shortly afterwards introduced locomotives. Initially passengers on the Caradon could travel on mineral wagons by the expedient of paying for the transport of a parcel, and receiving a 'free' pass. Passenger carriages were introduced on the Caradon line from 1860, and on the line to Looe from 1879.

The connection with the main line using a steeply graded and tight loop from Coombe Junction was opened in May 1901, and passenger traffic trebled almost immediately, but the ore and stone traffic was in sharp decline by this time. The Great Western Railway took over working of the Looe and Caradon lines in 1909, but the latter system was abandoned in 1916. The Liskeard & Looe Railway survived to be absorbed into the GWR in 1923. As late as 1935 a scheme was mooted for a new direct line from St Germans, which would have been easier to work, but this was not built.

Llanelly & Mynydd Mawr Railway

This was a small privately owned railway built by an Edinburgh railway contractor on the route of an old tramway, which dated from 1806, in return for a share of the receipts. He also provided the rolling stock. Although authorised in 1875, the line was not opened until 1883. It ran for 12 miles from Llanelly. Unusually, the locomotives all carried names without numbers.

Midland & South Western Junction Railway

Last to be absorbed into the Great Western, gaining almost nine months' extra independence, the Midland & South Western Junction provided an important link between the Midlands and the growing port of Southampton, but had a difficult early life.

Owing largely to the efforts of the London & South Western Railway, Southampton's importance as a port grew throughout the nineteenth century, so that it became a significant centre and worthy of consideration for a through line from the Midlands rather than having all traffic directed through London. As early as 1845 the initial plan was for a line from Cheltenham to Southampton, but in fact the line eventually had to be built in two stages, first as the Swindon, Marlborough & Andover Railway, authorised in 1873 and completed in 1881, and then as the Swindon & Cheltenham Extension Railway which opened in 1891, and reached Cheltenham over the Great Western Railway, by which time the two lines had merged to form the Midland & South Western Junction Railway. The 62 route miles proved costly to build, and the original Swindon, Marlborough & Andover received financial assistance from its contractors. Although not strictly speaking a contractor's line, once opened it passed into receivership, where it stayed until 1897.

The MSWJR was rescued by Sam Fay, who was seconded to the company in 1892 from the LSWR as receiver and general manager. Fortunately, Fay felt that the line held considerable potential and upgraded the system, including a new line to avoid the GWR at Savernake. Fay remained until after the company returned to solvency in 1897 and did not return to the LSWR for another two years, by which time one contemporary railway commentator credited him with having 'made an empty sack stand upright'. The MSWJR had branches connecting it to the GWR at Swindon and to the military base at Tidworth, the station on the line with the highest receipts. The value of the line lay in the potential for through carriages to run to and from Southampton, with Sheffield and Birmingham served in this way from 1893, followed later by Bradford, Leeds, Liverpool and Manchester, while for a period carriages ran from Whitehaven to Southampton carrying emigrants.

Disputes over the value of the Midland & South Western led to a delay in it being absorbed into the Great Western in 1923.

Neath & Brecon Railway

One of the least hopeful projects, the Neath & Brecon Railway acquired the powers of two predecessor companies, both unsuccessful, and opened its 72 route miles between 1867

The Midland & South Western Junction Railway resisted grouping for as long as possible, largely to obtain better terms from the GWR. This was that company's No. 24, renumbered 1008 by the GWR. It is seen here at Swindon in 1927, and was later rebuilt to conform to GWR specifications in 1930. (*HMRS/J. Minnis AAA820*)

and 1873. The line ran through sparsely populated country, with no towns of any significance, and even the coal traffic was relatively meagre. The N&BR passed into receivership in 1873, despite which by 1877 costs exceeded revenue by no less than 238 per cent. The line was only saved by the Midland Railway's ambitions, in this case to grow traffic from Birmingham and Hereford to Swansea by taking running powers over the N&BR, while at the southern end of the line, coal traffic was sufficient to be profitable.

Port Talbot Railway & Docks

Pressure for port space in South Wales during the nineteenth century saw the development of new dock facilities at a number of locations, including Port Talbot, where docks were built from 1835 to serve the copper industry at nearby Cwmavon. Coal traffic did not become significant until 1870. In 1894, to protect and encourage this traffic, the Port Talbot Railway was authorised and opened in 1897–8, with two lines from Maesteg and Tonmawr, to the north of Cwmavon. The railway also acquired the docks. The total route was just 48 miles, but the dock and railway company was profitable, and the Great Western took over operation of the railway in 1908, although the docks operated separately.

Princetown Railway

The standard gauge Princetown Railway took over the abandoned Plymouth & Dartmoor Railway above Yelverton in 1883, as the latter company was having difficulty in finishing the work. The Plymouth & Dartmoor had been promoted primarily for quarry traffic and used the unusual gauge of 4ft 6in. The route of the Princetown Railway, a subsidiary of the GWR, was over the 10½ miles from Yelverton to Horridge, much of it over former Plymouth & Dartmoor infrastructure, and while some traffic from the King Tor Quarry was carried, in practice the main business was transporting prison officers and convicts, and supplies, to Dartmoor Prison. It also attracted some excursion traffic.

Rhondda & Swansea Bay Railway

Yet another of the coal lines built to bypass the pressure on the docks at Cardiff, the Rhondda & Swansea Bay Railway ran from Treherbert to Briton Ferry with a 2-mile-long tunnel. Opened in 1890, the line developed into a small system of 29 route miles. The line passed into the control of the Great Western in 1906, but was not taken over completely until 1922.

The South Wales Mineral Railway

The South Wales Mineral Railway operated a short line just 13 miles in length, running from Briton Ferry to Glyncorrwg Colliery by way of Cymmer. Although nominally independent until 1923, it was taken over by the Great Western in 1908, and was operated using GWR locomotives.

Swansea Harbour Trust

Strictly speaking, this was not one of the railways covered by the Act. Nevertheless, its fleet of shunting locomotives passed into Great Western ownership in 1923. The trust itself was brought into existence by Act of Parliament in 1854 to develop the port of Swansea, and initially used contractors to operate the port. After several contractors had been experienced, or perhaps suffered since the relationships seem to have been unsatisfactory, the trust decided to operate the port itself, and acquired a stud of steam locomotives.

Teign Valley Railway

A number of plans emerged for an inland railway between Exeter and Newton Abbot, but it took two railway companies to provide this line, with one of them, the Teign Valley Railway, needing no fewer than nine Acts of Parliament to bring it to life, and another three afterwards, all for 7¾ route miles. While an alliance with the London & South Western Railway was considered, the bankrupt company was eventually brought into the GWR fold. Once opened between Heathfield and Ashton in October 1882, it was worked by the GWR. Heathfield was on the broad gauge Moretonhampstead line and the Teign Valley was standard gauge, so until the former was converted, the Teign Valley had an isolated existence with a single side tank locomotive and a handful of six-wheeled carriages. It was not until 1903 that the Exeter Railway, authorised in 1883, opened, giving a through route from Exeter to Heathfield. The line's full potential as a diversionary route when the Dawlish sea wall was closed because of bad weather was never realised as it suffered from severe gradients, and while the GWR persisted with this, the nationalised railway preferred taking the longer LSWR route via Okehampton.

Van Railway

Opened in 1871, the Van Railway was just 6½ miles in length and was worked from the outset by the Cambrian Railway. Opened to goods, mainly traffic from a lead mine, in 1871, and to passengers in 1873, it was closed on 4 November 1940 during the period of Railway Executive Committee control.

West Somerset Railway

Built to broad gauge, the West Somerset Railway was authorised in 1857, although work did not start until 1859. The company had difficulty in raising the £160,000 needed, so the line was not opened from Norton Fitzwarren to the small port of Watchet until 1862. A further extension, the Minehead Railway, had an even longer gestation period, being authorised in 1865, dissolved in 1870, revived in 1871 and finally opened in 1874. From the start, both lines were worked by the Great Western Railway, and the two railways were converted to standard gauge in 1882. The GWR took over the Minehead Railway in 1897, but the West Somerset remained independent until 1922.

   Traffic on the line was always light, partly as there was no connection with the West Somerset Mineral Railway at Watchet, and little onward railway movement of cargo arriving at the docks. It was not until the early years of the twentieth century that passenger traffic began to grow as Minehead developed as a resort. In 1933 the number of passing loops was increased from four to six, and in 1934 and 1936 stretches of the line were doubled.

Weston, Clevedon & Portishead Light Railway

This was not one of the grouped companies, as most light railways slipped through the net and retained their independence, doubtless to the relief of everyone, and especially the 'Big Four'. Nevertheless, under the control of the Railway Executive Committee, the companies were not quite their own masters. The GWR took over the Weston, Clevedon & Portishead Light Railway in 1940 and traffic was discontinued on 18 May. The line had been built using powers obtained in 1885 as a tramway to replace a horse bus service, but the 8½-mile stretch between Weston-super-Mare and Clevedon did not open until December 1897, and the rest followed later giving a 14½-mile route with no fewer than seventeen stopping places. In 1899 its own Act of Parliament authorised the conversion to a light railway, and at the time of the GWR acquisition there were five steam locomotives, of which three were immediately condemned, and a Fordson rail tractor, as well as an ex-Southern Railway Drewry petrol railcar. Passenger carriages included three with bogies, while the rest were four- and six-wheelers.

Joint Ventures

Hammersmith & City Railway

Opened in 1864, the Hammersmith & City Railway initially ran from Green Lane Junction (later renamed Westbourne Park) via Shepherd's Bush to Hammersmith, a distance of 3 miles. At Latimer Road there was a connection to the West London Railway. The line was built mainly on viaduct, and until 1868–9 it was mixed gauge. In 1867 the line was acquired jointly by the Great Western Railway and the Metropolitan Railway, with both companies providing locomotives and rolling stock until the line was electrified during 1906–7, when new jointly owned rolling stock was provided. That the line was a success was despite the fact that the two shareholders had suffered severe differences when the original Metropolitan Railway had been built, but by 1867 relations had improved considerably.

   Under the joint owners, Hammersmith & City Railway trains were extended eastwards in stages using the Inner Circle Line and then the East London Line to reach New Cross in 1884. Although through electric working between Hammersmith and New Cross began in 1914, it was discontinued in 1941, never to resume.

   When the London Passenger Transport Board was established in 1933, it took the Metropolitan Railway interest in what became the Hammersmith & City Line, but not that of the Great Western Railway, which in retrospect seems strange. The line continued to be operated jointly and did not pass completely into London Transport control until railway nationalisation in 1948.

Narrow Gauge Lines

Although only one narrow gauge railway was specifically mentioned as forming part of the 'Western Group' under the 1921 Act, Wales was for long the home of many such lines owing to the difficult contours that favoured the construction of narrow gauge railways, which were often the only form of railway that could be viable in such areas. It was no coincidence that Switzerland also spawned many narrow gauge lines, although in Switzerland the gauge generally standardised at a metre. One line, the Corris Railway, was not absorbed by the GWR until 1930.

Corris Railway

Authorised in 1858 as the Corris, Machynlleth & River Dovey Tramroad to carry slate from the quarries at Corris to the River Dovey, the line was built to a gauge of 2ft 3in and operations started in 1859 with horses pulling the slate wagons. The section between Machynlleth and Derwenlas was closed once the Cambrian opened its line from Machynlleth to Borg in 1863, while the title was shortened to Corris Railway in 1865. Steam locomotives were not introduced until 1879. Four years later the first passenger services were introduced between Corris and Machynlleth, and in 1887 these were extended to Aberllefeni.

The Bristol Tramways and Carriage Company obtained a controlling interest in the Corris Railway and so the company did not pass into the Great Western sphere of influence until the late 1920s, after the GWR had obtained powers to operate bus services and taken a majority holding in Bristol Tramways. The GWR absorbed the Corris Railway completely under an Act of 1930, and in 1931 replaced the passenger service with buses. The slate traffic continued, although in decline, and the line was finally closed after nationalisation in 1948.

Festiniog Railway

Authorised by Parliament in 1832 to construct a line from the harbour at Portmadoc to the slate quarries at Blaenau Festiniog, the 13¼-mile Festiniog Railway was the first of the narrow gauge lines and was built to a gauge of 1ft 11½in. Work started in 1833 and the line was opened in 1836. The line required extensive engineering works and costs would almost certainly have been prohibitive had it been built to standard gauge, with the line running for some distance on a narrow shelf cut into a hillside, spanning deep ravines on narrow stone embankments and burrowing through two tunnels.

At first the line was worked by horses and gravity working, with the first steam locomotives not being introduced until 1863. Passenger traffic had been established by 1850, possibly earlier. Between the two world wars growing competition from road transport saw passenger services suspended in winter. The company remained independent, but operations were discontinued in 1946, and not restarted until taken over by a preservation society in 1954.

Glyn Valley Tramway

Built to the unusual gauge of 2ft 4½in, the Glyn Valley Tramway was a roadside line running for 8¼ miles from Chirk in Denbighshire to Glyn Ceirog and Pandy. Its main traffic was slate, granite and silica from local quarries, and instead of running to a harbour its destination was the Welsh section of the Shropshire Union Canal. Authorised in 1870, the line used a combination of horse traction and gravity working when it opened in 1873.

Powers were obtained in 1885 to withdraw services from the Pontfaen–Chirk section in favour of a new line from Pontfaen to the Great Western station at Chirk, while powers were also taken to extend the line from Glyn to Pandy and use steam locomotives.

The line remained independent until its closure in 1935, while passenger services had been withdrawn in 1933.

Padarn Railway

A private mineral line built in 1848 and using two gauges, 4ft and 1ft 10¾in, in Snowdonia.

Snowdon Mountain Railway

The only rack-and-pinion railway in the British Isles, it was built as a tourist railway on private land, with work starting at the end of 1864 and completed in early 1896. It has remained independent.

Talyllyn Railway

The Talyllyn Railway was authorised by an Act of 1865 and was intended both as a slate line and as a passenger line from the outset, running from Bryn Eglwys, south-east of Abergynolwyn, to Towyn on the Aberystwyth & Welsh Coast Railway. It was built to a demanding specification with many cuttings, bridges and embankments, to keep the maximum grading to 1 in 75, and to a gauge of 2ft 3in to match that of the horse tramway in the Corris Valley (see Corris Railway). Unlike many such lines it was a narrow gauge railway but not a light railway.

Lacking any association with other railways, the line never passed to the Great Western but remained independent, and transferred into what must have been one of the first preservation societies when it was taken over by the Talyllyn Railway Preservation Society in 1951.

Vale of Rheidol Light Railway

The only narrow gauge railway to pass into the hands of British Railways, the Vale of Rheidol was opened in 1902. This 1ft 11½in-gauge line was initially operated by the

Tank locomotives were meant to work equally well running backwards, but with an open-backed cab, working 0–6–0PT No. 325, seen near Stourbridge in 1925, must have been uncomfortable. The carriage next to the locomotive looks as if it may have been an ex-Cambrian vehicle, still in green and white. *(HMRS/J.E. Cull AEQ827)*

Cambrian Railway. Running from a yard next to the Aberystwyth station of the Cambrian, the line ran for 12 miles to Devil's Bridge and was built to serve iron-ore mines. The Vale of Rheidol was finally purchased by the Cambrian in 1913, which is why it was not mentioned in the 1921 Act. Under Great Western ownership, it continued to operate and in the late 1930s received new passenger carriages. The line not only survived nationalisation to be operated by British Railways, but had the dubious distinction of carrying 'British Rail' blue and the 'coming and going' logo.

Welshpool & Llanfair Light Railway

The 2ft 6in-gauge Welshpool & Llanfair Light Railway was completed in 1903. Unlike most of the Welsh narrow gauge lines, it was not built primarily for mineral or slate traffic, although it did have traffic from the Standart Quarry, but operated through an agricultural area. The line was built to link the small town of Llanfair Caereinion to the nearest large (the terms are relative) town of Welshpool, and using the Light Railways Act 1896, a Light Railway Order was obtained in 1899. One term of the order was that the railway would have to be worked by an existing company, and so the following year it was leased to the Cambrian Railway for ninety-nine years in return for 40 per cent of the receipts. Only three passenger carriages and two locomotives were built.

Chapter Two

Paddington –
A Temple to Steam

Alone among the 'Big Four', the Great Western had just one London terminus, Paddington. This was the result of there being only one company among those grouped to make the 'new' Great Western with a London connection. The GWR did not have the problem of multiple termini that afflicted the others, and the Southern in particular, which even had two pre-grouping companies sharing two of its termini, Victoria and London Bridge. On the other hand, for travellers to London and to the City in particular, Paddington was probably the least convenient location at which to arrive in the capital. Not for nothing did the GWR value its stake in the Hammersmith & City Railway, or at one stage operate by a circuitous route through the west of London to Victoria.

Built to accommodate the broad gauge, Paddington acquired a natural spaciousness, and gave the impression of being built by an affluent railway, with none of the mean, low and even wooden structures of lesser railways, and the graceful roof provided by Brunel was cathedral-like, to the extent of having what almost amounted to transepts.

Yet, Paddington almost didn't happen. A location close to Victoria at Grosvenor Road was considered, as was sharing with the London & Birmingham Railway at Euston, reached through a junction close to what later became Kensal Green Cemetery. Either way, the proud Great Western would have been seen to take second place to other, lesser, railways that did not survive the grouping with their identity intact. To Brunel, this would have been both a humiliation and the end of his plans for a broad gauge railway. Going to Euston would have meant no broad gauge, for as far as Brunel could see, the *only* valid argument against broad gauge would have been if the Great Western was forced to share with the London & Birmingham, later the London & North Western. Being forced to accept what became standard gauge would have saved the Great Western much expense later, and its travellers and the shippers of freight much inconvenience and, certainly in the case of the latter, loss and damage in the meantime, but to Brunel's undisguised relief, negotiations with the London & Birmingham broke down. In later years the Euston option would have afflicted both railway companies with an overcrowded and congested terminus and approach lines, and the Victoria option could have placed great strains on the road and Underground system in the immediate area.

The First Paddington

Even the most ambitious could not know how the railways were to grow, not just in the case of the network, but in usage, and even the best-funded had to be careful at first. That said, confident as ever that all problems would be resolved, the Great Western began preparatory work on the approach to Paddington even before the approach line received parliamentary sanction in 1837. The line reached London from Kensal Green along the alignment of the Grand Union Canal towards Bishops Walk, subsequently renamed Bishops Road and then Bishops Bridge Road, using land leased from the Bishop of London. An immediate shortage of capital meant that a temporary station had to be built, mainly of wooden construction with the passenger facilities and offices in the arches of the bridge under Bishops Road, and with just an arrival and a departure platform separated by a broad vehicle roadway. The temporary station opened on 4 June 1838, on the

Paddington was one of the most attractive railway termini, but also had its fair share of goods traffic, including milk, with churns often found on some of the platforms. This is 4–6–0 29XX No. 2917 *Saint Bernard* at platform 8. *(HMRS/J. Tatchell ADD912)*

day that the line itself opened for business over the 22½ miles between Paddington and Maidenhead. The line extended to Reading on 30 March 1840, and the ambition of linking London and Bristol was achieved on 30 June 1841.

Temporary it may have been, but the early Paddington station was clearly regarded as being fit for royalty. Queen Victoria made her first railway journey on 13 June 1842, travelling from Slough, the nearest station to Windsor, behind the locomotive *Phlegethon*. Gooch drove the locomotive at an average speed of 44mph, which alarmed Her Majesty somewhat, so that Prince Albert was moved to request that future journeys be conducted at lower speeds. This request was observed by all railways subsequently, to the extent that Queen Victoria's fastest journey was that of her funeral trains, which her heir, Edward VII, impatient to get the proceedings over and done with as quickly as possible, had driven at the best available speed from Stokes Bay, near Gosport, to Victoria, and subsequently from Paddington to Windsor, on 2 February 1901.

The original station was perfectly adequate for the twelve trains or so on an average day, but the opening of the line to Bristol immediately put the temporary station under pressure. Enlargement of the temporary station had to be the immediate answer, and by 1845 there were three arrival platforms and two for departures to the south of the arrival platforms, as well as a further two tracks, while at the country end of the station lay a carriage shed, and beyond that an engine shed and workshops. A wooden shed for goods and offices were erected on land south of Bishops Road. However, these improvements soon looked short-sighted, for once authorisation was received for a permanent terminus in late 1850, the facilities had to be replaced and this caused delays to the construction of the new station. As an interim measure the Great Western directors initially authorised a departure shed, hoping that, despite the line nearing completion in South Wales and to Birmingham, the original temporary station would be adequate as an arrivals shed for a while longer. In 1853 the board bowed to the inevitable, and agreed that the permanent terminus could be completed in its entirety.

Facilities for the travelling public at the temporary station included the Prince of Wales Hotel, advertised as a 'commercial inn for families and gentlemen', on the south side of the station.

Brunel's Paddington

Brunel was one of that generation of engineers, effectively the first generation, who could turn his hand to anything and was expected to be able to do so. The differences between locomotive and civil engineering, between bridges and marine engineering, were discounted. Even so, he had the wisdom to engage one of the most eminent architects of the day, Matthew Digby Wyatt, as his assistant, officially to provide ornamentation. In his design for Paddington, Brunel was influenced by his time as a member of the building committee for Paxton's famous Crystal Palace, and also by the new main station in Munich, which led him to design a metal roof, the first for a large station. The buildings at the town end of the station had to be impressive as the platforms lay in a cutting, and the station offices were alongside the main departure platform. The splendid face of Paddington was the Great Western Hotel, later renamed the Great Western Royal Hotel, which opened on 9 June 1854. Designed by Philip Hardwick, as built the hotel had 103 bedrooms and 15 sitting rooms, and the impact of the frontage was literally raised by two towers at each end, both two storeys higher than the main building. A sculpture of Britannia surrounded by displays of the 'six parts of the world, and of their arts and commerce' stood above the pediment.

The new station was located more than 200yd south of the temporary terminus, much of it on the old goods sidings, and was 700ft long and 238ft wide. Offices some 580ft long were built on the south-western side of the station along what was then known as Spring Street, but is today Eastbourne Terrace, while a cab road was built on the north-eastern side. As with the original temporary station, arrival platforms were on the northern side and

Paddington in 1928, with 4–6–0 40XX No. 4045 *Prince John* having just arrived. On the far left, a steam lorry stands on a nearby platform. *(HMRS/J. Tatchell ADD934)*

departure platforms on the southern, and with royal patronage firmly in mind, the latter could be reached through a private entrance in the office building and a special royal waiting room, expensively furnished with French furniture. Above the royal entrance from the street, there was a crown, but the two doorways to the platform had one surmounted by the royal coat of arms, the other by that of the Great Western.

The greatest visual impact came from the roof, towering up to 55ft above the platforms and with glass and corrugated iron supported by wrought-iron arches. There were three spans, of 70ft, 102ft 6in and 68ft, separated by two 50ft transepts. The transepts were not intended to be purely ornamental, but had the practical function of accommodating large traversers to move carriages between the tracks, but these machines were never used.

Broad gauge tracks were complemented by wide platforms, with the main departure platform next to the offices being 27ft wide, and an adjoining track being supported by one of the two faces of the subsidiary departure platform, itself 24ft 6in wide. North of the subsidiary departure platform lay another track, then five more used for storing carriages, then two more on either side of an arrival platform 21ft wide, with a tenth track serving a further arrival platform which, including the cab road, was 47ft wide. This northernmost platform included offices for incoming parcels. The site of the temporary terminus was not abandoned, but instead became the new goods depot. To modern eyes, the unusual feature of the platforms was that the subsidiary platforms were all island platforms, as there was no main concourse and the tracks extended beyond the platform ends to nineteen turnplates (some tracks had two) for horses and carriages to be loaded and unloaded. Rather than build a subway or even a footbridge, access to the subsidiary platforms was by small bridges that rested on a truck and could be lowered and raised using hydraulic power. One of these survived in use between platforms 1 and 2 until 1920, and was only finally scrapped during the Second World War.

The departure side was brought into use on 16 January 1854, followed by the arrival side on 29 May. New engine sheds came into use at Westbourne Park during 1855, allowing those by the temporary station to be closed and the entire site to be taken over by the new goods depot. Westbourne Park had another function, for in common with many railways of the time, tickets were not collected as trains rumbled into the terminus, impractical given the lack of corridors on early rolling stock, or at the terminus barriers, but at a station close to the end of the line, and a call at the ticket platform at Westbourne Park was a necessity on trains inward bound for Paddington.

Signalling at first had consisted of the disc-and-crossbar type using revolving posts, and semaphore signalling did not appear until 1865, with block operation introduced the following year as far as Ealing.

The dream of a fast and spacious broad gauge railway was a nightmare for many users, and the GWR failed to make the most of its advantages either in the width of rolling stock or in achieving speed significantly higher than railways elsewhere. As early as 1861 the GWR agreed to amalgamate with the West Midland Railway, a standard gauge line, and so to enable its trains to reach Paddington, standard gauge track had to be laid between Paddington and the connecting junction 37 miles out of London at Reading West. By September 1870 Paddington's suburban services were mainly standard gauge, but it was not until early on 21 May 1892 that the services to Plymouth and Cornwall were finally converted to standard gauge.

Paddington may have compared well with many of the other railway stations being built at this time, both in space and amenity, but it was far away from the West End and even further from the City of London. Appreciative of this problem, the GWR decided to invest in the new North Metropolitan Railway to the extent of £175,000. The intention was that the railway should be built as a mixed gauge line, with standard and GWR broad gauge, and a connection to the GWR just west of Paddington, which was to prove a blessing once construction began as the spoil from the works could be removed by this route. Renamed the Metropolitan Railway in 1854, it reached Farringdon Street in 1863, although passengers from Paddington had to use a separate station, Bishops Road, to reach the Underground. Initially, the service between Paddington and Farringdon Street, a journey of just 15 minutes, was worked by the GWR, but this arrangement was terminated on 10 August owing to a number of differences between the two companies, of which, inevitably, money was one. The Metropolitan could not introduce rolling stock of its own until late 1864, and in the meantime managed to survive using locomotives from the Great Northern Railway and carriages from the London & North Western Railway, for which the standard gauge tracks proved a blessing. The Metropolitan's other priority, in addition to funding its own rolling stock and completing the line, was to buy out the GWR's stake in its business. This was not the only underground connection, as from June 1864, using Bishops Road station, the Hammersmith & City Railway commenced operations to Hammersmith. The Hammersmith & City left the GWR main line at Westbourne Park, but it was intended to act mainly as a feeder into the Metropolitan, and enjoyed the support of both companies, which by 1867 had recovered from their earlier differences and managed the Hammersmith & City through a joint committee. Initially the Hammersmith & City was worked by GWR broad gauge trains, but from 1 April 1865 the Metropolitan used its own standard gauge rolling stock over the entire route between Farringdon Street and Hammersmith, while GWR broad gauge trains eventually ran over Metropolitan tracks as far east as Moorgate until March 1869, and then, once standard gauge rolling stock was delivered, as far east as Liverpool Street.

In the other direction, GWR trains also ran to Kensington. Trains from as far away as Windsor, by this time a branch off the line at Slough, ran through to the Metropolitan, and between 1866 and 1868, slip coaches from these trains ran into Paddington. The growing Metropolitan Railway was extended to Gloucester Road, and in October 1868 a new station was opened in Praed Street directly opposite the Great Western Hotel. Even so, there was no footbridge providing direct access to the services from Bishops Road, later renamed Paddington (Suburban) until 1878, and no subway between Paddington and Praed Street until 1887.

This growing network of urban services continued to use the GWR main line between Bishops Road and Green Lane Junction, near Westbourne Park, until 30 October 1871, when separate suburban lines were opened with stations at Royal Oak and Westbourne Park, but the increasingly busy main lines were crossed by the local trains until a dive-under was commissioned between Royal Oak and Westbourne Park on 12 May 1878.

It was on the lines to the Underground that the worst accident occurred at Paddington, on 5 May 1864, when a Great Northern 0–6–0 locomotive leaving Bishops Road at 09.05 for Farringdon Street suffered a boiler explosion. A number of people were injured, two of them seriously, and the station was badly damaged, with one piece of debris falling 250yd away, penetrating the roof of the main-line station.

The Hammersmith & City was electrified on 5 November 1906, and once the Metropolitan Line was also electrified, GWR trains, by this time all standard gauge, were hauled to the City of London by Metropolitan electric engines.

Paddington's isolation was eased further by the building of the deep-level tube line, an extension of the Baker Street and Waterloo, or 'Bakerloo', proposed as early as 1899, but not actually agreed until 1911. To the dismay of the Metropolitan, which saw the new arrival as a competitor, the GWR drew the Bakerloo northwards from Baker Street with the inducement of a subsidy, and services started on 1 December 1913, with the line extended to Willesden Junction in 1915 and to Watford in 1917. The new deep-level tube platforms were more than 40ft beneath a new booking hall underneath the cab road close to the arrival platforms. The attitude of the Metropolitan Railway towards the Bakerloo is hard to understand, as the Bakerloo connected Paddington with the West End and the London & South Western Railway, and for that matter with the South Eastern Railway at Charing Cross, while the Metropolitan provided the link with the City of London.

The Growing Station

Meanwhile, as the network of underground lines around Paddington developed, change was taking place on the surface. The original arrangement of two tracks to and from Paddington was soon inadequate as traffic continued to grow, and by 1871 four tracks were in place between Paddington and Westbourne Park, but these did not reach Slough until 1879, and Maidenhead until 1884. The new arrangement was for the fast lines, known as the 'main lines', to be on the south side and the suburban lines, known as the 'relief lines', on the north. In 1878 a new arrival platform, No. 9, was commissioned, and a new cab road reached the station using a bridge over the approaches to the goods depot. A new section of roof sheltered the new platform and roadway, albeit less grand than the original. Two new departure platforms were introduced in 1885, and some time later were renumbered 4 and 5. This expansion was achieved by the simple expedient of reducing the number of tracks available for carriages in the main station or train shed, and new West London Carriage Sidings to the south of the main line were commissioned during the late 1880s. In 1893 further changes enabled platform 7 to be moved southwards, with another new arrival platform. Apart from the expansion of 1878, all of these changes were accommodated under the original Brunel roof, something that was made possible by the removal of the carriage sidings and the switch from broad gauge to standard gauge.

Extension of the station buildings towards the hotel also saw the steady disappearance of the horse and carriage facilities from 1881 onwards.

There were other changes too, as in 1880 Paddington became one of the first railway termini to use electric light, although with just thirty-four lamps and even these proving unreliable. Nevertheless, in 1886 a more reliable supply was introduced using three generators installed at Westbourne Park, which lit the terminus itself as well as the offices, goods sheds and yards, and the stations at Royal Oak and Westbourne Park. The generators had to be moved in 1906 to allow platform 1 at Paddington to be extended, and new facilities were installed at Park Royal with a fully fledged power station that also provided the Hammersmith & City Railway with traction current.

The goods traffic handled at Paddington's adjacent depot obviously included coal, the primary source of fuel for the Victorian and Edwardian household, but inevitably milk became an important traffic for Paddington given the nature of the GWR's territory and the needs of a thirsty capital. Milk traffic was so important that it used the main terminus, which doubtless improved the productivity of the operation as it mainly took place during what might otherwise be described as the 'quiet hours'. The 1878 platform had a milk arrival dock completed in 1881 at its outer end, and accommodation was also arranged for this traffic on the departure side. By 1900 more than 3,000 milk churns were being handled each day at Paddington, joined by trains handling meat, fish, newspapers and horses, while there were also special flower trains during the early spring, bringing produce from as far away as the Isles of Scilly via Penzance.

In response to the growing number of through workings between railway companies in the North and Midlands and those in the South, early in the twentieth century the GWR encouraged the London, Brighton & South Coast Railway, whose Victoria terminus it had used, to introduce a daily return service between Brighton and Paddington. The journey to and from Brighton reached Paddington using the Latimer Road spur and the West London Railway, with the through service taking 100 minutes, but the operation only lasted from July 1906 to June 1907, as it failed to attract sufficient custom. Later, a service was introduced between the Midlands and Victoria, but this also failed.

The GWR had started services to and from Victoria as early as 1 April 1863, with what was essentially a suburban service from Southall, where connections could be made with its main-line services. Trains running through to Reading, Slough, Uxbridge and Windsor were also provided at times over the years that followed, while there were experiments with slip coaches off trains from further afield, such as Bristol and Birmingham, special trains to Henley and to the Wycombe line, and finally, between 1910 and 1912, a daily train in each direction between Birmingham and Wolverhampton and Victoria. Wartime restrictions saw the end of the Southall service in 1915, superfluous with the opening of what is now known as the Circle Line between Victoria and Paddington in 1868.

Edwardian Heyday and Beyond

The new century saw the railways enjoying a boom, while trains were becoming longer and heavier, with corridor coaches having connections between the carriages, which especially on main-line duties increasingly were mounted on bogies. Once again Paddington was in danger of being outgrown by the traffic being generated. Before the problem could be resolved, a substantial amount of preparation had to be put in hand. In March 1906 a new locomotive depot was opened at Old Oak Common, allowing the earlier structure at Westbourne Park to be closed. New carriage sheds were also opened at Old Oak Common. There were other minor works as well, all of which contributed to the whole, so that in 1908 the main departure platform had an extension, numbered 1A, used primarily for excursion trains and, later, for Down milk traffic, although milk traffic was finally moved to the goods depot in 1923, probably reflecting the increasing use of tanker wagons. Later 1A became a platform for rolling stock waiting to be moved onto the main platform, cutting the interval between departures, and then it became a double-sided parcels platform. At around this time island platforms 2 and 3 were extended to around 1,000ft, while platforms 1 to 5 had a luggage subway built with lifts to the platforms.

All of this really consisted of tampering with the edges. In 1906 a more comprehensive scheme was approved by the Great Western's directors. The arrival side of the station was to be extended with the addition of three new platforms under a 700ft long and 109ft wide steel and glass roof, intended to be in sympathy with the original, with platform 9 extended to 950ft, while the Bishops Road platforms were also to be extended. The old overbridges with their brick arches were to be replaced by a new steel structure with long spans that would enable the tracks to be rearranged, and would allow greater freedom for such adjustments in the future. The most radical of these changes was the construction of a new goods depot to be built at South Lambeth, as the GWR termed Battersea, doubtless to avoid confusion with the LB&SCR (London, Brighton & South Coast Railway) station, which would ease the pressure on Paddington goods, and no doubt make interchange with other railways in the South easier.

These works took until the First World War to complete. The new overbridges alone took until 1914, but in the meantime the approach tracks were rearranged. As with many of the older termini, empty stock workings at Paddington for many years occupied the running lines and significantly reduced line capacity for revenue-earning trains. There had been some relief with new engine and carriage roads to serve the new engine and carriage sheds at Old Oak, but these only ran part-way on the north side of the line. Sharing of the main and suburban lines by goods trains made the problems worse. In 1911 work began on lines to segregate all empty carriage and light engine workings over the entire 3 miles between Paddington and Old Oak Common, hampered by the need to rebuild Westbourne Park station, but war intervened and work ground to a halt in 1916, was suspended for ten years, and was not finally completed until 1927.

The new layout meant that there was a Down empty carriage line all the way from Paddington to Old Oak Common north of the suburban or relief lines, shared by goods workings, while the old engine and carriage line was converted into a goods running line. From the junction with the subway or dive-under, a second Up empty carriage road was provided into Paddington. The result of these changes was that the last three-quarters of a mile into Paddington was arranged, from the north, as follows:

Up City
Down City
Down carriage
Up relief (suburban)
Up main
Up carriage
Down main
Up carriage

Ten years later, the Up main and Up relief lines were resignalled to enable them to be used to ease congestion on the Down carriage line, and then later the Down carriage line and one of the Up carriage lines also became running lines.

Meanwhile, Paddington itself was being transformed. The layout of the approach tracks was remodelled to provide improved connections to the Hammersmith & City lines and the Ranelagh engine yard on the south side of the lines at Royal Oak station, where locomotives from the provinces were turned. The old goods yard and its approaches were replaced by three new platforms with a roadway. While the new roof was not completed until 1916, the new platforms were brought into use in stages between November 1913 and December 1915, and introduced new features to the GWR, including hydraulic buffers. Passenger amenities improved, with space from 1910 beneath platform 1 for lavatories, bathrooms and a hairdressing salon. The new station had platforms 1 to 4 for departures on the main line, 5 to 7 for outer suburban trains, and platforms 8 to 11 for main-line arrivals. Until 1923 platform 12 handled milk arrivals, and other perishable traffics such as fish, as well as mail and parcels, while the opposite face of the platform opened out onto a sunken roadway so that these goods could be manhandled easily across the platform onto the backs of road vehicles.

The First World War had far less impact on Paddington than on the termini of the southern companies, but even so the number of troop movements meant that a free twenty-four hour buffet was introduced, staffed by female volunteer workers. There were also a number of ambulance trains, with a total of 351 over the four years or so of war. Spared air-raid damage, nevertheless some of the glass panels in the roof were broken by shrapnel from anti-aircraft fire. Postwar, a war memorial to members of the GWR who had fallen in combat was installed between the doors of the royal suite on the main departure platform.

Other postwar work to complete the 1906 programme of improvements saw Brunel's old cast-iron columns supporting the roof between platforms 2 and 3 and 7 and 8 replaced by steel columns on which Wyatt's original decorations were reproduced. Other columns had been replaced during the construction of the new roof for the extension. Paddington also became the terminus for the Post Office tube railway when it opened in December 1927, with a station beneath the Royal Mail's district office in London Street. Mail chutes were installed at the head of platforms 8 to 10, while platform 11 had a bank of no fewer than eight chutes, at the bottom of which were conveyors to take the mail to the tube. In the opposite direction, mail arriving on the tube was brought up by a conveyor that emerged on the departure side of the station behind the hotel.

Redeveloped Yet Again

Interrupted by the First World War, the 1906 programme of improvements had been barely completed when further work was put in hand, made possible by a combination of the removal of the passenger duty on railway travel and implementation of the Government Grants (Development Loans, Guarantees and Grants) Act 1929. Both measures were intended to reduce unemployment. The latter measure meant that the GWR's plans for a £1 million rebuild of Paddington had to be approved by the Treasury. Work began in May 1930, and was completed in 1934.

Once again, a significant feature was the extension of platforms, in this case Nos 2 to 11 to beyond Bishops Road bridge, giving lengths of between 980ft and 1,200ft, with veranda-type roofing rather than a new overall roof, while the construction of a new parcels depot in Bishops Road allowed a passenger concourse to be constructed between the head of the platforms and the back of the hotel. Platform extension is often seen as an easy way of improving railway capacity, but the need to reposition signalling and points, or lineside structures, and rebuild bridges, can mean that extensions are expensive and time-consuming, or bring shortcomings. In the case of Paddington, the site of the original station at the western end of the extensions meant that some tight curves were inevitable. There were also new office blocks and new cab and goods depot approach roads. The tracks outside the station up to a distance of three-quarters of a mile were reconstructed, with a new parcels line on the Down side, and the Ranelagh engine yard was improved.

Between 1929 and 1933 electric power signals (as opposed to electric light signals) were introduced on all lines between Paddington and Southall West Junction, while electric motors were installed at points and track circuiting was introduced. Colour light signalling was commissioned on the Hammersmith & City lines using just two aspects, since there was no need for single or double yellows on a line lacking heavy steam-hauled goods trains. New arrivals and departures signal-boxes were needed because of the platform extensions, with the new departure box at Westbourne Bridge opening on 9 July 1933. In addition to the Down main lines, it also looked after the parcels depot, Ranelagh yard and two of the carriage roads. The new arrivals box that opened on 13 August 1933, replacing both the Bishops Road and Royal Oak station boxes as well as the original arrivals box, was badly affected by fire on 25 November 1938, closing the suburban station and forcing emergency signalling on all other movements. A makeshift box had to be improvised until a new one could be commissioned on 2 July 1939, and in the meantime through trains did not operate to the City. Meanwhile, a fire had broken out in the Westbourne Bridge signal-box on 23 December 1938, so this also had to be replaced. Subsequently, all new boxes were fitted with carbon dioxide fire extinguishers and master switches to cut out the signalling in an emergency.

Of all the London termini, Paddington has always been the least troubled by suburban traffic. In 1903, when Liverpool Street on the Great Eastern had 136 suburban train arrivals between 05.00 and 10.00, Paddington had just eight. Reasons for this included the slow pace at which the GWR had built its suburban stations, and the overlap of the Great Central and the London & South Western suburban networks with the catchment area for Paddington, while the proximity of the Hammersmith & City and the Metropolitan reinforced this. The Birmingham route had brought additional suburban traffic, but this still remained small compared with that of the other London termini. After the First World War this began to change, although traffic was to remain modest by the standards set elsewhere. While the 1920s and 1930s did bring a considerable increase in Paddington's suburban traffic as speculative builders began extending the western suburbs outwards in Middlesex and the southern part of Buckinghamshire, this was nothing compared to the developments affecting many of the other London termini.

Even so, this steady growth in suburban traffic meant that new arrangements became necessary and the decision was taken to enlarge Bishops Road station as Paddington (Suburban) for terminating trains and those bound for the Metropolitan. The old Up and Down platforms were replaced by two island platforms, one for Up and one for Down traffic, each with two faces. These works were completed in 1933. The usual practice was for electric trains to use the outside platforms, 13 and 16, while terminating GWR steam trains used the inner platforms 14 and 15.

On the surface, the inner end of the main station had become known as the 'Lawn', possibly a reflection of the time when horses and carriages were handled on this spot, and had become something of an eyesore over the years as successive forms of business were carried out. Even the beautiful overall roof did not reach to this spot, which had become something of a no man's land under a lower roof with many supporting columns. All of this was ended with the 1933 reconstruction, with for the first time a broad new concourse extending across platforms 1 to 8, whose buffers were set back to provide extra space and a uniform ending, and stretching round to platforms 9 and 10. A new, higher steel and glass roof was provided over the concourse, although the name of the Lawn persists to this day. The office blocks on either side of the station were revamped and new steel-framed structures built at either end of the Lawn, while the hotel was also extended, being completed in the summer of 1936 with a new total of 250 bedrooms. An electrically operated train indicator board was installed on the Lawn in 1934, and in 1936 a loudspeaker system was introduced. A new parcels depot with two platforms was built on the site of the former platform 1A.

Wartime

Few looked forward to the Second World War with any degree of confidence. The view that had gained widespread acceptance between the two wars was that the 'bomber would always get through'.

Wartime enforced many changes, and through working of trains to and from the Metropolitan ended on 16 September 1939, by which time emergency cuts were being made to timetables. Paddington did not escape its share of wartime wounds, with a parachute mine demolishing part of the departure side building in 1941, while in 1944 a V1 flying bomb damaged the roof and platforms 6 and 7. Nevertheless, traffic was not disrupted for long.

The big problem was that with a restricted train service commuter traffic actually increased as many of the more affluent Londoners moved to the outer suburbs or even further out to escape the worst of the bombing. For holidays and for evacuees the West of England and Wales were seen as the best options, not least because most of the south coast was taken over for military purposes with beaches cordoned off behind barbed wire.

During the period before the Normandy invasion in 1944 only residents and those with special business were allowed near the south coast. The east coast resorts were not much better off. On the morning of 29 July 1944, a summer Saturday, Paddington was closed for three hours, and no Underground tickets were sold to Paddington, because the main concourse and platforms were blocked solid with people waiting to catch trains. The problems of wartime had been compounded by government restrictions on extra trains and even on extra carriages on existing trains, adding to the much-reduced frequencies and extended journey times. It took three telephone calls by the general manager, Sir James Milne, to the Ministry of War Transport, and the threat of a visit to Downing Street, before a man from the ministry arrived and authorised the use of the locomotives and carriages that were standing idle at Old Oak Common depot. The restrictions were eased somewhat after this, but even so, at August bank holiday weekend, then taken early in August and not at the end as today, mounted police had to be called in and the queues snaked along Eastbourne Terrace, which did at least have the advantage of allowing passengers to get to and from the trains.

There was disruption of a different kind on 16 October 1944. The locomotive of a Down empty carriage train was derailed outside Paddington close to the parcels depot. This was soon followed by two coaches of the Down 'Cornish Riviera' express being derailed at the same point, and although there were no casualties the line was blocked and normal working could not resume until the next morning.

Chapter Three

Great Western Destinations

The Great Western Railway was promoted by wealthy businessmen in both London and Bristol, then rival ports. Bristol had become the important port for Atlantic trade and also handled a considerable coastal traffic, but the Merchant Adventurers who had done so much to establish the city as a leading centre for shipping and commerce had initially been reluctant to invest in the new railways until they could be assured of a worthwhile return. Brunel, the GWR's engineer, however, saw his line as part of a London to New York route, and later even designed the steamships as well. Nevertheless, it was not long before the GWR looked beyond its early London to Bristol corridor, initially to Exeter and then to Plymouth and Cornwall, north to the Midlands, and across the wide estuary of the River Severn to Wales. Each of these destinations became important, often thanks to the railways, and it was the railways that eased the embarrassment of some of them, notably Cardiff as it struggled to handle the growing demand for coal, as the industrial revolution continued into an evolution.

Birmingham

Unlike many of the major centres nurtured by the advent of the railway age, Birmingham was already a growing industrial city, sometimes described as the 'workshop of the world', before the railways arrived. It was the hub of a canal network that served the Midlands and beyond, with the Grand Union Canal linking the city with London. Many of the canals were to pass into railway ownership. Birmingham was linked to London by rail in 1838 when the London & Birmingham Railway opened its line from Euston. The Great Western Railway's advance on Birmingham was abruptly checked when the Midland Railway acquired the Birmingham & Gloucester and Bristol & Gloucester companies, to the relief of the London & North Western Railway, as the London & Birmingham had become by this time, which had been concerned about the disruption that would be caused by broad gauge lines running into the city if the Great Western was welcomed by the Midland into its terminus at New Street.

The GWR was determined to serve Birmingham, however, and indeed aimed to go further north to Merseyside. Its ambitions were to be satisfied by the acquisition of first the Birmingham & Oxford Railway, which opened in 1852, and then in 1854 by the acquisition of the Birmingham, Wolverhampton & Dudley Railway. Unable to enter New Street, a new terminus was built for these broad gauge companies at Snow Hill, which was also in the central district of Birmingham but was approached through a tunnel to avoid demolition of valuable properties. All of the companies

Opposite top: Commuter services on the Great Western were not just confined to the London area, for whose commuter market the company was very much a minority player, but also operated around Bristol and, in this picture, Birmingham, where in 1929 2–6–2T class 45XX No. 4595 heads a busy suburban service near Bentley Heath. *(HMRS/D.H. Haines AEV000)*

Bottom: A suburban train from Birmingham Snow Hill is headed by 2–6–2T class 3150 No. 3156 in 1934. *(HMRS/D.H. Haines AEV431)*

serving Birmingham, which included the Grand Junction as well as the GWR, LNWR and MR, were slow to develop a suburban network for the growing city, and it was not until the 1860s that suburban branches started to open. In the case of the GWR, its Birmingham branch network concentrated on the towns to the north and west of the city, including Wolverhampton, Dudley and Kidderminster, and south to Leamington Spa, while other areas were reached with the acquisition of the Birmingham & North Warwickshire Railway, which was to become part of a GWR line competing with the MR between Birmingham and Bristol, finally opened in 1907–8. Although Snow Hill was rebuilt in 1912 and in its new form was a spacious and elegant station, local trains also had their own terminus at Moor Street. By this time a Paddington–Banbury direct route had been opened, in 1910, and the GWR's timings from Paddington were now competitive with those of the LNWR, whose route was in fact slightly longer. Great Western expresses were able to cover the 110½ miles between the two cities in two hours.

Bristol

New docks had opened in Bristol in 1809, but it was not until 1841 that the city was linked to London by the Great Western Railway. To be fair, the railway could not have been ready to coincide with the opening of the docks, and as many of the early railways, such as the Stockton & Darlington and the Liverpool & Manchester, were short distance and met local needs, the delay in building what was a trunk route seems understandable. At the start of the nineteenth century an entrepreneur wanting to link two major cities would have been more likely to consider building a canal.

Nevertheless, the GWR arrived in Bristol to find that the next stage of the railway westwards, the Bristol to Bridgwater section of the Bristol & Exeter Railway, was already

Bristol Temple Meads was one of the most rebuilt stations on the GWR, and was even relocated to some extent. This view shows the station in 1935. (*Kevin Robertson*)

opened. Both lines were built to the broad gauge favoured by Brunel, engineer to both companies, but it was strange that the meeting of the two at Temple Meads, about a mile from the centre of Bristol, was at right angles, and a tight curving line with a separate 'express platform' cutting across the approach to the Bristol & Exeter's station proved necessary. That Bristol was to be not simply a terminus but a major junction and interchange was soon confirmed by the opening of the Bristol & Gloucester Railway in 1844, again engineered by Brunel, but his ambition to continue the line to Birmingham was foiled when the Midland Railway suddenly acquired both the Bristol & Gloucester and the Birmingham & Gloucester railways in 1845. The first standard gauge trains to reach Bristol were those of the Midland Railway from Birmingham in 1854. It was not until after the opening of the Severn Tunnel in 1886 that the GWR could open its own route to the Midlands via Shrewsbury, followed in 1908 by a route to Birmingham Snow Hill via Stratford-upon-Avon.

Brunel's dedication to the broad gauge made both him and the GWR unpopular in Bristol, where the influential local merchants and the council felt that it isolated the city from the national standard gauge network. Feelings on the matter ran so high that as early as 1861 the first plans for a standard gauge rival line to London were being promoted, with the Bristol & South Western Junction Railway running 40 miles to join the London & South Western Railway line to Waterloo from Exeter. There was another scheme in 1882 and yet a third as late as 1902, by which time the broad gauge was history. Another factor in these schemes was the desire to build a central station in Bristol, although finding a suitable location for this would have been difficult.

Traffic between Bristol and South Wales had been strong for many years, with the distance between Bristol and Newport by sea being just 25 miles. A rail link between Bristol and South Wales was introduced in 1852, with trains running over the Bristol & Gloucester and South Wales railways, although this meant that the distance between Bristol and Newport by train was 82 miles. In 1863 the broad gauge Bristol & South Wales Union Railway opened a line from Bristol to New Passage, connecting with a steam ferry to Portskewett, which was on a short branch off the South Wales Railway. The BSWUR line was eventually adapted to provide the route to the Severn Tunnel, which opened in 1886. With a length of more than 4 miles, it was then the world's longest underwater tunnel. The opening of the tunnel meant that most of the traffic between London and South Wales worked through Bristol and Bath, a shorter and more direct route than that via Gloucester, with an avoiding line keeping through traffic away from Temple Meads.

Meanwhile, in 1878, an elegant new Temple Meads station was built by the GWR and MR, displacing the original station and that of the Bristol & Exeter. The original station became a goods station and then a car park, before being used more recently as an exhibition centre. Despite the construction of a spacious new station, more growth meant that Temple Meads continued to be congested, and several measures were taken, initially to ease pressure on the station and then, later, to reduce distances and journey times, ending the jibe that GWR stood for 'Great Way Round'. First, the Bristol Avoiding Line was built in 1892, close to Temple Meads, while the far more ambitious Castle Cary cut-off, opened in 1906, reduced the route from Paddington to Taunton by 20 miles. Before this, the South Wales & Bristol Direct Railway opened in 1903. Often referred to as the 'Badminton Line', it cut the Paddington to South Wales route by 25 miles compared to that via Gloucester and 10 miles compared to the line through Bath and Bristol, and journey times were better than these figures might suggest as the new line enjoyed an excellent alignment. Using the Badminton Line, even the route to Bristol was reduced by a mile, and enabled the GWR to offer a two-hour Paddington to Bristol schedule.

Other routes continued to grow out of Bristol, including one to Southampton and Portsmouth which also shared part of its route with the line to Weymouth. A relatively small port development at Portishead was linked by broad gauge track to the Bristol & Exeter Railway in 1867. Later, both the GWR and the MR built lines to the docks at Avonmouth, where new docks opened in 1877 as ever larger deep-sea ships could no longer reach Bristol up the spectacular, but narrow, Avon Gorge. Surprisingly, lines into the existing Bristol Docks did not enjoy the same urgency, although three short dock branches were built eventually. Avonmouth was also connected to the South Wales line.

The lines to Bristol benefited from quadrupling during the 1930s, and both the GWR and the MR's successor, the London, Midland & Scottish, were given powers to borrow money to finance improvements in the Bristol area and at Temple Meads.

Cardiff

Oddly, the lords of the manor for Cardiff were the Marquesses of Bute, whose business interests included Cardiff Docks. Originally a small town – smaller than Merthyr Tydfil, Newport or Swansea – Cardiff enjoyed considerable expansion at the outset of the industrial revolution when the Glamorganshire Canal, opened in 1794, brought first iron ore and then coal from Merthyr Tydfil and the Taff Vale for shipment. The old docks were soon overwhelmed by the new traffic, and a new dock was built by the 2nd Marquess and opened in 1839, by which time the traffic had overtaken the capacity of the canal and relief came with the opening of the Taff Vale Railway from Merthyr in 1841. From this time onwards, Cardiff enjoyed rapid growth, so that by 1881 it was the largest city in Wales. Meanwhile, a second new dock, the East Bute Dock, had been opened in 1859, and authorisation given to build a third, which was completed in 1887.

The railways played a considerable part in the development of Cardiff both as a port and as a city. The Rhymney Railway reached Cardiff in 1858, and with the Taff Vale was responsible for most of the coal and ore traffic. To ease congestion on its lines and at Cardiff Docks, the TVR also served the new dock at Penarth 2 miles away when it opened between 1859 and 1865. The broad gauge South Wales Railway had entered the town in 1850, but this played little part in the coal and ore traffic until after its conversion to standard gauge in 1872, allowing through running of wagons between the 'valley' lines and the main line.

Cardiff's success and the resultant congestion was almost the port's undoing as, previously mentioned in Chapter One, in 1882 the mine owners were behind the

Wisely, the Great Western did not centralise all of its locomotive work at Swindon, keeping a locomotive works at Caerphilly for the engines on the extensive network of lines in the Welsh valleys. This is the traverser, with the overhead crane on the upper left. *(HMRS/J. Tatchell ADC503)*

establishment of the Rhondda & Swansea Bay Railway intended to remove their business from Cardiff, while in 1884 others started to build a new dock at Barry served by the Barry Railway, which opened in 1889. Fortunately, with coal output doubling between 1889 and 1913, sufficient traffic existed to ensure that all of these railways and docks were kept busy.

Nevertheless, after the coal miners' strike and the related General Strike in 1926, coal production declined sharply, falling from 50 million tons to 35 million tons between 1922 and 1938. The postwar boom had been short-lived and the years of recession also affected demand, and many export markets for Welsh coal were lost during the strike and never regained. Being heavily dependent on the port and its coal and ore traffic, the recession affected Cardiff especially badly. By this time the GWR was the monopoly provider of railway services in and around Cardiff, and was accused of neglecting the area. Although there was little evidence to substantiate these claims, faced with sharply declining traffic and some duplication of routes, the GWR itself had to close some 25 miles of line to passenger traffic in the valleys.

Exeter

If Bristol was the gateway to the West Country, Exeter was the gateway to the south-west, and as such was to be served by both the Great Western Railway from Paddington and Bristol, and by the London & South Western Railway from Waterloo and Salisbury. The broad gauge Bristol & Exeter Railway reached the city in 1844, and the GWR arrived at the city over its tracks and then continued through the city's main station at St David's, on a riverside location on the outskirts, to Plymouth using the lines of the South Devon Railway. From Exeter, the South Devon lines also reached Kingswear, across the river from Dartmouth, while the rival LSWR headed north to North Devon, although it also built and operated the branch to Exmouth, which rapidly became what almost amounted to a suburban line.

By 1862 St David's had become an important junction and, for the next thirty years, interchange point between broad and standard gauge, which did little to expedite traffic through the city, although it was spared the worst of the problems that afflicted Gloucester, possibly because there was less interchange traffic given the overlap of the LSWR and GWR networks in the area.

While the LSWR station at Queen Street, later renamed Exeter Central, was in the centre of the city, it entailed a steep descent to St David's, and in the opposite direction a steep climb away from the GWR station. The opening of a competing LSWR line inland via Okehampton to Plymouth in 1876 produced the oddity of London–Plymouth trains through St David's travelling in opposite directions, with the GWR insisting on a compulsory stop for its rival's services.

St David's was rebuilt twice, once in 1864 and again between 1911 and 1914. The LSWR attempted to build a line bypassing the station in 1905, but was successfully opposed by the GWR. However, the Southern Railway did obtain parliamentary approval for a new route in 1935, but the Second World War and then nationalisation prevented this being built.

Gloucester

Although not a major centre, Gloucester achieved considerable importance to the Great Western as its first uninterrupted route into Wales and as a vital objective in its progress from Bristol to Birmingham, until foiled by the intervention of the Midland Railway. It became notorious in railway circles for the problems of transshipment between broad gauge and standard gauge. The city's significance in railway terms fell considerably after the opening of the Severn Tunnel and the conversion of the broad gauge to standard gauge, both of which meant that trains could run directly, with the Severn Tunnel route bypassing Gloucester altogether.

Truro in Cornwall was an important stop on the run westwards to Penzance, and the junction for the Falmouth branch. This was Truro West signal-box in 1930, with a breakdown spares van to the left. *(HMRS/J. Scott-Morgan ABX016)*

Truro also had its own locomotive shed, seen here also in 1930, with an 'Aberdare' class and possibly also a 'Hall' class visible. *(HMRS/J. Scott-Morgan ABX020)*

Penzance

While Falmouth with its important docks and ship-repair facilities was the objective of the Cornwall Railway running from Plymouth, the West Cornwall Railway linked up with the Cornwall at Truro. The West Cornwall had come into existence by acquiring the Hayle Railway and extending its line to Penzance, with services to Truro established in 1852, where the standard gauge line had an inconvenient break of gauge with the Cornwall Railway. In 1864, the Cornwall Railway demanded that the West Cornwall convert to mixed gauge track under legislation acquired in 1850, but the West Cornwall lacked the funds to carry out the work, and was compelled to transfer its assets to the Cornwall Railway, which was owned by the Associated Companies, the GWR, Bristol & Exeter and the South Devon, who between them had subscribed a fifth of the Cornwall's capital.

Both Cornish railways were impoverished as the county's mineral wealth was sent away by sea, and it was not until tourist traffic grew that either showed any potential. In later years Penzance became both the interchange point for the ferry to the Isles of Scilly and for early spring cut flowers from the islands on their way to London and other significant mainland markets.

Plymouth

An important naval base for many years with a less famous commercial port at Millbay, Plymouth was in fact three towns – Plymouth, Devonport (the naval base and dockyard) and Stonehouse.

Plymouth was reached by the broad gauge South Devon Railway running from Exeter in 1849, which the following year ran a short branch from its terminus at Millbay to the nearby commercial port. The South Devon joined up with the Cornwall Railway in 1859, a station was opened at Devonport and a branch to Tavistock was completed. In 1876 mixed gauge track was laid to allow the London & South Western Railway to reach Plymouth from Lydford, and much of the dockyard also had mixed gauge track. The LSWR was initially dependent on the GWR for access, but the opening of the Plymouth, Devonport & South Western Junction Railway in 1890 considerably improved matters.

In 1876 the GWR absorbed the South Devon Railway. Meanwhile, the Cornwall Railway had been authorised in 1846 to build a 66-mile line from Plymouth to Falmouth, with a connection to the West Cornwall Railway at Truro. The line was opened as far as Truro in 1859 and to Falmouth in 1863. The most significant engineering structure was Brunel's Royal Albert Bridge at Saltash, carrying the line from Devon into Cornwall, but there were many other structures along the route, although mostly originally built of timber to save money. The GWR took over the Cornwall Railway in 1889, at which time most of the line west of Plymouth was single track.

While Reading was passed through by more people than ever used this busy station, it was also an important interchange point and had sidings and shunting facilities. This was the backing signal. (*Kevin Robertson*)

Chapter Four

A New Great Western

Strictly speaking, the 1921 Act only created a 'Western Group' of railway companies, and by definition the Great Western was just one of those companies, but in fact Paddington predominated. As we have already seen, the new company might have been different, but it was the only substantial company among those grouped and the only one with access to London, and while companies such as the Cambrian had a substantial network, they had neither the balance sheet nor the reputation to influence events. The other grouped companies coped with the changes in different ways, but the Great Western was spared the infighting between Midland and London & North Western factions that did so much damage to the London, Midland & Scottish. And unlike the Southern, which sometimes seemed to pretend that grouping hadn't happened with its Western, Central and Eastern divisions and apparent reluctance to create improved access between different parts of London Bridge or Victoria, there was no doubt that the GWR was an integrated railway with an existing management structure and organisation that could easily absorb its constituent and subsidiary companies.

In one sense the 'new' GWR emphasised its identity by reverting to the 'old' GWR colours. Up to the 1860s carriages had been chocolate brown, and only then were cream upper panels introduced. In 1908 all-over chocolate was reintroduced as an economy measure, but dark red was introduced for passenger carriages in 1912, while goods wagons were either dark red or grey. The chocolate brown with cream upper panels was reintroduced in 1923, with white roofs. The company's coat of arms, a simple device showing the arms of London and of Bristol, was not amended to reflect any of the companies taken over, just as it had never been amended to demonstrate the GWR's own expansion to the south-west and into Wales and to the Midlands. The sole change was that the original coat of arms was encircled by a garter, and this was dropped during the 1930s.

Still the GWR

Yet, if the GWR of 1923 had taken everything in its stride, with most of the real work carried out during 1922 when the new management team led by Felix Pole settled down in anticipation of the formal transfer on 1 January 1923, it had not always been the case.

Much earlier, a critical point had been reached shortly after the turn of the century, when James Inglis, the chief engineer, was selected by the board to become the new general manager. In his previous role, Inglis had enjoyed considerable freedom, but he now found himself in a position where he could take a broader view, and virtually became poacher turned gamekeeper. Almost at once Inglis could see that there was no financial control and that his former department was a law unto itself. He knew that both the London & North Western and the Midland Railways operated a different system, of which the general managers were in overall charge, but at the GWR costs were out of control and the finances of the engineering departments were shrouded in mystery. He did not hesitate to take control. He was also able to compare costs, discovering that a 4–6–0 locomotive built in Swindon cost much more than one built of almost identical specification at Crewe. He tackled the new chief mechanical engineer George Churchward in front of the rest of the management team as to why his locomotives were so much more expensive, and allegedly received an offensive response. On his own Inglis could do nothing and the dispute between the general manager and engineering remained unresolved until 1908, when Viscount Churchill succeeded Alfred Baldwin as chairman, and under his leadership the directors eventually supported Inglis. A new organisational structure was issued to all departmental heads affirming the supremacy of the general manager, but it was too late for Inglis, who succumbed to the stress of the dispute and died in 1911. It was to take another ten years and the appointment of Felix Pole as general manager, almost coinciding with the retirement of Churchward, before the new structure began to work for the company and its shareholders.

The GWR was in a position to tackle the challenge of merging the other companies into its grouping, and having resolved its own structural problems it ensured that the 'Western Group' worked almost from the outset. However, not everything was as easy for the new company. No business fares well when its customers run into trouble, and for the Great Western its inheritance was a mixed blessing. It did indeed have some of the best railway lines in the country and linked London with Birmingham and Bristol, and the latter two cities together as well. On the other hand, the start of the once-prosperous South Wales coal industry's decline coincided with grouping, with output declining steadily from 1923 onwards, aided by a combination of recession and a damaging miners' strike. All of the companies faced years of depression, so that the volume of business anticipated by Parliament at the time of the grouping was never achieved, but for the GWR in South Wales and the London & North Eastern in Scotland and Yorkshire, these problems were aggravated by the collapse in the market for coal. The small companies that had fed coal to the South Wales ports from the valleys became liabilities rather than assets, and it is likely that had these companies with their short-haul and hugely local business not been absorbed into the new Great Western, some at least might not have survived. As it was, the GWR had to withdraw passenger services from some 25 route miles of railway.

There was a sense of triumph emanating from the GWR that may well have irritated many of those coming to the 'new' company from the smaller railways. The GWR had started its own employee publication, *The Great Western Railway Magazine*, as early as 1888, and the issue for January 1923 showed a cartoon, captioned 'A Survival of Title', of an explosion, with 'amalgamation' and 'upheaval' at its heart and railwaymen being thrown around, except for a man in GWR uniform saying: 'Hooray! Never even blew me cap off!'

Felix Pole, the general manager, was wont to give sometimes lengthy editorials. In this issue, after wishing every member of the GWR's staff a happy and prosperous new year, he continued:

Associated with this wish is a recognition of the estimable qualities of the Company's employees. The Great Western family has grown considerably in recent months and now exceeds a hundred thousand . . . the name of the Great Western has long been identified in the public mind with a courteous and efficient service.

Naturally, therefore, the Company's staff are proud of the fact that when, with the opening of the New Year, the titles of all of the other great railway undertakings in the country are changed, owing to the grouping . . . the name of the Great Western will continue . . .

The 'New' GWR

A highly profitable railway before the grouping, the GWR was to remain profitable overall for the difficult years between the wars, and indeed was the most profitable of the four grouped companies. Despite the large number of companies absorbed by the GWR, it was the third-largest of the groups, with only the Southern Railway being smaller. These were the only two of the so-called 'Big Four' that seemed to offer any real hope of long-term viability. Whether or not this was because they were smaller and more manageable or simply had the right markets, or perhaps because they were the most forward-looking, has to be a matter of conjecture.

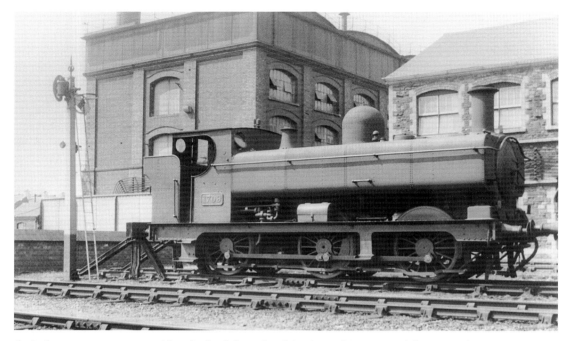

Swindon water tower provides the backdrop for this view of 0–6–0PT of the 1701 class, No. 1709, in 1934. *(HMRS AAD206)*

Grouping had indeed changed the GWR. Its route mileage had grown from 3,005 miles to 3,712 miles, while staff had grown from 87,000 to 108,000, and shareholders from 95,000 to 120,000. These figures show a very modest increase in the number of employees per route mile, from 28.95 to 29.09, which is interesting since many of the acquired companies would have had relatively lightly trafficked lines, including the light railways, although the exceptions were the heavily worked but short lines into the valleys of South Wales.

The famous named expresses are dealt with later, but while the GWR could match or even better the LMS and LNER in this field, like the Southern it was always concerned about the quality of its branch lines. The GWR was also the line least dependent on a heavy London commuter traffic, a business that brought many passengers but also many problems, with traffic concentrated into just a couple of hours in the morning and evening. When the London Passenger Transport Board was established in 1933 the receipts of all the suburban railway services within the area, less operational costs, were pooled with those of London Transport, which had taken over most of the Underground system. The GWR's share of the pool was just over 1 per cent, compared to more than 25 per cent for the Southern Railway with its large electrified suburban network.

In continuing its traditions, the GWR went much further than returning to its earlier brown and cream colour scheme. It was the only one of the major railway companies to continue the old tradition of allowing the chief mechanical engineer to retain control of locomotive operation, so that engine crews, or footplatemen, as well as the staff at sheds and works, were on his payroll. The CME's Locomotive Department was organised on a divisional basis, and the divisional locomotive, carriage and wagon superintendents enjoyed a very high degree of autonomy, with some of them actually having their own works. On many railways there was a tendency for a locomotive no longer to be assigned to a driver and fireman, with a permanent relief crew if a second shift was needed, but for all locomotives to be pooled so that a driver or fireman might not see a particular steam engine again for many months. The pooled system might have been more modern and productive, but it meant that crews were slower to recognise a developing fault, and had less interest in reporting it so that it could be corrected. Despite this pooling had its drawbacks, as the allocation of locomotives to more or less permanent named crews must have contributed towards the GWR having the lowest locomotive operating costs of any of the 'Big Four'.

Finance

For its last year as the 'old' pre-grouped Great Western, a dividend of 8 per cent was paid to shareholders, a worthwhile improvement on the 7.25 per cent paid for 1921, which had also included £125,000 from the government's compensation scheme. In fact, full control of the railways was not handed back to the companies until shortly before grouping. The period of state control had not been entirely beneficial, as control of wages had been lax while charges had been kept under tighter control.

In taking over the railway once again, managements were concerned about industrial stability. This was the theme of one of Felix Pole's editorials in the company magazine, for there were rumblings of discontent among the workforce that would ultimately lead to the famous strike by coal miners, and also the General Strike in support of them. It is important to bear in mind that in the democracies the period after the First World War was also that of the Bolshevik Revolution in Russia, which had a traumatic effect on many, not only in positions of power and authority, but also farmers and small businessmen, and those in between. The General Strike of 1926 was still far off, however, when the GWR had a strike by a number of its locomotive crews from 21 to 29 January 1924. On the other hand, a most unusual sign that the GWR's belief in the quality of most of its employees was justified came on 29 March of that year, when the season ticket holders at Weston-super-Mare gave a dinner for GWR staff at a café in the town, attended by 160 season ticket holders and railwaymen.

Concern about rising costs meant that economy was preached, and again the company magazine was used. Engine firemen were reminded that keeping full steam up after a locomotive had finished its work and was ready to be taken to the yard was wasteful, as the fires would have to be doused and coal in the fire-grate thrown out. It was pointed out that if every duty, or 'working', for a locomotive saved a shovelful of coal, it would amount to 10,000 tons of coal a year.

It was also important to dispose of old coaching stock as profitably as possible. Rather than scrapping redundant carriages, which at the time would have had relatively little metal content, these were offered for sale at prices between £18 and £27, with free delivery to anywhere on the GWR system. Those wanting delivery to another railway company's station, or delivery by road, had to pay the additional costs. As we will see in the chapter on rolling stock, following an initiative by the LNER, in the late 1920s an even better way of disposing of surplus passenger carriages was to establish camping coaches, or 'Camp Coaches' as they were known to the GWR.

There was government pressure to cut charges, with passenger fares reduced from 75 per cent to 50 per cent above pre-war levels, while goods rates were to be cut from 112 per cent to 75 per cent above. Nevertheless, traffic receipts started to decline alarmingly in 1924, although those for passengers recovered during the summer months. Part of the problem was simply the uncertain state of the economy, but this was compounded by the increasing use of road transport. The post-First World War growth in road transport reflected the greater reliability and sophistication of the vehicles, as well as many ex-military vehicles offloaded onto the market at near scrap rates, while many men had learnt to drive and maintain vehicles during the war years. In addition, there was another factor in the rising popularity of road transport that the railways could not compete with – the greater flexibility of road transport in responding to demand. For their part, the railways felt that they were discriminated against, with the GWR estimating that the company paid an average of £363 in rates and taxes for each of its locomotives, while the bus or lorry operator paid an average of £21. This discrimination extended to the status of the railways being classified as 'common carriers', which meant that they had a statutory duty to carry

In the Midlands, a 4–4–0 'Flower' class heads a train near Henley-in-Arden, 1920s. Apparently the leading carriage is still all-brown, the livery of the 1900s. *(HMRS/G.M. Perkins AAM212)*

whatever traffic was on offer, and there were controls over pricing as well, while the road haulier could refuse traffic or charge whatever the market would bear and competition allow.

While the Railway Rates Tribunal kept a strict control over what the railways could charge, one of the first acts of the Great Western's management on grouping was to bring the season ticket rates on the many lines in South Wales into line with its own charges. For most, if not all, of the commuters affected, this meant a reduction in the cost of their tickets.

Nevertheless, while overall receipts for 1924 were down by £315,000 and expenditure was up by £561,000, the dividend was maintained at 8 per cent for the year. The following year saw the dividend fall to 7 per cent, not helped by a dispute at many goods depots with workers refusing to accept certain shipments. On 3 May 1926, many GWR personnel joined the General Strike in support of the mineworkers, and volunteers were sought, many of them from the general public, to help run the railway. In the June issue of the company magazine, it was claimed that many novices had become proficient in just two days, but it was also true that the dispute had cost the company £1.8 million. Even after the return to work, the industrial situation remained uncertain, with losses as the mines stayed closed, while locomen and shunters at Swansea came out in strike again during August.

That not everyone was doing his best soon became clear, with the story in November 1926 of a goods locomotive that finished its rostered duty at 4.05 p.m. one day, and then spent the next 3¼ hours idle. Disciplinary action was taken against the driver, guard, signalman, shunter and the supervisor, who were all dismissed, but reinstated after a petition was signed by 3,000 of their colleagues, who also condemned their action. No doubt the GWR felt that relations could be improved through such a gesture.

Further evidence that all was not as well as it could be came from the fact that the regular monthly magazine feature, 'From People We Have Pleased', with letters from satisfied customers, was joined by one entitled 'From People We Intend to Please', featuring criticism. By December 1926 this had become a blunt 'From People We Have Not Pleased'.

The collieries had been stopped from May to November 1926, and the Great Western's traffic had fallen by more than £5.3 million up to 28 November. While everyone hoped that business would recover in 1927, the dividend for 1926 was chopped to just 3 per cent, not much more than an investor could get from a Post Office savings account. It returned to 7 per cent the following year, but goods traffic was struggling to recover as recession began to bite and the overseas customers for British coal had, naturally enough, taken their business elsewhere. A hopeful sign for the railways was that in August 1928 they received powers that allowed them to engage in road transport other than simply providing collection and delivery services to and from their own stations and depots. Even so, the dividend for 1928 fell once again, this time to 5 per cent. The pain was shared more widely than might be the case today, as in August 1928 employees had 2.5 per cent deducted from their gross wages. This continued until May 1930.

In 1929, the then Chancellor of the Exchequer, Winston Churchill, finally abolished the Railway Passenger Duty, a tax that had replaced that on stage-coaches and yielded the Treasury £400 million annually – about £25 billion at today's prices – and dated from 1832. Churchill was not so much concerned about the health of the railway companies or the wealth of the railway traveller, but instead wanted to help ease unemployment. It was a condition of the abolition of the duty that the railways spent the money thus saved on modernisation. The GWR decided on a programme of improvements to its stations and goods yards, while also doubling single-track stretches and quadrupling double-track stretches to ease points of congestion. It was already engaged in replacing many old wooden viaducts, and this extended not only to work on the main lines, but also to branches, including that to Falmouth in Cornwall. New goods wagons for ever-heavier loads were another area of investment. However, to the traveller, the GWR's programme may have seemed less obvious than the Southern Railway's electrification programme, which the abolition of the duty encouraged the railway to take from the suburbs and on to the main lines. The abolition of the duty was followed by a system of government grants and loans, partly so that the money saved by the duty could be more easily invested.

Sir Felix Pole was wooed away to manufacturing industry in 1928 and replaced by Sir James Milne, whose approach to editorials in the company magazine in his early days proved to be less concerned with preaching, although the steady stream of statistics about the company's business continued. As the investment in road transport continued to grow, so too did the dividend, returning to 7.5 per cent in 1929.

An express train for Leamington Spa at Birmingham Snow Hill behind 4–6–0 40XX No. 4064 *Reading Abbey*. A siphon vehicle is immediately behind the locomotive. (*HMRS/D.H. Haines AEV410*)

A new statistic introduced to GWR employees at this time was the performance ratio, which used as its base the average of the three years 1923–5, which was stated as 100. The GWR went from 97.4 in 1926, the year of the General Strike, to 101.39, the best of any of the companies. The Southern Railway went from 98.26 in 1926 to 100.93 in 1928, when the LNER achieved 100.49 and the LMS 99.8. The industry average was 98.48 in 1926 and 100.65 in 1928.

Productivity may have improved, but the dividend for 1930 went back to 5.5 per cent. There was also uncertainty in that the London Passenger Transport Bill was before Parliament and this would mean that passenger receipts, less expenses, for railway travel in that part of the railway companies' suburban network falling within the London Transport area would be pooled and the companies granted a proportion of the total.

In 1931 the Weir Committee on main-line electrification reported, but there was no formal GWR reaction, and it was not until just before the outbreak of the Second World War that the company commissioned consultants to look more closely at this issue. The dividend fell further to just 3 per cent in 1931, and remained at this figure for the following year, with passenger traffic down 3.5 per cent. To stimulate passenger traffic, summer return fares were offered just a third above those for the single journey, giving a third-class fare of 1*d* per mile. To enhance earnings from freight traffic, on those routes where there was competition with the LMS or the LNER, freight receipts were pooled.

Traffic improved considerably in 1933, but by the end of the year London suburban receipts were being pooled with those of the other main-line companies and London Transport. In the GWR's case this meant that the company, with its small suburban network, received just a little more than 1 per cent. The struggle to attract passengers continued, and the bargain rates offered to third-class passengers were extended to those in first class, who paid 50 per cent more than the third-class fare. In each case the minimum fare for the attractive new return rates to take effect was 2*s* 6*d* third-class and 4*s* first class.

Dividends of 3 per cent continued until 1936, and until 1935 this sum was being supported out of reserves. During 1931 employees had again been asked to take a pay cut of 2.5 per cent of gross earnings, but by 1937 this was reduced to 1.25 per cent and eventually abolished. Business had improved again during 1937, helped by increased passenger travel in the year of the coronation of King George VI, so that the dividend for the year rose to 4 per cent, while annual turnover rose to £32,586,547, up from £29,788,622 in 1935. The improvement was short-lived, however, as passenger travel slumped in 1938, the year of the Munich Crisis, when turnover fell to £31,039,727 and the dividend fell to ½ per cent. This must have been a time of considerable difficulty for retired shareholders, for whom the dividend was an important part of their income.

At first it seemed that worse was to come, as the dividend for 1939 had to be delayed while negotiations took place with the government over the compensation for its virtual takeover of the system. There were also the other uncertainties, for although the industrial dispute threatened on the eve of war had not taken place, a pay rise had been agreed and there were still further claims forthcoming as prices began to rise under wartime pressures. In the event, when the dividend for 1939 was declared, it was far better than for the previous year, at 3½ per cent.

From the operational point of view 1940 got off to a bad start, with what was described in one periodical as the 'worst winter on record', with heavy snow in January and February. Nevertheless, the guaranteed income after operating expenses meant that a dividend of 4 per cent was possible, and this was maintained for 1941. This was defended by the chairman on the grounds that it was an important part of their income for many shareholders who were retired, while the institutional shareholders were often pension funds. The shareholders were not the only ones to receive an increase, with a special wartime advance on wages for employees with a minimum of 4*s* a week and a maximum of 7*s*. While fewer trains were being run for the travelling public, the traffic for August 1940 was higher than that for August 1939. Such optimism had been evident in the spring that a new edition of *Holiday Haunts* had been published, but this evaporated with the invasion of

Denmark and the fall of Norway, the defeat of France and the Low Countries, and then the Battle of Britain.

The pressure on passenger services continued, and although those for the August bank holiday were curtailed the public still wanted to travel and severe overcrowding resulted. This situation continued throughout the rest of 1940 and the two years that followed, and may have been behind the Railway Executive's decision to suspend cheap-day tickets from 5 October 1942. At around the same time most of the remaining restaurant cars were withdrawn.

Early in 1943 the war advance on wages rose to 16s weekly. In an attempt to cope with the growing demand for freight wagons, a 'Q' campaign had been started earlier in the war in yet another attempt to turn wagons around more quickly. The next step, early in 1943, was to 'up-plate' wagons, so that they could carry a heavier load, and everyone was assured that the rolling stock and track engineers had examined the issue and found the increased weights to be safe. The dividend for 1942 was increased to 4.5 per cent, and held at that for 1944. While rising dividends seemed to suggest that not everything was going wrong, at the annual general meeting shareholders were told that the arrears in repairs and maintenance had reached £8.5 million, about a third more than the Great Western's guaranteed annual compensation for the use of its track and trains. The growth in arrears did not represent negligence on the part of the company, but instead it was a reflection of the shortage of materials and skilled manpower.

Some relief for the hard-pressed railway came with the arrival of 2–8–0 tender freight locomotives from the United States, to be pooled by the British Railways, a title that was being used repeatedly. Assistance in the reverse direction came when ambulance trains converted from its own rolling stock by the Great Western were handed over to the United States Army.

By January 1944 some 15,380 Great Western personnel were in the armed forces, about a seventh of the pre-war workforce. This was the peak, but as the year progressed, there were hopeful signs. Plans were prepared for the resumption of air services to the Channel Islands. However, these seemed premature. Many must have expected a German surrender of the islands at some time after the invasion of France, but instead the German commander of the forces in the islands held on to the bitter end. Nevertheless, Railway Air Services was able to restart services between London and Liverpool and between Liverpool and Belfast on Monday 13 November, while also maintaining a connection with Isle of Man Airlines at Speke. The needs of Irish workers in the UK on war work also led to a resumption of ferry services across the Irish Sea on 1 December. Later that month the Great Western contingents of the Home Guard were stood down.

The state of the railway in late 1944 was difficult. The American locomotives that had arrived in 1943 had been taken away to help the United States Army as it advanced through France. As for the Great Western's own locomotives, there was a two-year backlog for repairs and renewals. Yet passenger traffic in 1944 was 64 per cent up on 1938, and even 28 per cent up on 1923, which had been the busiest year for passenger traffic between the wars. All of this was carried on trains that travelled 23 per cent fewer miles than in 1938. Freight traffic in 1944 was double that of 1938.

The end of the war came as a relief, long expected after the invasion of France and seemingly often delayed. Unfortunately, the travelling public expected the service to return to normal as soon as possible, despite the damage and the arrears of maintenance and renewals which by this time had reached no less than £18 million. This sum was almost three times the annual compensation still being paid to the company. The annual compensation arrangement was intended to continue for at least a year after the cessation of hostilities. Nowhere was the continuing impact of the war more obvious than with the ferries, for as 1945 dawned there was just one Great Western ship not in government service.

Nevertheless, a dividend of 5 per cent was paid for 1945.

Chapter Five

The Managers

Churchward's influence on Great Western locomotive design continued well beyond his retirement, and in fact his successor seemed to be reluctant to make too many changes. *(NRM 2086/76)*

Happily the grouping came at a time when the Great Western itself had changed, with a new general manager Felix Pole, later Sir Felix, having settled into his post in 1921, and the brilliant but stubborn George Churchward having retired as chief mechanical engineer. Pole has been described as the first real general manager of the GWR. It had taken more than four decades to reach this point in the evolution of the company, which even before the grouping had been one of the world's most important railways. Indeed, as early as the 1860s one commentator had been moved to suggest that the GWR had a 'board of directors and an anti-board'.

Four men were responsible for shaping the new GWR, and while the first of these was Felix Pole, he owed his chairman Viscount Churchill much. His successor Sir James Milne built upon the foundations he had laid and was another general manager worthy of the title. Then there were the two great chief mechanical engineers, of whom Charles Collett was the more influential, being longest in post and the designer of the famous 'Castle' and 'King' class locomotives, among other achievements. Collett's successor, Frederick Hawksworth, was also forward-looking, but the scope for his imagination was limited by the requirements of maintaining a wartime railway and the shortness of his period of office before nationalisation. Nevertheless, he exacted improved performance from the company's locomotives by increasing the degree of superheating.

Viscount Churchill

Taking over in 1908, Churchill has been described as 'one of the greatest railway chairmen of the twentieth century'. When he arrived the railway was entering its most prosperous period, but then had to face the difficulties imposed by the First World War, and while these were as nothing compared with those encountered during the Second World War, state intervention meant that the railway could not be run as it needed to be, while there were manpower shortages and even locomotives and rolling stock were requisitioned to help with the war effort. Postwar came the challenge of the grouping, the miners' strike of 1926 and the related General Strike, and the years of the great depression.

Not everything was as wonderful at the GWR in 1908 as it might have seemed to outsiders. Churchill arrived to find a fierce internal battle between the general manager James Inglis and the highly respected chief mechanical engineer George Churchward. This was not simply a question of a senior officer of the company seeking to resist interference with his area of responsibility, it was nothing less than a question of who ran the company. Churchill sided with Inglis, himself formerly in charge of the GWR's engineering, and eventually persuaded his fellow directors to do the same. Sadly, the death of Inglis in 1911, and the demands of the First World War, meant that not much was done by Inglis's successor, and it was not until Felix Pole took over in 1921 that the way ahead seemed assured.

Inglis and Pole were the two greatest out of the five general managers serving under Churchill's chairmanship. Churchill retired from the board in 1934.

Charles Collett

Originally trained as a marine engineer, Charles Collett joined the GWR at Swindon as a draughtsman in 1893 when he was twenty-two years old. He became assistant works manager in 1900 and works manager in 1912, and became deputy to Churchward in 1920.

Collett took over as chief mechanical engineer in 1922, and his arrival coincided with that of Felix Pole as general manager. A protégé of Churchward, one can only assume that Collett was far easier for others to work with, and he was also an inspired CME. It was Collett who designed the 'Castle' and 'King' class 4–6–0 that for many were the finest examples of Great Western locomotives. Both these classes continued to follow Churchward's principles of locomotive design, since the 'Castle' was a development of the earlier 'Star' class. Collett also introduced further standard types, notably the 'Hall' and 'Grange' class mixed-traffic locomotives, again based on earlier types, in this case the 'Saint' class express locomotive. When they entered service the members of the 'King' class were Britain's heaviest and most powerful 4–6–0 locomotives, their operation only made possible by a relaxation in permitted axle-loadings on the company's main lines. Even so, they were not permitted to operate west of Plymouth.

Less obvious but perhaps even more important, Collett continued and developed Churchward's work on the standardisation of locomotive boilers and fittings, which must have reduced costs considerably and also shortened repair times. One of his achievements was to extend this work to the locomotives absorbed from the many smaller companies that passed into Great Western control. High-degree precision construction and repair work became the standard at Swindon, Wolverhampton and Caerphilly works, greatly extending the intervals between workshop visits, while the stationary testing plant was modernised, as was the company's dynamometer car. As a result, Collett set the accepted British standards for locomotive testing and research.

Safety was much improved by Collett's extension of the GWR's automatic train control system to all of the company's main routes, and in 1927 he became a member of the Pringle Committee that studied the use of such systems in Britain. Some have criticised Collett's later locomotive designs as being too conservative, perhaps owing too much to his mentor Churchward, but he was the first to consider complete dieselisation of the fleet, electrification being a less attractive option for the GWR as little of its route mileage experienced the heavy traffic flows and high-frequency services that made this option so worthwhile for the Southern Railway. It was also the case that Collett worked on a railway that no longer enjoyed the prosperity of earlier years. In addition to the desperate international economic situation, all of the railway companies were already suffering from the impact of road and even air competition. He retired in 1941.

Frederick Hawksworth

Hawksworth spent his entire working life on the GWR, starting during the Churchward era when he worked in the drawing office, and then under Collett as chief draughtsman. His drawings were used for *The Great Bear*, the GWR Pacific locomotive, and he supervised all of the design work for the 'King' class locomotives.

Frederick Hawksworth had a short tenure of office as chief mechanical engineer, but proved to be more radical than his predecessor, Collett. *(NRM 3210/64)*

Taking over from Collett in 1941, he kept the GWR rolling stock on the move in wartime when stations, works and lines were subjected to intense enemy aerial attack, while locomotives had to struggle to haul trains of extended length often while using inferior-quality coal. Later, despite resenting the interference of the British Transport Commission and the loss of much autonomy, he adapted the GWR's locomotives and practice to meet the new conditions, and introduced higher degrees of superheating to improve performance. Hawksworth conducted successful trials on oil-firing of steam locomotives and also was responsible for the introduction of the first gas-turbine locomotive to operate in the UK.

Sir James Milne

Like Inglis before him, Milne was an engineer. He trained and graduated in Manchester before joining the locomotive department of the GWR in 1904 at the age of twenty-one. In contrast to Inglis, however, rather than continuing to rise through the engineering ranks, Milne eventually moved to the company's head office and became involved in collecting statistics and gained operational and traffic experience. He moved to the new Ministry of Transport when it was formed in 1919, becoming director of statistics, but returned to the GWR in 1922, on the eve of grouping, as assistant general manager.

On Pole's departure in 1929, Milne took over as general manager. He inherited a company suffering from the after-effects of the miners' strike that had resulted in lost export markets for coal, with output in South Wales in decline, while wider economic depression was also taking its toll, along with growing road competition for both goods

and passengers. Milne was forced to find ways of reducing costs, but he consistently took a longer-term view, and after railway companies were allowed to invest in road transport in 1929, he took the GWR into a greater involvement in bus operation and road haulage, while later he invested in air services both through Railway Air Services and Great Western Air Services, including collaboration with the Southern Railway. He also considered main-line electrification for the GWR, but on closer examination this proved to be too costly for its less densely trafficked network, and further analysis was interrupted by the outbreak of the Second World War. He was knighted in 1932.

Sir James Milne carried the railway through the war years, and then retired rather than run the nationalised railway. As the next choice to head the railways executive found, it was a wise move. *(NRM 446/62)*

During the Second World War Milne was deputy chairman of the Railway Executive Committee, but since the Minister of War Transport was the chairman, he was *ipso facto* chairman. As plans for the railways postwar began to be discussed, including the strong possibility of nationalisation, which was Labour Party policy, Milne made clear his strong opposition to state ownership. Even so, no doubt because of his war service on the REC, he was offered the chairmanship of the Railway Executive of the British Transport Commission, but declined it, leaving the post to be offered to his counterpart at the Southern Railway.

Sir Felix Pole

Sir Felix Pole was responsible for making the 'new' post-grouping Great Western work, and was judged such a success that he was lured away to manufacturing industry. Nevertheless, his memoirs were overwhelmingly devoted to his time on the railway. *(NRM 445/62)*

A protégé and great admirer of Sir James Inglis, Felix Pole spent most of his working life with the GWR. At the age of just fourteen he joined the company as a telegraph clerk in 1891, and later worked under the civil engineer before moving to the general manager's office in 1904. For many years while he was working in the general manager's office, Pole edited *The Great Western Railway Magazine*, working on this part-time, while he had already gained a reputation as a writer on railway matters.

Appointed general manager in 1921, inevitably Pole spent most of the following year preparing for the grouping. In contrast to some of the other groupings, which were mergers of equals or near-equals, and there were two or three possible candidates for the general managership of the post-grouping company, there was no doubt that Pole of the GWR would run the new railway. His new responsibilities included taking over no fewer than twenty-one Welsh companies, as well as a network of ports and docks, many in South Wales. He introduced the GWR to the concept of regular interval main-line services out of Paddington in 1924, so that passengers did not have to carry a timetable. He was also very conscious of the importance of a good public image for the company, and had also done much earlier in his career to improve communications with employees by revamping *The Great Western Railway Magazine* while working in the general manager's office. He was knighted in 1924.

The railways were not the only industrial sector to undergo mergers in the 1920s (other companies emerging at this time included Imperial Chemical Industries, ICI), and in 1928 Pole was persuaded to leave the GWR and assume the chairmanship of another large industrial grouping, Associated Electrical Industries, AEI, where he remained. This type of move, commonplace today, was most unusual at the time.

In later life Pole was afflicted by blindness, but even so he managed to write an autobiography, most of which was devoted to his time on the railways, clearly much more exciting to him than running factories.

Chapter Six

Steam on the Great Western

Although the Great Western Railway was renowned for its preference for the 4–6–0 wheel arrangement, the company had the distinction of building Britain's first powerful 4–6–2 Pacific locomotive, No. 111 *The Great Bear*. Many believe that Churchward built this large locomotive for prestige purposes, and while it seemed to be prized by the GWR management, possibly because of its novelty value, the designer's dislike of it was well known. Judged objectively, *The Great Bear* was the wrong type of locomotive for the GWR, as its heavy axle loading confined it to the line between London and Bristol. It was not surprising that soon after grouping, it was rebuilt as a 'Castle' class locomotive.

While innovative in so many ways, the GWR was also prone to be conventional in many others, especially after the grouping when the company became much less aggressive in its style. While the three other 'Big Four' companies built Pacific locomotives, with the Southern being the last to do so, the GWR stuck steadfastly to its 4–6–0 locomotives. The GWR was also conservative in its use of superheating, and although older locomotives were modified to have superheating and this was standard in new locomotives, the degree of superheating was far less than that adopted by other railways. Despite much progress being made in this area by the chief mechanical engineer for the Great Western's final years, Frederick Hawksworth, it was not until after nationalisation that the superheating in many former GWR locomotives was improved.

The first 4-6-2 steam locomotive in Great Britain was the Great Western's No. 111 *The Great Bear*, but it was also the company's last as its designer, Churchward, did not like it. It was rebuilt as a 'Castle' Class locomotive. (*HMRS ABL105*)

An express near Gwinear Road behind 4–6–0 No. 4077 *Chepstow Castle*, c. 1930. *(HMRS/D.H.Haines AEV035)*

Part of the problem was that when Churchward retired his role was taken over by his former assistant, Charles Collett, who seems to have remained in the shadow of his guide and mentor. In fact, much of Charles Collett's work as chief mechanical engineer could be said to be refinements of Churchward's designs and especially his 'Star' class locomotives, which first appeared in 1907. The result was clear. After the grouping an exchange of locomotives in 1925 with the London & North Eastern Railway showed the GWR contenders in a good light, with better economy than their LNER counterparts,. However, after nationalisation, the reverse was the case. This judgement may have been unduly harsh, as, to be fair, the ex-Great Western locomotives were given poor-quality coal and had always been designed to use the best-quality Welsh steam coal. It was not until Collett retired and was replaced by his deputy, Frederick Hawksworth, that superheating began to improve, with notable results, especially when locomotives were forced to use poorer-quality coal.

Appendix IV on page 187 gives details of the main classes of GWR steam locomotives, including those built by the company before the Grouping, while Appendix VI on page 218 provides details of the locomotives absorbed by the company from the other constituent companies and the subsidiary companies. Many of the locomotives inherited from elsewhere were withdrawn over the space of a few years, but the rest were rebuilt in the GWR pattern, including replacement tapered boilers. In addition, a number of the smaller lines were in any case worked by the GWR before the grouping. A substantial number of small 0–4–0 tank locomotives worked in the marshalling yards and in the extensive docklands that fell into the company's hands on grouping.

Post-grouping, as well as rebuilding the absorbed locomotives, the inherited locomotive sheds were rebuilt along GWR lines. This was a clever move in standardisation of locomotives and maintenance facilities, but it also drove home to the former employees of the many small Welsh companies that they were now part of the Great Western 'family', as the general manager Felix Pole liked to call it. Everything would have to be done the Great Western way. At the same time an air of practicality ensured that the Welsh valley lines had their own workshops at Caerphilly, recognising the sheer number of mainly small locomotives working in the Welsh valleys and docks, which could have strained the resources of Swindon considerably, as well as increasing congestion on the busy main line, had they been sent away for major overhauls or rebuilding.

Churchward was, probably with Daniel Gooch, one of the two most influential GWR chief engineers. He bought three 4–4–2 Atlantic compound locomotives from France and converted the GWR's 4–6–0 No. 171 *Albion* to the same wheel arrangement for comparison, and also constructed a further Atlantic at Swindon. After trials, Churchward decided that the 4–6–0 wheel arrangement and four cylinders was better suited to the GWR's requirements and the result was the 'Star' class.

No substantial railway can be served by one type of locomotive alone, and Churchward also designed 4–4–0, 2–6–0 and 2–8–0 tender locomotives for the GWR, as well as 4–4–2, 2–6–2 and 2–8–0 tank engines, all with two cylinders. The 2–6–2T s were the famous GWR Prairie tanks, built in both large and small variants. Later 4–6–0 locomotives had three or four cylinders.

One unique characteristic of GWR locomotives was that they were mainly 'right-hand drive', that is the driving position was on the right of the footplate rather than on the left, as on other British railways. The conversion from broad gauge to standard gauge had left sufficient space between the lines for signals to be placed.

Of course, to even the casual onlooker the profusion of brass and the copper-capped chimneys were the hallmarks of the GWR, but also on many of the locomotives, and not always the fastest or most powerful, were the elegant tapered boilers. Except for two experiments with domed front ends, the GWR did not go in for streamlining as such, doubtless regarding it as a vulgar fad. Bearing in mind that the 'Coronation' class Pacifics of the LMS and many of the air-smoothed (as opposed to streamlined) 'Merchant Navy', 'West Country' and 'Battle of Britain' classes of the Southern Railway were rebuilt after nationalisation, the GWR may have had a point.

The GWR's dalliance with streamlining was simply to adapt two locomotives, one from the 'Castle' class, No. 5005 *Manorbier Castle*, and another from the 'King' class, No. 6014 *King Henry VII*,

April 1931, and 4–6–0 No. 2941 heads a Birmingham to Bristol express near Leverton Halt. *(HMRS/D.H. Haines)*

STEAM ON THE GREAT WESTERN

in 1935. These were fitted with partial streamlining consisting of a bullet nose to the front of the smokebox and coverings over the external cylinders, air-smoothing of a number of other items, including the chimney and safety valve cowling, a long splasher and a wedge front to the cab. The streamlining remained on the 'Castle' until 1947, and on the 'King' until its withdrawal.

Probably of more use to the efficient running of steam locomotives was the introduction some years earlier, in 1928, of a new style of steel tyre for locomotive wheels, with a redesigned flange that increased the area of contact with the railhead. This improved traction across the full range of locomotives, not just the expresses, and also provided greater stability and safety on tight bends.

Despite its growing interest in diesel railcars, in 1932 the Great Western introduced new 0–6–0T locomotives for 'accelerated auto services', so improvements were not confined to the main lines.

There was another characteristic of the Great Western express locomotives as the Second World War approached. This was that many of them were fitted with speedometers. An initial 100 were fitted during the late 1930s and many believed that the programme should be extended to most, if not all, locomotives. Today, when every inch of track is subject to a speed limit, often with sharp reductions at junctions and stations, it seems surprising that on the railways speed was once left to the judgement and experience of the driver.

Away From Home

The popular myth has grown up that the pre-grouping railway companies operated in self-contained units, but the opposite was the case, with many long-distance trains running efficiently through the territories of several companies. Neither the west coast nor the east coast routes from London to Scotland would have worked without close collaboration, and there were many other examples, of which the most ambitious was Britain's longest railway journey, Aberdeen to Penzance, via York, Birmingham and Bristol, a distance of some 860 miles.

The Great Bear after rebuilding as a 4–6–0 'Castle' class in 1924, still retaining its number but renamed *Viscount Churchill* after the company's chairman. *(HMRS/J.P. Gill ABL001)*

There were also many joint lines. For every example of insularity there were others in which railwaymen were obviously interested in pursuing what would today be regarded as 'best practice'. In fact, some companies developed close working relationships, such as the London & South Western and the Midland, later the Southern and the LMS, while the GWR and LNER found they had much to gain from liaison, in addition to the Aberdeen–Penzance service.

One of the first acts of the newly nationalised railway was to organise a system of locomotive exchanges between what had been the former companies, so that the best-performing design might be recognised, or the special qualities of each identified. The objective was to provide the basis for a new standardised design, and while the British Railways standard designs that eventually emerged were certainly handsome locomotives, owing much to LMS practice and design, one might question why they bothered as the days of steam were clearly numbered.

However, there was nothing novel about the exchanges. It had all been done before.

Stung by criticism from the new general manager of the Great Western that his 4–6–0 locomotives were the most expensive of any on the country's railways, Churchward had proposed an exchange to his opposite number, C.J. Bowen Cooke of the London & North Western Railway, in 1909. The GWR locomotive No. 4005 *Polar Star* worked LNWR expresses between Euston and Crewe, and showed its superiority by low fuel consumption and trouble-free running. In exchange, an LNWR 4–6–0 running on Great Western tracks was found to be less powerful and was also hampered by the low water capacity of its tender and the greater distances between water troughs on the GWR.

A little more than a decade later, in 1920, the North British Railway was deciding whether to build an 0–8–0 tender locomotive for its heavy coal and iron-ore traffic, or to see what performance could be gained from the locomotives of other companies. The North British had a design of its own that had been available since 1908, but had never been built, and had also sampled a North Eastern Railway 0–8–0 in 1916. The NBR's traffic

Double-heading was not as much a feature of the Great Western as it was on the Midland Railway, but even so, this was necessary at times with heavy trains and severe gradients, or it could be the means of avoiding a light engine working over a busy stretch of line. Here 4–4–0 No. 3252 *Fowey* pilots a 2–6–2T No. 45XX through Matley in 1923, which is probably why the carriages are still in lake livery. *(HMRS AEQ808)*

superintendent, Major Stamp, was attracted by the GWR 2–8–0s of the 'E' group. On the North British the company's most powerful goods locomotives had to be double-headed when the train reached twenty-eight wagons, but Stamp knew that the GWR 2–8–0s regularly managed such loads on their own over the steeply graded line between Lostwithiel and Liskeard.

Anxious to test a GWR 2–8–0 on its lines, the NBR approached the southern company and permission was given. The main obstacle in fact was finding a suitable route for one of the locomotives, No. 2846, to make its way to Scotland, but this was resolved and the test was fixed for 12 January 1921, with a run set for the 6 miles between Bridge of Earn and Glenfarg.

The day of the trial dawned with poor weather conditions. There were strong gales and blizzards, while the section chosen for the test lay under snow. The North British sent forward one of its 0–6–0 tender locomotives with twenty-three loaded 16-ton wagons with a total weight of 437 tons, plus two brake vans, but the locomotive stalled after steaming a short distance up a steep gradient and the entire train had to be pulled back to Bridge of Earn. The GWR locomotive was given a load of twenty-nine wagons with a total weight of 552 tons, plus two brake vans, and set off, climbing easily to reach Glenfarg in the 25 minutes allotted for the run. A further test saw another five wagons added to the train, and while No. 2846 got away easily, after 2 miles it began to slip on the icy rails and eventually stalled.

At the British Empire Exhibition at Wembley in 1924, adjacent stands had one of the London & North Eastern Railway's new A1 4–6–2 Pacific locomotives on display and a GWR 4–6–0 'Castle' class, proudly proclaiming its higher tractive power. Despite some reluctance on the part of the LNER's locomotive department, an exchange was organised for 1925. The GWR 'Castle' class No. 4079 *Pendennis Castle* worked well, pulling heavy expresses between King's Cross and Doncaster, and impressing observers by making good, slip-free, starts from King's Cross and through the steeply graded tunnels leading away from this terminus. On services from Paddington the LNER A1 Pacific No. 4474 also proved to be a good reliable locomotive and was perfectly capable of handling the maximum load for the 'Cornish Riviera' express, but its one weakness was its much heavier coal consumption.

The LNER was at least as convinced that Pacifics were the right answer to its problems as the GWR was convinced that the 4–6–0s were right for the lines of the West of England and Wales.

The London, Midland & Scottish Railway was born into far less happy and decisive circumstances, with differences over just what the right express locomotive configuration would be. Part of the problem was that one of the predecessor companies, the Midland Railway, had a tradition of building and operating small locomotives, making frequent use of double-heading, while at the London & North Western larger locomotives were the order of the day, and it was felt that double-heading was uneconomic, which it certainly was in manpower terms.

The newly knighted general manager of the GWR, Sir Felix Pole, proposed the loan of a 'Castle' class to the LMS, which doubtless welcomed this as a way round the factional fighting that had continued after the grouping. In late October 1925 No. 5000 *Launceston Castle* was transferred on loan to the LMS. Once again the 'Castle' class locomotive was put through its paces and proved capable of handling single-headed even heavier trains than the former LNWR locomotives when running between Euston and Crewe. Nevertheless, this was as untypical of the overall LMS network as running between Paddington and Bristol was for the GWR. When the 'Castle' class was sent further north to work around Carlisle in the worst of the winter weather, its sanding gear proved to be inadequate. Despite this, the LMS had been impressed with the low coal consumption of the 'Castle' class and bore many of its design features in mind, even though they went for three cylinders rather than four when designing the 'Royal Scot' class, which was referred to internally as an 'Improved Castle'. Despite the LMS later building further 4–6–0s such as

There is an air of antiquity about this 0–6–0, No. 1188, heading a goods train in 1923. *(HMRS/D.A. Bayliss AEP501)*

the highly successful Stanier 'Black Five' 4–6–0 mixed-traffic locomotives, in the long run only the GWR remained faithful to the 4–6–0 for its heaviest and fastest locomotives.

Always publicity-conscious, the GWR accepted when the Baltimore & Ohio Railroad issued an invitation to send a locomotive to the United States to take part in that company's centenary celebrations in 1927, known as the 'Fair of the Iron Horse'. No. 6000 *King George V* was sent to Baltimore and was exhibited between 24 September and 15 October, each day joining the procession of locomotives past the viewing stands. After the fair the locomotive was run on the Baltimore & Ohio's metals, with a train as heavy as the 'Cornish Riviera' plus a dynamometer car, and without the relief of slip coaches to be cast off along the way, so that the full load had to be hauled over 272 miles, almost 50 miles further than Paddington–Plymouth by the Castle Cary route. The big disadvantage faced by the footplate crew was that the Welsh steam coal on which GWR locomotives thrived was not available and a hard gas coal had to be used instead, which produced a considerable volume of clinker in the firebox.

For its visit to the American railway system *King George V* had to be modified with a cowcatcher, headlamp and bell, but much of this paraphernalia was abandoned when it returned home, except for the bell. Thereafter, the locomotive was always referred to by railwaymen on the Great Western as 'The Bell'.

The Americans were said to have been impressed by the performance of the locomotive, including its smooth ride and the absence of black smoke. Indeed, later on *The Great Western Railway Magazine* was to see similarities between new Baltimore & Ohio locomotives and those of the GWR. One advantage that the 'King' class would have had, compared to American locomotives, was that it was much smaller and lighter, having less of its own weight to pull around, but American locomotives were built that way on purpose to cover that country's much longer distances.

While the Great Western never attempted an official steam record, leaving that between the wars to the impoverished London & North Eastern Railway, as the achievement of the *City of Truro* had shown much earlier, when it became the first locomotive to set a speed record, albeit unofficial, of more than 100mph on 9 May 1904, it was not averse to pushing

By contrast this humble 0–6–0, class 2251 No. 2204, looks modern, smart and well cared for, despite the dust and the filth of the coaling stage. *(HMRS AAD202)*

the limits whenever it could. Shortly before the outbreak of the Second World War, on 31 July 1939, No. 4086 *Builth Castle* managed to run at a speed of 100mph on an ordinary Paddington to Worcester express, staying at this speed for 4½ miles near Honeybourne. The train had seven carriages at the time, giving it a load of 243 tons. This was, of course, of far more use than many of the official records, but it also lacked the publicity value and it seems strange that the company did not make more of this. The performance was even more noteworthy as this was not a new locomotive, having been built at Swindon in 1925.

While the Great Western was proud of its record in building its own locomotives, and Swindon even built a number for other railways including, in pre-grouping days, the Taff Vale, the company was not opposed to buying locomotives from elsewhere, especially if it thought that there was a bargain to be had. The best example occurred when a number of surplus locomotives built for the War Department became available during the 1920s. The first batch of these locomotives had seen little or no service, but the same could not be said of those received later, which were in poor condition, having seen considerable service abroad with little of the attention that a steam locomotive needs to remain efficient. The story of these locomotives is covered at the end of Appendix VI (page 227). There is the impression that some of the less well-maintained locomotives must have been an embarrassment to the company, and even a 'punishment' duty for their crews, as they were given little attention and were in effect run into the ground before withdrawal, which followed whenever they failed.

The Second World War saw thirty-nine Great Western locomotives requisitioned by the British Army for service overseas. Wartime losses and the increased traffic, with freight traffic in 1944 double that of 1938, was meant to be relieved by the arrival of US-standard 2–8–0 locomotives. These were modified for use on Britain's railways by the Great Western, but were intended to operate as a 'pool' among the British railway companies. Known as the S160 class, the first arrived in early 1943. The Allied invasion of Normandy soon changed this plan, and the locomotives were taken back by the United States Army and promptly sent abroad. In all, they only served in Great Britain for about a year.

Some idea of the layout of a coaling stage can be gathered from this view of 0–6–0 class 2301 No. 2439 in 1930. The coal is taken from the wagons on the raised line and transferred by small wagons to the locomotive tender: a time-consuming and labour-intensive activity. *(HMRS/J. Scott-Morgan ABX113)*

Automatic Train Control and Communication

The Great Western was one of the pioneers of automatic train control, although as the accident at Norton Fitzwarren showed it was not always proof against an accident. Between the wars the then chief mechanical engineer, Charles Collett, extended the GWR's automatic train control system to all of the company's main routes. In 1927 he became a member of the Pringle Committee that studied the use of such systems in Britain.

Traditionally, when operating in fog, the railways called out fogmen, railway workers who had been trained to stand beside each distant signal and place two detonators on the line when the signal was at danger, giving the driver enough time to stop at the next home signal. This was an extra duty for the permanent way staff, and it was both labour-intensive and costly. As the detonators had to be removed once the signal stood at clear, it could mean that a driver went some considerable distance without having any indication of the signalling, and doubtless there must sometimes have been the nagging suspicion that perhaps the fogman hadn't had time to put down the detonators if the fog had only just come down and he hadn't arrived at his post. It was also possible if fog had been a problem for some time that the fogman had succumbed to fatigue or even been taken ill. Before the clean air acts after the Second World War, in the industrialised and heavily built-up parts of the British Isles, thick fog could persist for days.

This system was so obviously unsatisfactory that a primitive form of fog warning device had been developed in the 1890s, but on the North Eastern Railway, not the Great Western. The NER's locomotive superintendent, Vincent Raven, designed and installed a stop arm which was placed in the middle of the track and linked to the signal arm. When the signal was set at danger, the stop arm would be raised and strike a pendulum lever mounted under the cab of the locomotive, which when struck blew a whistle in the cab. This was a vast improvement as it removed the need to get fogmen into position quickly, but it still suffered from the drawback that it did not reassure a driver that all was truly clear ahead. Nevertheless, the NER did well to get this system into position at every signal on its system, but as a link in the east coast route from London to Scotland, and with trains running across country to get to the Humber ports, it must have had many locomotives from other companies running through its system that were not fitted with the stop arm pendulum.

It was recognised by the Great Western that whenever visibility was poor it was as important to give drivers the reassurance that the line ahead was clear as it was to warn them of danger. The Signal and Locomotive departments cooperated on developing a system that would give an audible warning, letting the driver know whether a distant signal was in the clear or the warning position by using different sounds for the two positions. To ensure reliability, the actuating device laid in the track should have no moving parts and not be mechanically linked to the signal arm. It should also be failsafe, so that any failure of the equipment would sound a warning in the locomotive cab. In about 1905 the solution was developed, with a ramp varying in length between 40 and 60ft, depending on the line speed, set between the tracks some way ahead of the distant signal, and sloping at both ends but rising to 4in above track level. The top of the ramp was an inverted 'T' bar, electrically energised when the distant signal was set at clear, but dead when the signal was at caution, or if the equipment had failed for whatever reason.

Underneath the locomotive, a plunger hung 2½in above the level of the rails, but was spring-loaded so that whenever it passed over the ramp it lifted 1½in. The apparatus for the warning signals was placed in the driving cab. Every time the plunger made contact with a ramp, it opened a small air valve in the warning apparatus, and if there was no electrical current, the air valve caused a warning siren to sound. If the ramp was energised, the electrical current would pass up the plunger and electromagnets in the warning apparatus would in turn be energised, closing the air valve and ringing a bell for the brief period that the plunger was in contact with the ramp. This meant that the audible signals were so different that there could be no misunderstanding, while the driver and fireman had the comfort of actually knowing that all was clear on the line ahead. As a further safety measure the driver had to cancel the siren, or warning signal, whenever it sounded.

The GWR then took the working of the system a step further by incorporating a safety device, so that when the air valve opened to operate the siren, it also admitted air to the brake pipes. This ensured that if the driver didn't acknowledge the siren, the vacuum in the braking system was broken and the train quickly brought to a halt. Not only did the driver now have the assurance that all was well ahead and that his train hadn't been forgotten, but there was also a safeguard in case the driver was incapacitated or negligent.

Equipping all of the Great Western's lines and locomotives was a major task. The Signal Department fitted the equipment at distant signals while the Locomotive Department equipped the engines. By the outbreak of the First World War 180 route miles of track and ninety locomotives had been equipped. Further progress was delayed by the First World War and the inevitable shortage of materials and skilled manpower, but postwar the work continued, so that by late 1931 the track devices were in place on 2,130 route miles. The withdrawal of the duty on railway passenger travel in 1929 and the availability of government-guaranteed loans during the 1930s meant that the GWR was able to allocate some of the funds available to extend the system, and the work involved was such that signalling contractors had to become involved as well as the company's own resources. The entire main-line network and 3,000 locomotives were involved in the scheme.

A demonstration given for senior managers of the London & North Eastern Railway in 1938 showed that an express headed by a 'Castle' class locomotive and drawing ten carriages could be brought to a halt from 69mph in 900yd. The distant signal was set at caution and the driver instructed to ignore the siren. The ramp was set 318yd ahead of the distant signal, which in turn was 1,032yd ahead of the home signal, so that the train in question was stopped 450yd ahead of the danger point.

That the system was not adopted earlier and more widely by the other railway companies was partly a reflection of their poor financial situation, and partly a question of it being 'not invented here', or NIH, as the instinctive reaction of most senior railway officers was that their way was the best.

Colour light signals were becoming increasingly commonplace even before the Second World War, and the system needed to keep pace with these changes. Although on some lines, colour light signalling showed just three aspects, red, yellow and green, most installations used four aspects – red, single yellow, double yellow and green. In October 1947, a little more than two months before nationalisation, a modified system capable of coping with colour light signalling was successfully demonstrated. The bell still sounded if the signals were set at clear showing a green light. At caution or a double yellow, a horn sounded, while at the next stage, a single yellow, the siren sounded, and if this was ignored the brakes were applied.

Another system that must have helped safety came with the experiments just before the start of the Second World War for a means of communication between the driver and the guard of a train. Guards could only hope to catch the attention of the driver once a train was on the move by signalling, and hoping that the driver would occasionally glance back to see that everything was in order. A new invention, the 'laudaphone', brought telephonic communication to the guard's compartment and the driving cab. The noise of a locomotive travelling at speed was such that a conventional telephone would have been almost useless, and in any case 'hands-free' operation was necessary, at least on the footplate. The 'laudaphone' attracted the driver's attention by flashing a luminous indicator and by a loud high-frequency continuous buzzing, while voice communication was considerably amplified. The main value of this lay in the guard being able to communicate with the driver if a passenger was taken ill, rather than suddenly applying the brakes as the train neared a station.

Water Troughs

For the longer-distance railway companies, water rather than coal was the limiting factor in steam locomotive range. Stopping to take on water or change a locomotive took time, and especially on competing routes the companies were anxious to cut journey times as much as possible. It was also true that a locomotive pulling away from a standstill used more fuel than one steaming at a constant high speed.

The solution was quite clearly one that would allow a steam locomotive to collect water without stopping, and the solution was found by John Ramsbottom, the then locomotive superintendent of the London & North Western Railway, in 1860. This consisted of a trough between the rails from which a locomotive fitted with a scoop beneath its tender could pick up water. Part of the fireman's duties was to lower the scoop and raise it again, while the speed of the locomotive needed to be sufficient for the water to be forced up a vertical pipe and into the tender. The first working trough was at Mochdre in North Wales.

The obvious dangers of such a system were that the fireman could lower the scoop too soon or raise it too late, and this was overcome by putting lineside boards to indicate when to lower and raise the scoop. Far less obvious as locomotive speeds increased was that a massive volume of water could be forced up the pipe under such pressure that the tender's water tank would soon be filled to overflowing. It was not that uncommon for the carriage behind the locomotive to be soaked, and on one occasion water overflowed from a tender with such force that it smashed the eyeglass of a locomotive passing in the opposite direction.

Among the longer-distance companies in England, only the London & South Western failed to introduce them. This meant that its expresses, which were meant to compete with the Great Western, had to have locomotive changes or water stops on their way from Waterloo to Exeter, usually on Down journeys at Wilton, the first station after passing Salisbury, little more than 80 miles from London. The Southern Railway, preoccupied with

Essential elements for high-speed long-distance railway services in the days of steam were the water troughs. These examples are at Goring on the main line west from Paddington. *(Kevin Robertson)*

A Churchward-designed Mogul , aka a 2–6–0 tender locomotive, picks up water from a trough. Only tender locomotives could use troughs, as tank engines were found to split their tanks when picking up water in this way. *(Kevin Robertson)*

electrification, did not correct this omission, doubtless looking ahead to the time when it would introduce diesels on its West Country services.

The Great Western installed its first water troughs at Ludlow in 1896, and in 1898 installed them on the relief lines at Goring. In due course other locations were to include Keynsham, Rowington Junction, Creech, Chipping Sodbury, Exminster, Westbury, Aldermaston, Magor, Charlbury, Denham, Ferryside and Aynho. Some companies had water troughs every 30 miles or so, but on the Great Western the interval between troughs varied between 21 miles, between Chipping Sodbury and Magor in South Wales, near Severn Tunnel Junction, and 91 miles between Magor and Ferryside. There was also a water trough between Denham and Ruislip, just 12 miles out from Paddington. The usual distance between water troughs on the company's network was between 40 and 70 miles. The distance between water troughs on the Great Western put 'foreign' locomotives at something of a disadvantage when running on Great Western lines.

The actual troughs themselves also varied in length, probably to some extent because of the prevailing line speed, as slow-moving goods trains might require a longer run through the trough to obtain the required volume of water. Most seem to have been 560yd in length, rather more than a quarter of a mile, but Ferryside was 620yd, as was Keynsham, and Ludlow was 615yd, while Chipping Sodbury was just 542yd.

An obvious weakness of water troughs was that in cold weather the water froze. If the ice was thin enough, the scoop could break through and no damage was done, but it was soon the rule that an eighth of an inch of ice would mean the closure of the water trough and a stop to take on water, with an obvious knock-on effect on schedules. Because the act of scooping up water meant that a quantity was always splashed around the adjoining tracks, it then became the rule that water troughs could not be used if there was an inch of ice on adjoining sleepers, otherwise large accumulations of ice could build up and potentially cause a derailment.

The Great Western had to warn its track gangers not to break the ice as they were passing a frozen water trough, as their good intentions could cause damage to the surrounds of the trough. In fact, water troughs were severe in the strain they placed on the surrounding track, and as a rule the troughs themselves needed an overhaul every ten years or so.

Tank engines were unable to use water troughs, as it was soon discovered that the pressure of water tended to split their tanks.

While water troughs looked simple, the supply of water to them required some costly arrangements. No less important was the quality of the water itself. Any user of water for industrial purposes preferred soft water, as hard water caused limescale which reduced efficiency and was costly to remove. Steam locomotives were never an exception to this, and while most of the water sources in the West of England and Wales were soft, those in the Midlands and towards London were hard. Water for the troughs had to be softened, which was usually done by adding small quantities of lime, soda or ash.

Fuel

Even at the time of the grouping 'fuel' in railway terms usually meant coal, and this was the other basic ingredient of a steam railway. The railways were massive consumers of coal, with a typical Great Western tender locomotive carrying a load of 6 tons when full.

The GWR used a system of coal stages, with loaded coal wagons shunted onto a line that ran through the upper part of the coaling stage, from which its load was transferred to trolleys, each of which could carry 5 or 10cwt (250 or 500kg, approximately) of coal, and the trolleys carried the coal across a platform to be tipped over the side into the tender of a waiting locomotive.

Coaling tank engines needed considerable care, as the tight confines of their small bunkers meant that damage to the rear of the driving cab and its windows was all too easy, hence the modifications that gave rise to the 'Birdcage' locomotives that are mentioned in Appendix IV (page 187).

There were a number of major problems with coal as a fuel, even though during the period under review air pollution was not seen as one of these. Locomotive performance varied considerably depending on the quality of the coal provided, although superheating minimised this to some degree, and performance was also affected by the skill of the fireman, perhaps even more than the skill of the driver. Coal was bulky to move, difficult and dirty to handle, and also required considerable manpower. Much of the coal being carried over the lines in the Welsh valleys and beyond was for the railway's own needs.

At the end of the Second World War the Great Western started to experiment with the use of oil for its steam locomotives. With so many of its firemen away on active service, and many of those returning having been out of practice for some years, the lack of skill on the footplate was becoming noticeable, while in the chaos and shortages of the immediate post-war period no customer could be sure of getting their first choice of coal. Much of the coal supplied to the railways was completely unsuited for their requirements.

In 1947 a number of Great Western locomotives, mainly of the 'Hall' class and including No. 4972 *Saint Brides Hall*, which had been built in 1930, were converted to oil-firing. The experiment was an immediate success, so much so that the company, with government support, began to install oil-storage tanks at some of its locomotive sheds while the government began to encourage other companies to follow the GWR's lead. The GWR maintained that the scheme would also save good-quality coal for other industrial applications unable to convert to oil, while reducing the number of coal trains on its network. It even envisaged completely converting its services in Cornwall to oil-fired locomotives.

Nevertheless, the infrastructure of the railway was based on its locomotives using coal, and to extend oil-firing meant that refuelling depots, each of 36,000 gallon capacity, had to be built, with the first at Llanelly and Severn Tunnel Junction. Locomotives also had to be adapted to the new fuel while their tenders were fitted with 1,800 gallon tanks. Comparative figures showed that an oil-fired 2–8–0 freight locomotive burned 6.5 gallons per mile working under a heavy load, compared with 72lb of coal: in practical terms, this meant that the range of an oil-fired locomotive was roughly half as much again as for one using coal. An added bonus to the more reliable performance was that scarce labour was saved in the running sheds as ash no longer had to be removed.

Despite the promise that oil-firing held out to the railways and the massive investment in new or altered facilities, the scheme came to an abrupt end in 1948, when the government realised that the country's dollar reserves were almost exhausted and that there was insufficient currency with which to purchase oil. This was a monumental blunder and a waste of resources at a time when even the day-to-day maintenance needs of the railways could not be met because of the shortage of essential materials.

Chapter Seven

Diesels and Gas Turbines

By 1923 the internal combustion engine was no longer a novelty, and was increasingly reliable and better understood, largely owing to the First World War where many of those in the armed forces had encountered it. At the same time another major issue was that of railway electrification. Electrification had been proven to bring massive benefits to the travelling public and to the railways on busy suburban routes, and was by this time also extending to the outer suburbs, but the question now being asked was whether or not it had the potential for main-line work?

Early in 1923 *The Great Western Railway Magazine* carried a shortened version of a paper delivered at a conference in London on the subject of main-line electrification. For its readers, mainly although not entirely Great Western railwaymen, the advantages were examined in some detail, as were the disadvantages of steam power. Among the advantages were that the electric, or for that matter diesel, locomotive did not consume fuel while sitting idle between duties, unlike a steam locomotive that had to maintain steam. Both the new forms of propulsion were capable of being started and operational within a couple of minutes, while the steam locomotive needed to be attended by a fire-setter some three hours before its crew turned up, and when they did arrive, it took them a further hour to get the locomotive ready.

There were other advantages as well. Using steam locomotives, if a heavy train needed to be double-headed, each locomotive needed its own two-man crew, while using electric or diesel locomotives, only the leading locomotive needed a crew. It was interesting to note that the electric or diesel locomotives were still regarded as needing a 'crew' rather than just one man, even on a train with a guard. The fact that having a double-ended locomotive meant that time did not have to be wasted turning the locomotive round, with the attendant use of fuel and the need to find a path through the approaches to a busy terminus, was not mentioned. Nevertheless, when electric engines were built for the Metropolitan Railway in 1907 these were double-ended, although just a little earlier locomotives had been built with a central driver's cab and sloping ends so that there was a view in both directions from the cab.

The cost of coal was rising and a campaign to cut waste was introduced early in the life of the grouped GWR. At the end of a shift, a locomotive had to be cleaned, and before that could happen the fires had to be put out and the locomotive allowed to cool. Coal still burning in the firebox had to be raked out and was wasted. Diesel and electric propulsion simply meant switching off and no fuel was wasted.

There were other advantages that may to us today seem less obvious, but to the railwaymen of the day were all too real. Much of the coal hauled along the lines of the railway companies was for their own use. Having the coal go straight to a power station would free up many lines for other revenue-earning traffic. There was also at this stage some concern about the development of power station capacity, and railway electrification was seen as a means of encouraging this. Coaling a steam locomotive was also a dirty and labour-intensive business that took longer using the coaling stages than refuelling a diesel, while, of course, this was not a problem with an electric engine. Later, massive coaling apparatus lifting an entire goods wagon at a time would reduce both time and manpower, but these were not in general use at the time.

In its relatively short lifespan the 'new GWR' was to play an important role in the development of diesel power for passenger and parcels use with its railcars, and for shunting use as well. It was also to look forward not to diesel but to the still more modern gas-turbine propulsion for main-line passenger use, although, sadly, by the time the first two prototypes came into service the GWR was but a memory.

The Early Railcars

The problem of serving sparsely populated rural areas has been a perennial one for the railways, which have to bear the full cost of their infrastructure. Responsibility for the infrastructure can be a good thing on a busy route where the railway can dictate the standard of the infrastructure and how and when maintenance is carried out to minimise disruption, but infrequent use and very short trains can be expensive and can really only be justified if a branch line provides sufficient long-distance traffic to and from a main line to enhance its profitability. While the GWR has become associated with railcars in the public mind, the concept did not start with the company but with the Eastern Counties Railway in 1847, which had a steam railcar named *Express*.

Many of the first steam railcars were used for inspection work, but those for the travelling public were becoming increasingly common by 1900, by which time the railways were not simply attempting to improve the economics of rural branch lines, but were also combating the growing competition from street tramways, most of them by this time electric-powered. The trams were more frequent than railway travel, often cheaper, and even if not faster, overall journey times were often quicker as they tended to run closer to the departure points and destinations of their passengers.

The early railcars usually consisted of a small, generally four-wheeled, locomotive incorporated into the structure of a passenger carriage, with the unit capable of being driven from either end. Many of them suffered from being underpowered, while others generated so much traffic that they had to be replaced by push-pull trains. Nevertheless, those that managed to cope with the traffic available still suffered from one major disadvantage, which was that they needed a three-man crew of driver, fireman and guard, the same as a much longer train, but, of course, lacked the longer train's carrying capacity and revenue-earning potential. In addition to the other drawbacks already mentioned

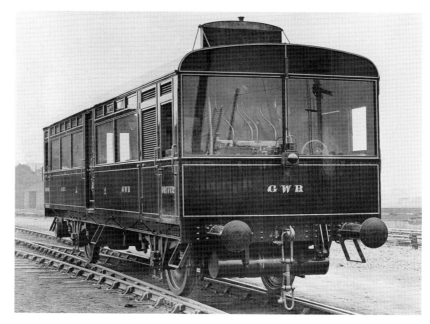

The Great Western was among the pioneers of motorised railway vehicles, although before the First World War this petrol-engined railcar, which ran between the main line at Slough and Windsor, was not as successful as the company liked to pretend. It was also too small. It is shown here at Windsor. (*Kevin Robertson*)

concerning the time and manpower spent in preparing a steam locomotive for the day's work, steam railcars presented maintenance problems as maintenance in a steam depot and coaling meant that the passenger accommodation was more difficult to keep clean. Despite these difficulties, those railway companies operating steam railcars were determined to make the most of them, and the GWR in particular ensured that many unstaffed halts were built along lines served by the railcars to ensure that as many people as possible could make use of their services.

The cost of electrification meant that it was only a viable solution for busy lines. For the quieter lines, the internal combustion engine was the only solution. As early as 1911 the GWR took delivery of a petrol-engined railcar built by the British Thompson Houston Company. This was a very small vehicle, just 33ft 3in long, roughly half the length of the railway carriages being built at the time, although longer than the maximum permitted length of contemporary buses. Petrol propulsion was chosen because the diesel engine was even more novel, and indeed for some years Britain lagged behind Germany in the development and production of diesel engines. To enhance its reliability, the railcar's 40hp Meadows petrol engine had two carburettors, although only one was in use at any one time. Maximum speed was 32mph.

In February 1912 the new railcar, No. 100, with its two axles more akin to a railbus than a railcar, started to operate between Slough and Windsor, along the short branch of 2.7 miles, taking just under 8 minutes for the journey. It seems that the forty-four seats on a three and two a side layout were not enough at peak periods, when a push-pull steam train had to be substituted.

The service was short-lived, and although public reports struck an encouraging note, privately the GWR seems to have been disappointed. It could be that too much was being expected of too little, as experiments with railbuses by British Railways also proved disappointing, with these being underpowered and undersized. It could also be that the branch was the wrong one for the experiment, and only chosen because of its proximity to the GWR's headquarters so that a close eye could be kept on it.

An 0–4–2T with an auto-trailer and even a goods van coming off the branch. This is Churston Junction in 1930, with a train arriving from Brixham. *(HMRS/J. Scott-Morgan ABX024)*

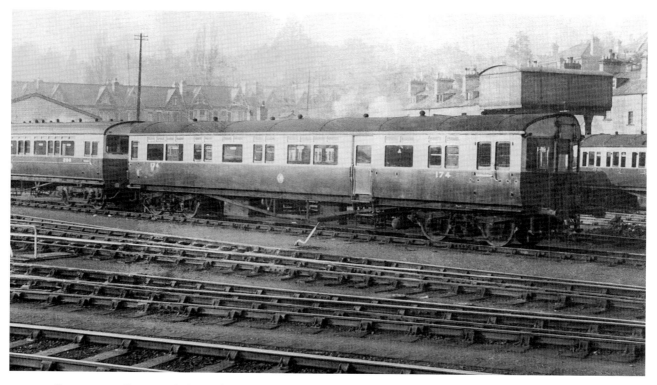

Two auto-trailers coupled together in 1938 at an unidentified location. (*HMRS/G. Hemingway ABH401*)

At the lower end of the scale were the autotrains, with a locomotive and a carriage or carriages fitted with controls so that the locomotive could be driven remotely, designed for lightly trafficked routes. Here a class 48XX is seen with two autotrains. (*Kevin Robertson*)

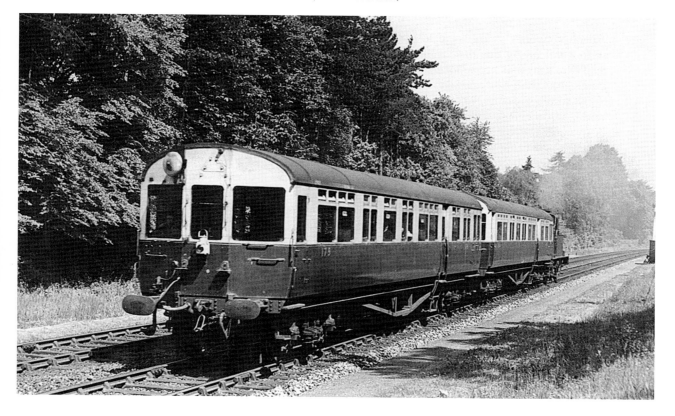

The great expresses are one of the romantic memories of the Great Western, but equally evocative waiting to take passengers along a Cornish branch line would be something like this 2–4–0T and an auto-trailer coach. This is Lostwithiel in 1930, complete with palm trees and china clay wagons. *(HMRS/J. Scott-Morgan ABX035)*

The Later Railcars

Another twenty years were to pass before the GWR once again ventured to experiment with a railcar. By this time reliable British diesel engines were available, including the AEC 8.85 litre that had proven itself in the demanding operating conditions endured by London buses. AEC had a subsidiary, Hardy Railmotors, and at the International Commercial Motor Show at Olympia in November 1933 they displayed a streamlined railcar, 62ft long and 9ft wide, with 2+3 seating for sixty-nine passengers and capable of speeds up to 63mph. Bodywork was by Park Royal, one of the leading bus body manufacturers. This attracted so much interest that it was estimated that more than half the visitors to the show went aboard the railcar, which had been bought by the GWR as Railcar No. 1. There was further publicity at the end of the show when the railcar was moved by road from Olympia to Brentford.

This was a far more sophisticated design than the railcar for the 1912 trials. It used a diesel mechanical drive system with a pre-selective gearbox, again reminiscent of London Transport practice, and seems to have seized the public imagination. The manufacturer and the GWR vied with one another to gain favourable publicity from the vehicle, and its press run from Paddington to Reading on 1 December 1933 was proclaimed by AEC as a 'triumph'. On 4 December the railcar entered revenue-earning service operating from Slough to Windsor, once again, and also to Reading and Didcot. Nevertheless, as could only be expected with a prototype, by the end of the year the railcar was out of service for attention to the engine mountings and brakes, while the opportunity was taken to adapt it for the Great Western's automatic train control system. When it returned to service in February 1934 it performed reliably and during its first year carried 136,000 passengers and accumulated more than 60,000 miles in service. It seems that part of the appeal of the railcar for passengers was the light and airy body design, which put it on a par with many

Much more successful were the diesel railcars introduced during the 1930s. This is one of the later models with space for luggage and parcels. *(HMRS M20002)*

observation cars, especially since passengers could see through the driving cabs at both ends.

Even at this early stage the Great Western was sufficiently convinced that it had discovered a winning formula that it ordered six more railcars in February 1934. These had two of the proven 8.85 litre AEC diesel engines and a maximum speed of 80mph. This was hardly traditional branch-line performance, although it could enable a fast-accelerating railcar to 'sprint' between smaller stations on the main lines, running between expresses. It could also allow the GWR to introduce fast express services between towns that might not otherwise justify such a service. This must have been very much in mind as the first three of the new railcars, Nos 2 to 4, were each equipped with toilets and fitted with a buffet bar capable of serving hot and cold drinks as well as snacks, and 2+2 seating with removable tables for forty-four passengers. These were intended to provide a fast business express service between Cardiff and Birmingham. In effect, with seating that was below first-class standards, this seems like the first instance of a 'business class' in transport. The GWR itself seems to have realised that it was perhaps in danger of racing ahead of the market, and the body layout for the remainder of the six vehicles was put on hold pending the outcome of operational experience with the first three vehicles.

The three new railcars were delivered during July 1934 and were shown off to the press as well as undertaking what might be described today as proving runs. Possibly realising that 2+2 seating could not command a premium, standard third-class fares were charged when the Birmingham and Cardiff express service was introduced, taking 2 hours 20 minutes for the 117½ miles, an average speed of 50.35mph. No doubt most, if not all, of the third-class fares were at full rates rather than off-peak fares, and the need to limit numbers indicates a reservation fee as well, so revenue per seat was probably well above the average for normal third class.

Starting on 9 July, there were morning and late afternoon/early evening services in each direction, which ran as shown overleaf:

Birmingham dep:	9.05 a.m.	3.40 p.m.
Gloucester arr:	10.17 a.m.	4.52 p.m.
dep:	10.19 a.m.	4.54 p.m.
Newport arr:	11.10 a.m.	5.52 p.m.
Cardiff arr:	11.27 a.m.	6.10 p.m.
Cardiff dep:	9.10 a.m.	4.50 p.m.
Newport dep:	9.27 a.m.	5.06 p.m.
Gloucester arr:	10.21 a.m.	5.55 pm.
dep:	10.23 a.m.	5.56 p.m.
Birmingham arr:	11.35 a.m.	7.15 p.m.

Given that there were three railcars, allowing for two in service and one as a spare or for maintenance, this was hardly intensive utilisation, but it was a low-cost means of providing an additional service, even if the lack of first-class accommodation meant that it was not a premium service. As we will see later it proved to be very popular.

The remaining three railcars were bodied by the Gloucester Railway Carriage and Wagon Company, which continued with the streamlined design of the prototype and the business expresses. In fact, the GRCWC design was more modern than the originals, and in addition to deeper windows to improve the view and better ventilation for everyone, including the driver, it also had sliding doors to speed boarding and alighting at stations. Before work on the bodies began, however, the underframes were modified and strengthened in the light of the experience already gained. Seating reverted to 2+3 with a total of seventy seats in Nos 5–7. In this form, these remaining three railcars of the 1933 order entered service in July and August 1935, working between London, Hereford, Worcester and Birmingham.

Once again the railcars proved popular with passengers, and the GWR capitalised on this by introducing summer Sunday evening 'mystery tours', known as 'half-crown tours',

The introduction of a diesel railcar to the Lambourn branch did provide a modest improvement in timings between 1922 (upper) and 1938 (lower), but perhaps less than might have been expected at just 2 minutes. Often the railcar would have been pulling a horse-box. (Bradshaw)

through the countryside around Worcester and Great Malvern. This really was a case of the railways venturing onto the preserve of the coach operator, taking the commercial battle to the enemy, road transport.

Before these railcars were delivered the GWR had already decided in February 1935 to order another ten railcars, again with bodywork by the Gloucester Railway Carriage and Wagon Company, although Nos 8 to 17 were to have three different styles of bodywork. Whether this reflected the continued need to try different layouts in a search for a successful formula, or that the GWR was simply taking advantage of the relative ease with which the lightweight bodies could be altered, is not clear, but it seems that the latter was the case. Nos 8, 9 and 13–16 were effectively copies of 5–7, while 10–12 had seating reduced to sixty-three as a result of installing a lavatory, while No. 17 was an express parcels van. There were some technical changes, such as the substitution of cast-iron cylinder heads in place of the aluminium alloy of the standard AEC 8.85 litre diesel, while oil coolers were added as the engines had been noted to run at high temperatures during continuous high-speed running. The earlier railcars also had these modifications incorporated in due course. Each of the railcars had a gearbox for each engine.

The next stage in the development of the railcar was No. 18, also ordered in February 1935. This had seating reduced to forty-nine and included a baggage compartment. The most significant feature was that No. 18 was designed to haul a load of 60 tons, and had two more powerful 13 litre diesel engines. With its standard buffers and couplings, it lacked the completely streamlined route of the earlier railcars. Initially, it was thought that the trailer would be an unpowered version of No. 18, but this was abandoned and a standard auto-trailer coach was used instead. This meant modifying the auto-trailer controls for a diesel rather than a steam power unit, and also installing equipment on the railcar to provide steam heating for the auto-trailer coach. Introduced to service in April 1937, No. 18 was set to work the Lambourn branch, with an early morning newspaper and mail service for stations between Reading and Basingstoke. It appears that not only did it sometimes work with an auto-trailer coach, but also on a number of occasions it pulled horse-boxes as well – scarcely surprising given the location of the branch in an area renowned for training racehorses and with a course not far away at Newbury.

The railcars had proven in a very short period that they could stimulate traffic on branch lines and to smaller stations on main lines, as well as cutting costs. Indeed, on a number of routes they had to be replaced by steam trains as traffic grew. By this time the GWR was sufficiently confident to start building its own railcars, depending on AEC for the running units, but building underframes and bodies at its Swindon works.

In September 1938 a further batch of twenty railcars was ordered, and again the order was split among a number of different versions. Nos 19–33 were designed for operation on branch lines, while No. 34 was to be another express parcels car. Most significant of all, Nos 35–8 were to be operated in pairs, being in effect two-car diesel multiple units with buffets and toilets for the Birmingham–Cardiff business express, giving a clear indication of just how successful this had been. There were a number of technical changes with derated engines, down from 130 to 105bhp, giving a maximum speed of 70mph. Surprisingly, once again there was less streamlining, as well as an extra 3ft to the body length, while each of the first batch had forty-eight seats in 2+2 abreast arrangement. Oddly, the first to enter service was No. 20 on 4 June 1940, while Nos 19 and 21 followed on 11 July. No. 34 followed the mechanical specification, but had hinged doors rather than the sliding doors of No. 18.

Meanwhile, in 1938 the total mileage run by the fleet of diesel railcars had risen by 97,000 miles over the previous year to 976,000 miles. The parcels car was put to good use, starting its day by carrying supplies from the catering company, Lyons, which at the time owned a nationwide chain of teashops, from Addison Road, London, to Reading and Oxford. On its Up return working it picked up parcels, stopping at all stations from Oxford to Paddington.

The first of the twin-car units arrived in 1941. Seating was provided for 104, however a standard corridor coach could be inserted between the two cars to give 184 seats.

In November Nos 35 and 36 took over the Birmingham–Cardiff service, while 37 and 38 joined them in February 1942. No. 37 was damaged by fire on 17 April 1947, so No. 33 was modified with one driving cab replaced by a corridor connection to operate with No. 38. Meanwhile, their success on the Birmingham–Cardiff service meant that at peak periods they had to be replaced by steam trains.

It is interesting to note that construction of these later diesel railcars was allowed to continue, as work on many railway and bus manufacturing projects was frozen at the outset of the war, and when limited production was allowed to resume out of necessity to cover war losses and increased demand for transport caused by the rapid growth in the numbers of service personnel, it was usually to a tight utility specification. Moreover, they used diesel rather than home-produced coal, as did steam locomotives and, indirectly, electric trains.

Shunters

Limited British expertise in building diesel engines meant that mechanisation of shunting initially saw the introduction of a small number of petrol-engined shunters, usually for lighter work moving just a few wagons at a time and mainly for use in private sidings. Some of these were in service during the early 1920s. Nevertheless, in 1933 a diesel-electric shunter, GWR No. 1, was delivered from John Fowler of Leeds for use in Swindon Works. This was obviously successful, as in 1935 GWR No. 2, supplied by Hawthorn Leslie, was put to work in the major goods yard at Acton in West London. This was yet another instance of classic GWR design, as it was the forerunner of the 0–6–0 08 class shunter that became the standard locomotive for shunting operations in the British Railway modernisation programme.

Gas-Turbine Locomotives

Strictly speaking, gas-turbine power does not belong in this book, as the first of the two prototypes was not delivered until the early 1950s, firmly in the era of British Railways. Nevertheless, the plans for gas-turbine operation were made by the Great Western, which deserves due recognition for being forward-looking and willing to experiment.

The LMS had experimented with a turbine-powered steam locomotive which survived from 1935 until withdrawal in 1952. Turbine power had worked well at sea, and in power stations. Indeed, as early as 1910 there had been steam turbine-electric locomotives, effectively miniature power stations on wheels, but these were too heavy and produced too little power to be attractive as railway power. The dawn of the jet age led to the development of the gas turbine for power station and, possibly, railway use, providing high power with great reliability from a compact installation, and with the power transmitted to the wheels through electric motors.

Having first considered whether or not the steam turbine offered any potential, the GWR ordered two prototype gas-turbine locomotives, or, strictly speaking, turbine-electric locomotives. The first, delivered in 1950, was from the Swiss pioneers of this form of propulsion, Brown Boveri, and was nicknamed 'Kerosene Castle' by the then Western Region railwaymen, while the second, delivered in 1952, was from Metropolitan Vickers. They were numbered 18000 and 18001 in the British Railways numbering scheme. Sadly, progress in jet propulsion was such that on delivery their turbines were already obsolete. Despite this, both locomotives provided a satisfactory and reliable performance – more than could be said for many first-generation diesel locomotives – but they were withdrawn in 1960. Reasons for their short service life included the fact that they used out-of-date technology, so the lessons to be drawn from them were limited, while there was the inevitable problem of having two non-standard locomotives with completely different technology, making maintenance and spares holdings difficult and uneconomic. The factor that worked most against them, however, and dissuaded British Railways from pursuing

Looking ahead, the Great Western ordered two prototype gas turbine locomotives before nationalisation, but when the first of these, numbered 18000 by British Railways, arrived from Switzerland after nationalisation, it was already obsolete. It was also thirsty and noisy. *(Kevin Robertson)*

the technology, apart from a prototype of the abortive Advanced Passenger Train project, was that fuel consumption was relatively high – higher than that for a diesel – and, worse still, did not reduce much when operating at low speed or as a light engine. Running with a part load, the Metrovick locomotive used 2.97 gallons per mile, roughly three times that of a diesel-electric under similar conditions. They may also have taken slightly longer to reach their operating temperature when started from cold than a diesel, and would have needed to 'cool down' by idling before the engines were turned off. Both locomotives were noisy and unpopular with their drivers. No. 18000 returned to Switzerland to become a rail adhesion testing unit, but was brought back to the UK in 1995 for preservation.

Chapter Eight

Carrying
The Goods

'Goods' or 'freight' might be the question. It is not simply a case of 'freight' being American or modern and 'goods' British and traditional. The term 'goods' was inherited from canal practice and terminology in the UK, but it is significant that going back almost a hundred years one finds that Great Western people more often than not talked about their 'freight traffic', and even 'freight trains'.

Certainly, the role of freight loomed large in Great Western thinking and planning. While the Great Western is best remembered for its famous passenger trains and for its experiments with diesel railcars, it was also a railway that was a major conveyor of goods traffic. Indeed, several of its constituent and subsidiary companies were primarily goods lines, with passenger traffic almost as an afterthought. That many of them bothered with passenger traffic at all was a reflection of the time they were first built, when road transport was slow, unreliable and costly, and people would take a train for journeys that would today be regarded as the province of the bus – even for a journey of just a mile or two.

The period after the grouping coincided with growing industrial instability, while traffic fell

Grouping or not, nothing was done to rationalise the vast number of private owners' wagons over which the railway companies had little control. This is an 0–6–0 goods locomotive with a train of private owner wagons. (*Kevin Robertson*)

from the artificial peaks of the war years. Anxious to stimulate traffic, in 1923 freight rates were reduced from 112 per cent above the pre-war rate to just 75 per cent above. Nevertheless, costs had risen considerably during the period of state control, and traffic was falling. Estimates for Britain's railways as a whole suggest that total railborne freight reached 367 million tons in 1913, went on to peak at more than 400 million tons during the First World War, and then, except for a recovery during the Second World War, went into steady decline from 1919 onwards.

For most of Britain's railways freight was the main business, with the only exception among the 'Big Four' being the Southern Railway. Yet, at one stage passenger traffic was almost as important for the Great Western since, in 1912, well before the grouping, the company received almost 52 per cent of turnover, some £7.5 million, from freight, against £6.95 million for passenger traffic. Grouping changed this, and almost a quarter of a century later, in 1936, freight accounted for 58 per cent of turnover. This reflected the impact of absorbing the many mainly freight lines in the valleys and the docks, but the ratio of freight to passenger turnover would have been even higher in 1936 had it not been for the years of recession and also the loss of many export markets for coal during the miners' strike of 1926.

Freight Problems

Freight brought many problems to the railways, which had gained a 'common carrier' obligation, meaning that they were forced by law to accept any traffic offered to them provided that it could be carried by rail. There was nothing so simple as a charge of X per ton per mile travelled, as different rates applied to different categories of goods. This common carrier obligation was to become an increasing burden as road transport competition developed, able to charge what it liked and carry whatever suited that mode of transport most, often leaving the railways with the less economic loads. It is hard for us today to fully understand the importance of freight to the railways and vice versa.

Another mixed goods, with 2–8–0 47XX No. 4706 heading this train, c. 1930. (HMRS/J. Scott-Morgan AAA233)

Private-owner wagons were commonplace throughout the pre-nationalised railway system, as this photograph taken in 1925, with Cardiff Cathays locomotive shed behind, shows. *(HMRS/J. Tatchell ADC511)*

Virtually every railway station (halts were another matter) had its own goods yard, often shared by one or more of the local coal merchants who would bag and distribute coal to their customers from the premises. If a farmer wished to move farms, his entire stock of animals and equipment would travel in a train specially hired for the purpose. People moving house over anything other than a short distance would often have their belongings loaded into a demountable container aboard a lorry, which would take it to a railway station where it would transfer to a flat truck for the rest of the journey. The circus usually arrived by rail rather than by road, with the final procession from the railway station through the streets.

Freight, or goods, traffic was classified either as 'full load', taking a whole wagon or goods van, and what was variously known as 'smalls' or 'sundries', smaller consignments but different from parcels, which were carried by passenger train and charged at a higher rate. The smalls traffic suffered delays while waiting to be consolidated into mixed loads, in which a van or wagon full of these smaller consignments would be 'grouped' together, all travelling to the same goods station or depot, but for a number of consignees. Bulk traffics such as coal often provided a full train load rather than just a wagon or two, and many goods wagons were owned by industrial customers of the railways and could be seen around the system carrying their owners' names and in some cases their colours as well. The coal mines were major owners of goods wagons, but so too were many of the larger coal merchants.

Private wagons were the bane of many a railway manager's life. They could not be used for other traffic and had to be returned to the premises of the owner, as well as being generally looked after by the railway while away from their owners' premises. Long trains of empty coal wagons that could not be used for anything else did little for railway productivity, the railwaymen would argue, although having sent a train of fifty or more coal wagons to a coal merchant, it is hard to see what could be sent back.

There was another problem with private wagons, which was that they were built to the specification of the owner, rather than the railway. So while the railways, including the

While all of the railways had mixed-traffic locomotives, especially useful for fast freight trains, most of the traffic was handled by heavy goods locomotives such as this 2–8–0 class 28XX, No. 2803, seen here with a pannier tank behind in 1930. *(HMRS/J. Scott-Morgan ABX136)*

A classic mixed-goods train with a variety of wagons pulled by 2–6–2T class 44XX No. 4408, *c.* 1930. *(HMRS/J. Scott-Morgan AAA234)*

Another locomotive with eight driving wheels, but in this case a 2–8–0T of class 42XX, No. 4288 is seen in Swindon workshops in 1930. *(HMRS AAD107)*

GWR, might want to increase the size of their goods wagons and introduce continuous braking to permit higher speeds, a typical wagon owner such as a coal mine would want to persist with short-wheelbase two-axle wagons because of the tight curves on its premises. Many wagon owners wanted the cheapest and simplest wagon possible. Handling in many industrial sites, and especially collieries with tight curves and limited clearances above the mines (the surface goods wagons were too big to go underground), was often primitive and only the unbraked wagon, operated loose-coupled, was acceptable. When new 20-ton coal wagons were introduced, despite the offer of a 5 per cent cut in freight rates for using them, the mine owners largely ignored them as they were too big for the lines in their collieries.

If productivity seemed less important than simplicity to many industrial customers, this was a recurring theme in the Great Western's relations with its business customers almost from grouping onwards. The lack of investment during the war years and the loss of many wagons to the military meant that there was often a wagon shortage. There were pleas to industrial customers not to leave wagons waiting to be unloaded in their private sidings, and once empty wagons were loaded, there were further pleas that the GWR should be told at once so that they could be collected.

While special arrangements were made for whole trains for a particular freight customer, and some of these had regular timetables, for wagon load and less than wagon load freight, a steam locomotive and guard's van would operate what was known as a 'pick-up' freight, calling at station sidings and collecting whatever wagons or vans that were ready to move. There were also other goods trains that went from one station to another dropping off wagons and vans. Unless the station was busy enough to justify its own shunting locomotive, the locomotives of these goods trains would spend much of their time shunting wagons, something that was made more difficult and time-consuming as they always had to ensure that the guard's van was at the back of the train before continuing with their journey, just in case a wagon coupling failed, so that the guard would have time to alert the nearest signalman and place detonators on the track to protect the train.

Obviously the wagons collected by the 'pick-up' freight would need to be sorted and sent onwards to their destinations. This was done in marshalling yards, and during the period covered there was a move to a new style of marshalling yard, with humps so that wagons could roll using gravity and be directed into different sidings depending on their final destination. In the older yards locomotives would push the wagons into sidings, often letting them roll away. Wagons were stopped by simply bumping into another wagon. Damage to wagons was often severe, and their contents often fared badly as well, but measures were put in hand between the wars to minimise this damage, with growing use of steel wagons and even shock-absorbing underframes.

Goods trains were classified as either 'fully fitted', that is with many of the vehicles having vacuum brakes that could be controlled by the locomotive driver, or 'unfitted', that is with no continuous braking system. On 'unfitted' goods trains, each wagon had only a simple handbrake that could be applied in a siding or if the train was checked on a steep gradient. Otherwise braking was left entirely to the locomotive and, in an emergency, the guard's van. Such trains ran at speeds of around 5 or 10mph. Stopping would be accompanied by a clatter as the wagons ran into one another. Fully fitted freight trains were allowed to travel much faster, provided that the rolling stock could do this safely, and the permitted speed depended on the proportion of wagons or vans fitted with the vacuum brake, which automatically applied the brakes once the vacuum was broken, as would happen if the wagon became uncoupled from the rest of the train. Not all wagons were necessarily fitted with vacuum brakes on express goods trains and there were some variations, with those trains having between one-third and one-half of the wagons fitted with vacuum brakes allowed to run at speeds of up to 45mph, while on those with less than one-third of the wagons fitted with vacuum brakes the speed was reduced to 35mph. This was still an improvement over the speed of an unfitted goods train.

Many smaller customers had their goods collected or delivered from the goods station or depot by the railway's own fleet of vehicles, and even between the wars many of these were still horse-drawn, although petrol and diesel vehicles were steadily taking over. Two of the

Another aspect of freight working when most goods were sent by rail to even the smallest country station was the 'pick-up' freight, a slow goods train stopping at every station for whatever wagons awaited it, and clearly again some of these are private-owner wagons. This 0–6–0 of class 2301 near Churchdown. (HMRS/D.H. Haines AEV015)

A 20-ton 'Toad' brake van in a siding at Worcester, with cattle wagons to its left on the next track. *(HMRS/D.A. Bayliss AEP426)*

The GWR tried in vain to get the customers providing its mineral traffic, including coal, to use larger-capacity wagons to enhance productivity, while the use of fully fitted rolling stock would aid this further by raising speeds. This is what the company had in mind – a 20-ton wagon carrying coal to the GWR power station at Park Royal in 1929. *(HMRS AEL804)*

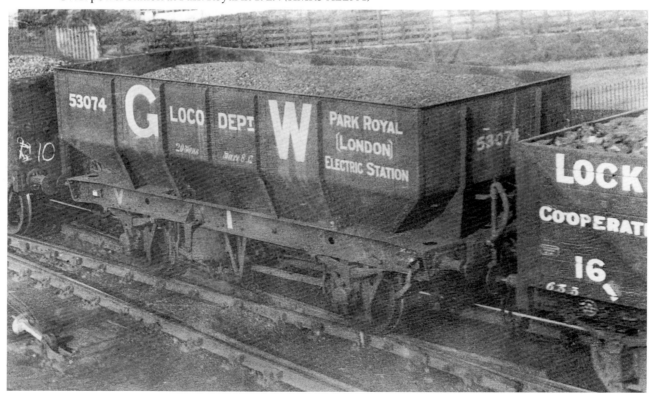

most practical of the new vehicles were designed with handling railway work in mind. These were the Scammell Mechanical Horse and the Karrier Cob, both of which were three-wheeled tractors with incredible manoeuvrability introduced in 1930. On nationalisation, the new British Railways inherited some 6,000 of these vehicles from the 'Big Four' railway companies.

In common with the other railways, the Great Western employed salesmen who canvassed for business from firms that were likely to become freight customers. Through running of trains or wagons between the different companies produced a fair volume of accounts to be settled, and as with passenger traffic this was done by the Railway Clearing House. There was overlap and competition at various points on the GWR's network with the London, Midland & Scottish in particular, and also occasionally with the London & North Eastern Railway, and so an agreement was reached between these companies that they should coordinate their activities as far as goods business was concerned. The Southern Railway was not a party to these arrangements, but as already mentioned was a comparatively minor player in the freight business.

Goods on the Great Western

While it is tempting to think of the Great Western as being primarily a haulier of coal from the South Wales valleys, this was only part of the business – fortunately, as it turned out. The company's territory was also agricultural, and a considerable volume of perishable traffic needed to be moved, so the Great Western became a major user of vacuum-fitted freight rolling stock, with many fast freight trains.

The fast goods trains gave the company an opportunity to market these to its major customers, and from the late 1920s it did so actively, doubtless because rates for consignments carried by such trains were well above the minimum set by the Railway Rates Tribunal. It was also the case that on longer distance fast freight the railways had an advantage over a road haulage industry that had no motorways, and in fact until the late 1930s hardly any arterial roads, and whose vehicles were limited to a maximum speed of 20mph.

Many of these trains had informal names given to them by GWR employees, such as 'The Flying Pig', the 10.45p.m. goods from London Old Oak Common to Exeter, which dated back to the days of the broad gauge. Another was named 'The Grocer', while the 'Didcot Fly' was supposed to take 12 hours for the 24 miles to Swindon, which must have qualified as some kind of record. Another train rejoiced in the name of 'The Tip'. Not at all discouraged by this levity, *The Great Western Railway Magazine* ran a competition seeking staff nominations of trains and suitable names, for which a first prize of £5 was offered, with a second prize of £3 and a third prize of £2. In fact, the title of 'The Flying Pig' was taken up by the company for the 4p.m. Exeter to Old Oak Common express goods. Other names given to freight trains included 'The Northern Flash', 'The Drake', 'The Bacca', suggesting a connection with the tobacco industry at Bristol, 'The Mopper Up', 'The Spud', 'The Western Docker' (Bristol to Wolverhampton), 'The Cocoa' (Bristol to Paddington), 'The Cotswold' (Gloucester to Paddington), 'The Carpet' (officially the 8.20p.m. from Kidderminster to Paddington), 'The Biscuit' (Reading to Plymouth) and the 'Up Jersey' (Weymouth to Paddington).

As much as possible of the Great Western's freight traffic was sent overnight, partly to avoid delaying passenger traffic, but also because the express goods trains travelling overnight could offer next-day delivery for premium traffic. Between 8.05p.m. and 12.35a.m. every evening no fewer than twelve express freight trains left Paddington goods station for points throughout the network, with trains for Birkenhead, Bristol, Cardiff, Carmarthen, Fishguard, Newton Abbot, Plymouth, Westbury and Wolverhampton. These Down trains were balanced by Up trains leaving in the late evening for Paddington Goods. These services included many long non-stop runs, including the 9.10p.m. Paddington to

The common carrier obligation meant that the railways had to carry unusual loads, for which a wide variety of wagons was available, such as this 25-ton low-loader 'Crocodile', seen with a truss load in 1937. *(HMRS/J.E. Cull AEP535)*

Birkenhead, which took the 145.1 miles from Greenford to Shrewsbury at an average speed of 38mph. This didn't compare with passenger express speeds – it did not need to do so – but it did compare well with the 5 or 10mph of ordinary goods trains. On good stretches of line the express goods trains could reach 60mph, the self-imposed speed limit that the GWR regarded as suitable for their rolling stock. The Birkenhead train was also far heavier than a passenger express, and could represent a gross load of 800 tons, for which a class 47XX 2–8–0 locomotive was needed. These locomotives were also used on the night goods to Newton Abbot and Plymouth.

It followed too that London was not necessarily the most important point for the Great Western's goods traffic, even if it did need more of its fast goods trains as the capital drew in food and milk for its people from the country districts. Coal was vital, not only for the railways themselves, but because it was the dominant fuel for private household heating, and also required for the town gas industry in the days long before North Sea gas began to be piped ashore. One of the main goods yards for handling coal was Severn Tunnel Junction, where the long and heavy coal trains from South Wales waited to be taken through the Severn Tunnel. The tunnel was not simply long, it also had steep gradients on both sides, with 1 in 90 descending from the Welsh side, and then a 1 in 100 climb to the English side, followed by a brief run on the level before the 1 in 100 climb in Cattybrook Tunnel. The widespread use of unfitted loose-coupled wagons meant that assisting engines were needed, which had to be coupled ahead of the train's own locomotives rather than simply banking at the back. The full braking capacity of these locomotives was needed in the descent.

The GWR spent some considerable time developing new rolling stock for its goods trains. As already mentioned, in 1923 it introduced new 20-ton wagons for coal trains, and tested trains with a gross load of 1,000 tons. This compared well with the 8 or 10 tons of the traditional coal wagon, and trains made up of the new larger capacity coal wagons would,

Full and empty private-owner wagons in a siding somewhere in South Wales. (*HMRS/P.E. Matthews AAX405*)

it was estimated, require up to 35 per cent less siding space. Unfortunately, the mine owners regarded these as too big and wouldn't invest in new sidings. That, coupled with the miners' strike in 1926, followed by the collapse in the export market for Welsh coal, meant that the thousand large steel coal wagons ordered by the GWR were largely wasted.

There were also special wagons for special loads, mainly with the railway's own telegraphic communications in mind, so that a 'Mogo' was a 12-ton motorcar van, or the more obvious 'Vent-Insulmeat' was an insulated van for the carriage of meat. It seemed appropriate to name a long-wheelbase fishvan a 'Bloater', but a long van with doors at each end being called an 'Asmo' seems much less obvious, even though one of its loads would have been new motorcars. Calling a 73ft-long flat bogie wagon for carrying rails and girder sections a 'Macaw' also seems fanciful. An open carriage truck was a 'Scorpion' and a covered bogie van with end doors a 'Python'. Wagons for heavy bulky loads were known as 'Crocodiles', with several different versions of which the 'Crocodile L' was the largest, capable of carrying a 120-ton load and needing twenty-four wheels. Given the technology available, true refrigerated rolling stock was out of the question, but with the trade in imported frozen meat from Australia and New Zealand growing, the GWR did its best with insulated vans kept cool using dry ice.

Some of the more difficult loads exceeded the track clearances, and so had to be run at quiet times, such as Sundays, so that they would not interfere with trains running on the adjoining track.

To encourage the use of railway freight, the GWR published its *Guide to Economical Freight*, which listed the express services available. Not all of the trains radiated out from London, as there were some fast cross-country goods trains as well. Typical of these was 'The Spud', which left Cardiff at 9.45p.m. for Chester, and 'The Moonraker', running at 4.20a.m. from Westbury to Wolverhampton.

Wartime saw efforts to improve productivity through the introduction of new freight rolling stock continue. These included 40-ton bogie coal wagons to carry the GWR's own supplies of locomotive coal.

Another special wagon was this 30-ton bogie bolster 'Macaw', seen here carrying tree trunks in 1924. *(HMRS/J.P. Richards AAJ900)*

Traffic, New and Traditional

While coal was the traditional traffic that was to prove the big disappointment during the inter-war years, it was not the only one. In particular, the Great Western had a substantial number of perishable traffics, and some of these, such as milk, were handled on a daily basis with the trains given a high priority.

The Great Western had the distinction of carrying more milk into London than any other railway, bringing in almost ¼ million gallons daily. Instructions were issued to expedite the handling of milk churns at stations, with many of them collected by milk vans attached to passenger trains. Safety was an issue, as trolleys carrying churns needed to be close to the platform edge to speed up loading, but far enough away not to interfere with the doors of trains arriving and departing. Between the wars, the move was away from the traditional milk churn, carried by the GWR in special semi-open-sided milk vans sometimes described as 'prisons on wheels', towards special 3,000 gallon tank wagons with glass-lined tanks, about 25ft long and still with six wheels even though weighing about 28 tons when fully laden, but intended to travel at near passenger train speeds. Some of the milk trains had long journeys, with one running daily from Whitland in Carmarthenshire to Paddington with eighteen tank wagons hauled by a 'Castle' class locomotive.

Another new system was the use of 2,000 gallon demountable tanks that could be transferred to and from railway wagons and lorries, ideal if the source or destination of the milk was some distance from the railway.

Other perishable traffics were highly seasonal, such as the annual harvest of broccoli from Cornwall to London and the Midlands. This was a new traffic, as commercial growing of broccoli in Cornwall had not started until 1925, but by 1928 the traffic had grown to 13,481 tons and by 1938 to 41,474 tons. By 1943 the total moved by rail had grown to more than

A goods train checked by signals at Birmingham Snow Hill in 1947. The presence of a 25-ton 'Toad' brake van in the middle suggests that perhaps the train will be divided at some point. *(HMRS/P.J. Garland AEL228)*

A new traffic for the Great Western was the motorcar. Here a Rover car is strapped safely into a 'Mogo' car van in 1936. *(HMRS/J. Tatchell ADC502)*

50,000 tons. The management of such trains was made all the more difficult by the weather affecting the date of the harvest. A mild spell late in winter could advance the crop, but heavy frost in March would delay it. The fast goods trains handling this crop were given priority, and so too were the empty vans on their return to Cornwall for the next consignment.

A new traffic for the railway, however, was the movement of motorcars. Several manufacturers, notably Morris at Cowley near Oxford, and Rover at Solihull, used the railways to deliver new cars to the distributors if these were some distance from the factory. Singer cars were taken from the Midlands by railway to the ports for export. These were the traffic for the Mogo, but there were also 45ft-long covered vans that could carry up to nine motorcar bodies from companies such as Pressed Steel to the motor manufacturers.

As the motor vehicle came to play a greater part in the nation's transport, oil wagons became an increasingly common sight. At the outbreak of the Second World War the GWR already had many six-wheeled oil wagons, and its oil-carrying capacity was boosted during the war by the arrival of eight-wheeled bogie oil wagons from the United States. These carried 40 tons of oil. The barrels and the bogies were shipped as dismantled units and assembled by the Great Western after arrival in the UK.

Livestock also presented a major traffic for the Great Western, and given its lines through the Thames Valley, the top end of this market included horse-boxes, which were often conveyed by passenger trains and even hauled by the Lambourn branch diesel railcar. Far larger were some of the animals carried by the Great Western when it moved the Bertram Mills Circus from one location to another, including a special type of van for the elephants.

One unusual and hazardous traffic was gunpowder, for which special vans were provided, each with a pair of gunpowder boots that had to be worn by railwaymen handling these consignments, so that sparks would not ignite the gunpowder. The present-day trains carrying radioactive material almost seem safe by comparison.

Wartime saw the Great Western pushed to the limit to handle the freight traffic demanded by the war effort. Many were the means employed to enhance productivity, including renewed pressure to unload wagons immediately so that they could return to

A 40-ton steel wagon for coal, seen in 1935. Widespread adoption of wagons such as this could have done much to improve the viability of freight services, but many collieries had such tight curves in their sidings that the wagons were impractical without relaying the track. *(HMRS AEL116)*

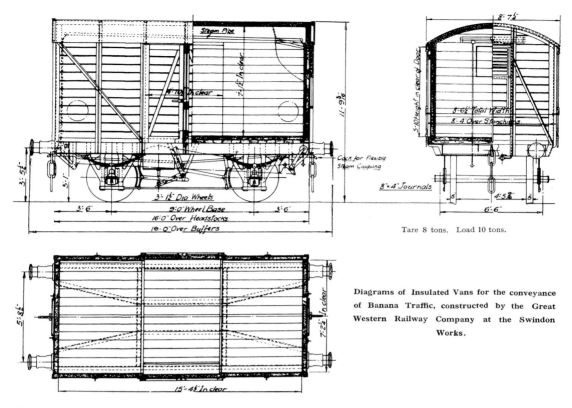

Tare 8 tons. Load 10 tons.

Diagrams of Insulated Vans for the conveyance of Banana Traffic, constructed by the Great Western Railway Company at the Swindon Works.

Goods, or 'freight' as the GWR had it, traffic was changing during the years between the wars, demanding new types of rolling stock. This is a design for insulated vans to carry bananas from the docks to the markets.

An 8-ton fruit van with a siphon van on the right. *(HMRS/D.A. Bayliss AEP428)*

traffic, while many wagons were 'up-plated' to be allowed to carry heavier loads. War brought new traffic to the railways, with one of the most obvious examples being trainloads of tanks, but there were some loads that were completely unique, as when a worn-out steam hammer block had to be moved on a 'Crocodile L' wagon as part of the scrap metal drive. Aircraft were also moved by rail, saving considerable quantities of aviation gasoline, but they first had to be dismantled before being moved in covered wagons. As with everything else, maintenance suffered, and wooden wagons were often patched with nothing more substantial than plywood or boxwood, with no attempt to conceal the patching.

Show Trains

Before the motorway network put most inland transport onto the highways, the railways had to meet every need and this involved them in some unusual activities. Bristol was important to the Great Western and one of that city's manufacturing industries was chocolate, with the then still independent Fry's of Bristol being one of Britain's major manufacturers. With the help of the Great Western, bogie freight vans were converted to

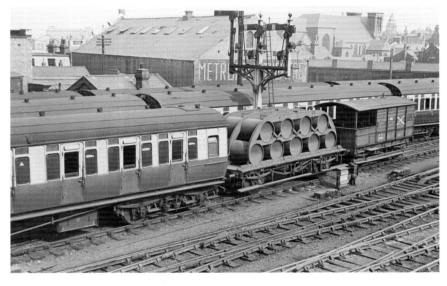

A nine-tank gas wagon shunted against passenger carriages in the siding at Birmingham Snow Hill in 1947. For safety reasons, it is unlikely that this wagon would have been attached to a passenger train. *(HMRS/P.J. Garland AEL219)*

Horses were another traffic that often travelled with passenger trains, but again in specially built wagons such as these, each with a compartment at the end for the groom. These were photographed in a siding at Tyseley in 1947. *(HMRS/P.J. Garland AEL200)*

Rather more demanding than horses were elephants. This is a 'Python' strengthened to 8 tons for carrying circus elephants, seen at Stourbridge in 1947. *(HMRS/P.J. Garland AEL202)*

become a three car 'Fry's Show Train', which made a 3½ month tour of the national railway network, calling at stations and usually using the parcels platform where visitors were welcomed.

This was not the last GWR-supported show train, and after the Second World War, a similar two-car train was provided to educate people about the new wonder pharmaceutical penicillin, and was promptly nicknamed the 'Penicillin Express'.

Chapter Nine

Travelling Great Western

While it lacked the massive commuter flows that made life so difficult and uneconomic for the Southern and the London & North Eastern railways, the Great Western Railway had a major peak period problem of its own – the summer holiday traffic. Summer days were busy ones for the railways before the days of mass car ownership, but to make matters worse, holiday-makers were even more likely to start and finish their holidays on a Saturday than is the case today. It was also true that the holiday season was far shorter than today and was largely concentrated on the school holiday period. On a winter weekday the departures from Paddington to the West Country were barely hourly; on a summer Saturday there could be as many as eight departures an hour. When destination codes were introduced for the expresses (see Appendix I), allowance was made for the fact that an express could have as many as five parts. The 'Cornish Riviera' not only had a relief, as mentioned in the chapter on named trains, but also an additional train in the form of the 'Cornishman' that served its all-year stops. All of the trains on these longer-distance services had restaurant cars.

Exactly how any railway company could cope with such pressures for some ten weekends a year and still remain profitable is hard to understand. Even allowing for the displacement of rolling stock and locomotives, and train crews, from business expresses, a substantial quantity of rolling stock must have been sitting idle for most of the time. An idea of the pressure placed on the company during the summer months was that, compared with its winter timetable, the 1938 and 1939 summer schedules required an extra 800 trains on a weekday and an extra 600 trains on a Sunday.

These were days when passenger train punctuality was not measured as it is today, on whether or not a train is more than five minutes late. Between the two world wars a train was either spot on time or it was late! The Great Western may have been publicity conscious, but it did not go in for what today would be described as 'spin', nor did it need to do so. Despite the company's best efforts, at peak periods there could be severe congestion on the way west, with stations and layouts not capable of handling the volume of traffic that was put upon them. There were occasions when not everything worked as well as it might, and then delays could build up, in rare instances to as much as two hours. Just before the grouping took effect, punctuality in late 1922 for express trains saw them running an average 3.6 minutes late, while other passenger trains ran an average of 2.3 minutes late.

It is hard to believe, given the legend that the Great Western has become, that at first third-class passengers were only conveyed in goods trains, and it could take all day to travel between London and Bristol. As already mentioned, for a company whose name became synonymous with service and style, it is also hard to believe that when the GWR suffered its first major accident on Christmas Eve 1841, third-class passengers were travelling in open trucks. The train ran into an earthslip in Sonning Cutting, east of Reading, and was derailed, with eight passengers killed and another seventeen injured.

Opposite: A very attractive end of the line for holiday-makers was Looe station in Cornwall. This picture was taken from the cliffs above the station in 1947. *(HMRS/J.E. Cull AEP527)*

Mail traffic was important for all of the railway companies, and required specially built vehicles such as this 54ft clerestory parcels van seen at Birmingham Snow Hill in 1947, and used on services to and from Paddington. Mail traffic included special trains, but was also often attached to passenger expresses. *(HMRS/P.J. Garland AEL408)*

This was a defining event as it encouraged Parliament to take an interest in regulation of the railways.

There was, nevertheless, even towards the very end a slight stinginess towards third-class passengers on the Great Western, given the long distances that its expresses covered. Both the LMS and the LNER provided third-class compartments with armrests that could take six people, but the GWR didn't provide armrests and always squeezed eight in. Perhaps that was one reason why it could afford to run those holiday extras.

While the Great Western had cut journey times considerably during the early years of the twentieth century with its 'cut-off' lines such as the Badminton Line for Cardiff trains and the Castle Cary route to the south-west, both of which avoided Bristol, major reductions in journey times generally came at widely spaced intervals. The next big step forward came in 1932, with the summer timetable introduced on 18 July. This saw the best timing between Paddington and Penzance for the 'Cornish Riviera' cut by no less than 120 minutes. The 7.32a.m. from Swindon to Bristol and stations to Taunton had 74 minutes cut off its schedule. Even cross-country services benefited, with the summer Saturday 8.10a.m. from Manchester to Ilfracombe taking 73 minutes less. The accelerated services were across most of the main-line network, and included the 9.45a.m. from Paddington to Wolverhampton, which took 48 minutes less. In introducing these accelerated schedules, the usual method was to start trains later so that they still arrived at their destination at the time passengers and those waiting to meet them had come to expect.

Reliability on summer Saturdays was also enhanced by quadrupling the line through Taunton and introducing a flyover to prevent trains coming from the direction of Bristol, including those from the Midlands and beyond, interfering with those running towards London via Castle Cary and Westbury. Westbury and Frome were also bypassed with new avoiding lines.

The reductions in journey times for the expresses were accompanied by the introduction of a new class of 0–6–0T locomotive for 'accelerated auto services' on branch lines. Nevertheless, not a few have pointed out that a lively performance by a Great Western locomotive was often countered by excessive times spent at railway stations, especially on branch lines.

New Trains for a New Era

Grouping saw the railways back under company control and away from that of the Railway Executive Committee, although fares were still subjected to the approval of the Railway Rates Tribunal. One of the first actions was to reduce passenger fares from 75 per cent above pre-war levels to 50 per cent, despite wages for GWR employees being on average 136 per cent of pre-war levels and the cost of supplies and other materials at 70 per cent above. This was not the only reduction. Season ticket holders on the lines in South Wales operated by other companies before the grouping found that the cost of these was reduced to the standard Great Western level.

An example of a more humble working was this class 45XX 2–6–2T with a Gloucester– Cheltenham local train which included a horse-box, parcels vehicle and a rake of four clerestory carriages in 1930. *(HMRS/D.H. Haines AEV013)*

A contrast to the generally dirty and run-down condition of many locomotives immediately after the Second World War was 0–6–0 No. 3204 at Cheltenham, clearly ex-works in 1946. Note the changed style of company name on the tender. *(HMRS/D.H. Haines AEU929)*

Churchward had been famous for wanting to create a standardised series of locomotives for the Great Western, but this was reversed to a great extent by the grouping that brought in locomotives from other companies. The same happened with passenger rolling stock, and although bogie carriages had been around since the late nineteenth century there were still many six-wheeled carriages in service. In any case, of the companies absorbed into the new GWR by the grouping only two, the Cambrian and the Midland & South Western Junction, had a main line of any distance.

Old carriages were initially offered for sale, as mentioned earlier, at prices ranging between £18 and £27, delivered free to any station on the Great Western, but what might be described as the 'carriage' costs of delivery to stations on other lines had to be paid by the purchaser. Later, the company followed the LNER in converting its redundant carriages into 'Camp Coaches'.

Churchward's contribution to railway carriage design was his new design of 1904, which was no less than 70ft long and 9ft 6in wide, without the clerestory roof of earlier GWR carriages and had an air of spaciousness. The design's arrival more or less coincided with the new battleship HMS *Dreadnought*, a ship that was the pattern for all future battleships and which had made earlier battleships obsolete overnight, so the new carriages were given the name 'Dreadnoughts'. This was appropriate because these were also to be the pattern for railway carriages in the future, but they were before their time and ahead of the preferences of the travelling public. The 'Dreadnought' carriages had end doors and corridors, but passengers preferred a door from the compartment onto the platform. In the detailed design, much had been neglected that might have convinced the passengers that there was some advantage in the new carriages. On the corridor side there were large windows, but the compartments still had three windows just as if a door had been fitted. A large picture window from which to admire the view might have won the passengers round.

Three years earlier two trains with open saloon carriages with a central gangway had been built for the Irish Sea boat trains, but these were so unpopular that afterwards the only open carriages built by the Great Western, apart from their diesel railcars, were for excursion traffic.

It followed therefore that when new stock was built by Collett for the post-grouping Great Western he initially reverted to the concept of having doors into each compartment, even on corridor stock, and indeed modified his initial design for new corridor carriages to have a number of additional doors on the platform side of the corridor.

The new passenger carriages introduced in 1923 were 70ft long and 9ft wide, indicating that they would not only run on converted broad gauge routes, for which Churchward's 'Dreadnoughts' had been designed, but on many of the lines that had been built to the standard gauge as well. There was some slight variation on this length for different versions of these carriages. The big innovation was the introduction of automatic buck-eye couplings. These carriages first went into service between Paddington and Swansea. They seem to have been the first carriages to be built with the new livery of brown with cream upperworks and white roofs. The choice of white for a roof colour was attractive, but it must also have said much about the quality of the Welsh coal used by the Great Western, not to mention high standards of cleaning.

The influence of the LNER was to be seen in the next batch of new passenger rolling stock, introduced in 1925. These were articulated carriages, and six sets of three carriages each were built for what would be described today as commuter services, but referred to officially as the 'Main Line and City Articulated Train'. Two sets each of three carriages made one train, but passenger comfort was limited by the tight dimensions, with just 5ft 10in between the bulkheads for third-class passengers, although first class provided 7ft. To the casual observer the carriages looked little different to what had become the new standard for local and suburban rolling stock, that is bogie carriages with non-corridor compartments. This arrangement did at least have the advantage of providing the maximum number of seats, while the doors into each compartment meant that station

LONDON, BICESTER, OXFORD, BANBURY, LEAMINGTON SPA, WARWICK, and BIRMINGHAM.—Great Western.

Week Days.

Miles	Miles	Down.	mrn	mrn	mrn	mrn	mrn	mrn	mrn	mrn	mrn	mrn	mrn	mrn	mrn	mrn	
		Notes	Except Monday mornings.														
		PADDINGTON dep.	1215														
5¾	5¾	Ealing (Broadway)															
26½	—	High Wycombe															
34¾	—	Princes Risboro'															
40	—	Haddenham															
47½	—	Brill & Ludgershall A 575															
50½	—	Blackthorn															
53¾	—	Bicester §§ 434 arr.															
		Bicester dep.															
57½	—	Ardley															
[illegible]	—	Aynho Park Platform															
—	—	130 Bournemouth Cen. dep	7 57														
—	—	148 Portsmouth	8 15														
—	—	130 Southampton Town	9t5														
—	—	47 Basingstoke	1130														
—	—	32 Reading	1 15														
—	—	17 Bristol (T.M.) 103															
—	—	7 Weymouth (T.)															
—	—	17 Swindon															
—	53¾	Didcot dep.															
—	56¾	Culham															
—	58¾	Radley 107															
—	63½	Oxford 46, 94, 95, 434 arr.	1 55														
		Oxford dep.	2 10														
—	69	Kidlington 53															
—	71	Bletchington															
—	73½	Heyford															
—	78	Fritwell and Somerton															
—	80½	Aynho ‡‡															
[illegible]	82	King's Sutton 104															
[illegible]	86½	Banbury † 104, 434, 590, 699 arr.	2 41														
		Banbury dep.	2 51														
[illegible]	89½	Cropredy															
[illegible]	95	Fenny Compton 590															
[illegible]	100	Southam Road and Harbury															
[illegible]	106	Leamington Spa § 438, 440 arr.	3 17														
		Leamington Spa dep.	3 27		7 0						7 15			8 0	8 7	8 25	
[illegible]	108	Warwick (Coventry Road) ‖			7 5						7 21			8 5	8 12	8 30	
[illegible]	112½	Hatton 108 arr.			7 13						7 30				8 20	8 38	
[illegible]	120½	108 Stratford-on-Avon arr.			7 35										8 45		
		108 Stratford-on-Avon dep.			Stop						7 5				Stop	8 0	
—	—	Hatton dep.									7 35					8 40	
[illegible]	116	Lapworth						6 50			7 44				mrn	8 49	
[illegible]	119	Knowle and Dorridge				6 5		6 57			7 53		8 12		8 30	8 56	
[illegible]	[illegible]	Widney Manor											8 17		8 35		
[illegible]	[illegible]	Solihull				6 12		7 6	7 30	7 42		8 10	8 23	8 33	8 39		
[illegible]	[illegible]	Olton [Yardley				6 17		7 11	7 35	7 47		8 15	8 29	8 38	8 45		
[illegible]	[illegible]	Acock's Green and South				6 20		7 15	7 38	7 50		8 19	8 33	8 42	8 49		
[illegible]	[illegible]	Tyseley 107			mrn	6 25	m	7 19	7 41	7 53		8 22	8 37		8 52		
[illegible]	[illegible]	Small Heath & Sparkbrook		5 20	6 10	6 26	6 33	7 22	7 44	7 56		8 26	8 41		8 57		
[illegible]	[illegible]	Bordesley		5 25	6 14	6 30	6 37	7 26	7 48	8 0	8 9	8 30	8 46	8 49	9 1	9 11	
[illegible]	[illegible]	Birmingham (M'r. St.) ‖‖ arr.				6 33								8 51			
[illegible]	[illegible]	Birmingham (Sn. Hill) ** 84 arr.	4 1	5 28	6 17	....	6 40	7 30	7 52	8 6	8 12	8 34	8 50	....	9 5	9 15	

Down.	mrn	mrn	mrn	mrn	mrn	mrn	mrn	mrn	mrn	mrn	mrn	mrn	mrn	mrn
Notes								Through Train, Taunton to Birmingham, see page 17.		Birmingham and North Express. Breakfast and Luncheon Car. Thro' Carriage to Pwllheli, see pages 84, 110, and 583.				Oxford, Worcester, and Malvern Express, see pages 94 and 100.
PADDINGTON dep.				5 30	5 45		6 30			9 10			7 30	8 45
Ealing (Broadway)					5 59								7 40	
High Wycombe					7 8	m				9 42				
Princes Risboro'					7 30	7 48								
Haddenham					7 39	7 58								
Brill & Ludgershall A 575					Stop	8 11								
Blackthorn						8 17								
Bicester §§ 434 arr.						8 23					m			
Bicester dep.						8 31					1020			
Ardley						8 39					1029			
Aynho Park Platform						8 47					1037			
130 Bournemouth Cen. dep														
148 Portsmouth														
130 Southampton Town														
47 Basingstoke													7 55	
32 Reading				6 18			7 43		8 0				8 42	9c30
17 Bristol (T.M.) 103				4 5				8 35					7 45	
7 Weymouth (T.)														
17 Swindon				5 13			6 40						9 0	
Didcot dep.				6 52			8 10		8 46				9 40	10 2
Culham				6 59			8 17		8 53				9 49	
Radley 107				7 7			8 26		9 0				9 56	
Oxford 46, 94, 95, 434 arr.				7 16			8 35		9 10				10 5	1017
Oxford dep.				7 27			8 43		Stop				10 12	
Kidlington 53				7 40									10 24	
Bletchington				7 47									10 31	
Heyford				7 57									10 39	
Fritwell and Somerton				8 4	mrn								10 47	
Aynho ‡‡				8 10	m								10 54	
King's Sutton 104				8 16	8 46	8 53					1042		11 0	
Banbury † 104, 434, 590, 699 arr.				8 23	8 53	9 0	9 11			10c24	1050		11 7	
Banbury dep.				8 32	Stop	Stop	9 17				Stop	11 0	Stop	
Cropredy				8 41								11 9		
Fenny Compton 590				8 50								11 18		
Southam Road and Harbury				8 59								11 27		
Leamington Spa § 438, 440 arr.				9 7	mrn		9 43		mrn	10 45	mrn	11 37		
Leamington Spa dep.		9 0	9 5	Stop	9 15		9 48		1015	10 48	11 0			
Warwick (Coventry Road) ‖		9 5	9 10		9 20		9 53		1020		11 5			
Hatton 108 arr.		9 13	9 18		9 29				1028		1113			
108 Stratford-on-Avon arr.			9 40					10 20			1135			
108 Stratford-on-Avon dep.	8 30	8 45						10 23						
Hatton dep.		9 14			9 30				1029					
Lapworth					9 38	mrn			1038				mrn	
Knowle and Dorridge					9 45	9 57			1045				11 23	
Widney Manor				mrn		10 2							11 28	
Solihull	9 11			9 20	9 52	10 6			1052				11 33	
Olton [Yardley				9 25		1011							11 37	
Acock's Green and South				9 29		1017							11 41	
Tyseley 107				9 33		1022							11 44	
Small Heath & Sparkbrook				9 37		1027							11 47	
Bordesley	9 20	9 37		9 42	10 1	1031	m		11 2				11 51	
Birmingham (M'r. St.) ‖‖ arr.														
Birmingham (Sn. Hill) ** 84 arr.	9 25	9 40	....	9 46	10 5	1036	1028	10 55	11 5	11 15	....	....	11 55	

** For Local Trains and intermediate Stations

BETWEEN	PAGE
Paddington and Princes Risboro'	42
Paddington and Didcot	32

For other Trains

BETWEEN	PAGE
Paddington and Oxford	46
London and Haddenham	690
King's Sutton and Banbury	104
Leamington and Birmingham	440
Stratford-on-Avon, Tyseley, and Birmingham	106

LONDON, BICESTER, OXFORD, BANBURY, LEAMINGTON SPA, WARWICK, and BIRMINGHAM.

Week Days.

Miles	Miles	Down.	mrn	mrn	mn	mrn	mn	mrn	mn	mn	mrn	mrn	mn	mn	mn	mn	mrn	mrn
		Notes	Except Monday mornings.	Connects with Isle of Man Boat. Arr. Douglas about 20 aft (1 30 aft on Sats.)		Saturdays only. Connects with Isle of Man Boat. Arr. Douglas about 20 aft.												
		PADDINGTON dep.	1210	1 30														
5¾	5¾	Ealing (Broadway)																
26½	—	High Wycombe																
34¾	—	Princes Risboro' ¶																
40	—	Haddenham ¶																
47½	—	Brill & Ludgershall																
50½	—	Blackthorn																
53½	—	Bicester 468 arr.																
		Bicester dep.																
57½	—	Ardley																
61½	—	Aynho Park																
—	—	159 Bournemouth Cen. dep.	7 50															
—	—	187 Portsmouth and S.	8 3															
—	—	159 Southampton Cen.	9 54															
—	—	50 Basingstoke	1135															
—	—	36 Reading	1 15															
—	—	20 Bristol (T.M.) 131																
—	—	8 Weymouth (Town)																
—	—	20 Swindon																
—	53½	Didcot ¶ dep.																
—	56½	Culham																
—	58½	Radley 130																
—	63½	Oxford 48, 50, 63, 116, 468 arr.	1 55															
		Oxford dep.	2 10															
—	69	Kidlington 93																
—	71	Bletchington, for Kirtlington ¶																
—	75½	Heyford																
—	78	Fritwell and Somerton																
—	80½	Aynho, for Deddington																
64	82½	King's Sutton 136																
67½	86½	Banbury (Bridge St.) 136, 468, 727, 844 arr.	2 40	2F58														
		Banbury dep.	2 50	3F2														
71	89½	Cropredy																
76½	95	Fenny Compton 727																
81½	100	Southam Road and Harbury																
87½	106	Leamington Spa (W.O. Rd.) 473, 474 arr.	3 15	3F26														
		Leamington Spa dep.	3 21	3F32			625	7 10			7 30		740	8 0			8d10	8 28
89½	108	Warwick (Coventry Road)					630	7 20			7 34		744	8 4			8d15	8 32
93½	112½	Hatton 130 arr.					638	7 28			7 43		753	812			8d25	8 39
102½	121½	130 Stratford-on-Avon arr.						7 47									8d46	
		131 Stratford-on-Avon dep.						Stop			7 0		732				Stop	
—	—	Hatton dep.					639	mrn			7 44		754	813				8 40
97½	116½	Lapworth					647	7 13		m	7 52		8 2			825	mrn	8 46
100½	119	Knowle and Dorridge			6 5		653	7 19		745	7 58		8 8	823		831	8 46	8 52
102	120½	Widney Manor			6 9		657	7 23		749			813			835		8 56
103½	122½	Solihull			613		7 1	7 28	740	754	8 4	8 10	817	830	834	840	8 47	
105½	124½	Olton [Yardley			617		7 6	7 32	744	758		8 14	822	834	838	844	8 51	
[illegible]	125	Acock's Green and South			620		7 9	7 36	747	8 2		8 17	826	837	841	848	8 54	
[illegible]	[illegible]	Tyseley 132			623	7 0	714	7 39	750	8 6		8 20	829				8 57	
[illegible]	[illegible]	Small Heath & Sparkbrook			626	7 3	718	7 42	753			8 23	833		847		9 0	
[illegible]	[illegible]	Bordesley			630	7 6	721	7 46	757		8 13	8 28	836	842			9 3	9 10
[illegible]	[illegible]	Birmingham (Moor St.) arr.			633									845				
[illegible]	[illegible]	Snow Hill 198 arr.	3 50	4F0	..	7 10	725	7 49	8 1	812	8 16	8 30	840	..	852	857	9 7	9 13

Down.	mn	mrn	mrn	mn	mn	mrn	mrn	mn	mrn	mrn	mrn	mrn	mrn	mrn	mrn	mrn
Notes	Mondays only.	RC Oxford to Blenheim and Woodstock, see page 93.						Saturdays only.			Birmingham and North Express RC London to Pwllheli, page 108. Connects with Isle of Man Boat. Arr Douglas about 7 0 aft. RC for Birmingham and beyond.	RC London to Didcot except Sats				Saturdays only. Cambrian Coast Exp.
PADDINGTON dep.			5 30		545		6 30		7 10		9 10	7 30		8 40	9 10	1020
Ealing (Broadway)					6 5				7 20					8 50	m	RC
High Wycombe					710	m					9 43			RC	9 50	
Princes Risboro' ¶					730	7 50									10 5	
Haddenham ¶					742	8 1									1016	
Brill & Ludgershall					Stp	8 16									1031	
Blackthorn						8 21									1036	
Bicester 468 arr.						8 27									1040	
Bicester dep.						8 32									1043	
Ardley						8 40									1051	
Aynho Park						8 47									1058	
159 Bournemouth Cen. dep.																
187 Portsmouth and S.														6 0		
159 Southampton Cen.														6T57		
50 Basingstoke														8N32		
36 Reading			6 18				7 33		8 2			8 14		9 27		
20 Bristol (T.M.) 131	415		4 15											7X50		
8 Weymouth (Town)																
20 Swindon	550		6Y20				6 55							9 0		
Didcot ¶ dep.			6 52				8 12		8 28			8 55		9 51		
Culham			6 59				8 18					9 3				
Radley 130			7 6				8 24					9 9		10 1		
Oxford 48, 50, 63, 116, 468 arr.	630	m	7 15				8 32		8 44			9 17		10 9		
Oxford dep.	Stp	7 10	7 20				Stop		8 52			9 40		10 15		
Kidlington 93		7 20	7 31									9 50				
Bletchington, for Kirtlington ¶		Stop	7 35									9 55				
Heyford			7 44									10 5				
Fritwell and Somerton			7 50									1011				
Aynho, for Deddington			7 55									1019				
King's Sutton 136			8 0			8 52						1025			11 3	
Banbury (Bridge St.) 136, 468, 727, 844 arr.			8 7			8 59			9 20		X1025	1031		10 44	1110	
Banbury dep.			8 15			Stop			9 25			Stop		10 48	Stop	
Cropredy			8 22													
Fenny Compton 727			8 31													
Southam Road and Harbury			8 40													
Leamington Spa (W.O. Rd.) 473, 474 arr.			8 50		mn	mrn	mrn		9 50		X1043	mrn		11 12		1150
Leamington Spa dep.			Stop	9 0	910	9 15	9 25	940	9 55	10 5		1050	1055	11 15		1152
Warwick (Coventry Road)				9 4	914	9 19	9 29	944	9 59	10 9		1054	1059	11 20		
Hatton 130 arr.				912	921	9 27	9 36	952		1017		11 1	11 7			
130 Stratford-on-Avon arr.	mn				940			109				1120				
131 Stratford-on-Avon dep.	835			843	Stp	8 43	8 43			9S25		Stop	1035			
Hatton dep.			mrn	913		9 28	9 37			1018			11 8			
Lapworth			9 6		mn	9 34	9 44			1026		mrn	1116		mrn	
Knowle and Dorridge			9 11		922	9 40	9 50			1032		1053	1122		1140	
Widney Manor		mrn			926		9 54			1036		1057	1126		1144	
Solihull		9 10			930	9 46	9 58			1040		11 1	1130		1148	
Olton [Yardley		9 14			934	9 51	10 2			1044		11 5	1134		1152	
Acock's Green and South			9 21		937		10 5			1047		11 8	1137		1155	
Tyseley 132					940		10 8			1050		1111	1140		1158	
Small Heath & Sparkbrook					943		1011			1053		1114	1143		12 1	
Bordesley	914	9 20	9 26	934	946	9 57	1014		1022	1056		1117	1146		12 4	
Birmingham (Moor St.) arr.																
Snow Hill 198 arr.	917	9 23	9 30	937	949	10 1	1017	..	1025	11 0	1110	1121	1150	11 46	12 8	1220

Local Trains and intermediate Stations

Paddington and Princes Risboro'	46
Paddington and Didcot	36

Other Trains

Paddington and Oxford	48
London and Haddenham	844
King's Sutton & Banbury	136
Leamington Spa and Birmingham	474
Stratford-on-Avon, Tyseley, and Birmingham	134

Birmingham was an important destination for two railways before and after the grouping, and between 1922 (upper) and 1938 (lower) 5 minutes was shaved off the timetable to offer a commercially attractive two-hour schedule. *(Bradshaw)*

dwell times were kept to the absolute minimum. This rolling stock survived the war years and was kept in service until the late 1950s.

The commuter articulated carriages were joined by what amounted to a complete train of articulated carriages for express use. Once again the train was made up of more than one set of articulated stock, with a two-coach articulated unit with a brake first and a first-class carriage, while another had three coaches including two third-class carriages and a brake third. There was also a three-coach dining set, with first-class and third-class dining cars on either side of a kitchen car. These express articulated sets were used for some years in their original form, until they were converted to conventional rolling stock in the mid-1930s.

Clearly the GWR had decided that articulated carriages were not for it. The problem was that while articulation cut both the cost and weight of railway carriages, as well as improving the ride, the rolling stock maintenance team found it more difficult to work on. This was one reason for not having the entire train as a single articulated unit. Another drawback was the concern that if there was a problem with one carriage, any others linked to it by articulation would also need to be withdrawn. Such was the logic of the pre-multiple-unit railway.

As main-line stock was replaced the older carriages were cascaded onto the longer branches and non-express cross-country routes, so that eventually many had either corridor stock or at least toilet compartments.

The next generation of passenger rolling stock arrived in 1935, and was probably the most famous of the interwar Great Western rolling stock, often known as the 'Centenary Riviera'. This could only be used on former broad gauge routes with its width of 9ft 7in, although the length was only 60ft. These carriages were true corridor stock with large picture windows, which dropped continental-style for ventilation, and the doors recessed at the ends to avoid problems with the loading gauge on bends. A typical train would include two composite brake carriages, each with thirty-six seats, and two third-class brakes, each with sixteen seats, three third-class carriages with fifty-six seats each and a composite carriage of forty-eight seats, while there was also a twenty-four-seat first-class dining and kitchen car and a third-class dining car with sixty-four seats. Less well known, but

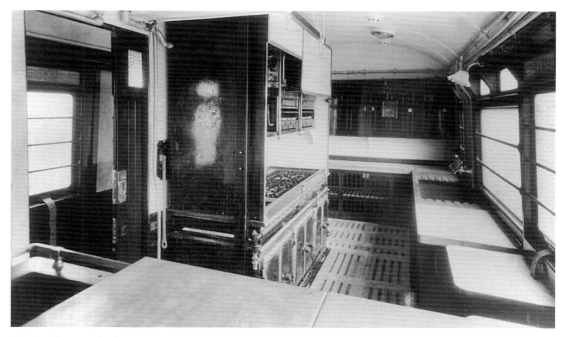

The kitchen end of a dining carriage of 1929 stock. No food preparation was done away from the train. Everything was prepared and cooked in these areas. (HMRS/J. Tatchell ADC518)

introduced at about this time, were new open carriages for excursion trains, each with eight bays, and with doors at the end and two lavatory compartments at one end.

The extra width of the 'Centenary Riviera' carriages must have made them very comfortable, but the next series of rolling stock, the last to be introduced before the outbreak of war, retained the large windows, but opted for sliding window ventilators of the kind seen on the post-nationalisation British Railways Mk I rolling stock. Clearly, passengers had come to accept the concept of end doors on corridor carriages, possibly won over by the large windows. It also seems likely that having been introduced to the new style of rolling stock, for every passenger who objected to not being able to gain access to his compartment straight from the platform, others appreciated not having their fellow passengers stepping over them with their luggage when calling at stations en route, and the absence of draughts from the doors.

While the name of the Great Western was synonymous with comfort and service, the company did not have great success with Pullman carriages. As mentioned in the next chapter, these had been tried on the 'Torbay Express' in 1929 but were soon discontinued. The next attempt was on the boat trains between Plymouth and London, with carriages 9ft 7in wide and 61ft 4½in long, complete with wide comfortable armchairs arranged at tables for four or two, all of which had a lamp. As with the 'Cornish Riviera' rolling stock, the doors were recessed into the sides at the end of the carriage. While these were not officially Pullman cars, passengers could reserve seats in carriages with a meal service at their seat.

Quite why the GWR could not make a success of Pullman cars is difficult to judge. The most likely reason could be that the journeys were too long, and that a dining car with two sittings made greater economic sense and more productive use of staff than having passengers tied to a table for an entire journey. Pullmans made sense on Waterloo to Bournemouth, a comfortable distance for a leisurely meal, but not on Paddington to Torquay.

Other developments were taking place at this time. Not only was the Great Western carrying cars on its goods trains for the motor industry, it was also carrying cars on passenger trains at the charge of 3d per mile as long as the car was accompanied by at least two adult passengers and subject to a minimum charge for 50 miles.

Possibly of even greater importance than this, the Great Western, along with the LMS and LNER, introduced third-class sleeping cars in 1927, initially on services to the West Country, and soon after on services to South Wales. Previously, sleeping cars had only been available for first-class passengers. The first third-class sleeping cars were converted from day passenger carriages, with each compartment sleeping four persons in bunks.

The other major advance in amenities for third-class passengers during the 1920s was when the Great Western introduced buffet cars. Although first-class passengers were not excluded, the third-class passengers were seen as the main market, enabling a greater number of these to take refreshments. Initially, buffet cars were conversions from older carriages so that different approaches could be tried and a standard style evolved. It was not until 1934 that the first new buffet cars were built, including one type with a 40ft counter with twelve stools, followed by another type with a shorter counter and eight stools, but with seats for twenty at tables. Later, a smaller buffet occupying half the carriage length was introduced and found to be successful, although it was realised that many passengers would be taking their food and drink back to their seats. Shortly before nationalisation, the Great Western experimented with a buffet that was fully automated, with passengers using vending machines, but this venture does not seem to have entered service.

Other than completing those railcars on order before the outbreak of war, the Great Western did not have to build any passenger carriages during the war years, so there was no need for a utility design. In 1947 Hawksworth introduced a new design of bow-ended carriages 64ft long, but while a number of these entered service, what would have been a normal production run was limited by the introduction of the British Railways Mk 1 standard carriages a few years after nationalisation.

A bright day and a rake of smartly turned-out carriages in 1930 with the train in the charge of an unidentified 2–6–2T of class 44XX. *(HMRS/J. Scott-Morgan ABX001)*

Slip Coaches

One feature that was always associated with the Great Western, although by no means unique to it, was the slip coach. This was a carriage attached to a train with its own guard's compartment and special coupling apparatus so that the guard could disconnect the coach while the train was travelling at speed, and by skilful handling of the brake bring the carriage to a stand at a station. This meant that many more stations could have a direct service while the train was not delayed unduly by the need to stop, since steam trains took some time to accelerate to the line speed. The first slip coaches were those introduced by the GWR in 1858 to serve Slough and Banbury.

Some trains had more than one slip coach, with the 'Cornish Riviera' at times having as many as three. Slip coaches lacked a corridor connection to the rest of the train, which would have complicated uncoupling at speed and also risked having passengers in the main train, but Ilfracombe justified a slip portion of no fewer than four coaches including a restaurant car, which was 'slipped' at Taunton. Working trains with slip carriages or portions demanded a number of special features, including a tail lamp system that enabled the slip to be distinguished from the main train, which itself had to have its own tail lamps otherwise, after the rolling stock at the back had been slipped, an alert signalman would assume that carriages had broken away. It also required special training and skill on the part of the guards involved, as too much braking could mean stopping short of the station platform, and too little could see the slip coach passing through the station and beyond the platforms.

The big drawback of slip coaches was, of course, that it was a one-way system. Passengers might arrive in fine style, having been slipped off an express, but they had to catch a stopping train back.

While slip coaches were first used on the Great Western and survived nationalisation, not finally being withdrawn on the Western Region of British Railways until 1960, their use was already in decline. In 1914 the GWR had seventy-four trains with slip coaches, but this fell to twenty-seven in 1921, just before the grouping, and despite rising to forty in 1929, by

The same year, but a less shiny rake of four carriages, one of which seems to be still in lake livery, headed by 4–4–0 class 33XX No. 3366 Earl of Cork, near Bilston. *(HMRS/D.H. Haines AEV014)*

1935 there were just twenty-two left. By comparison, the LNER and its predecessors had nineteen in 1914 and four in 1935, while the predecessors of the LMS had fifty-one in 1914 and seven in 1921, but none by 1929. The Southern Railway and its predecessors had twenty-nine in 1914, twenty-four in 1921 and just two in 1929, after which there were none left by 1935.

The superior acceleration of electric and diesel trains accounted in no small part for the demise of the slip coach, but so too did the improvement in road transport, as it became easier to travel to and from a more important station. At a time when growing emphasis was being placed on safety, including automatic train control, slip carriages were also something of a nuisance for the train operators, and, of course, they had to be returned to the main termini after use, usually as part of a stopping train.

'Camp Coaches'

During the 1930s old railway carriages had relatively little metal in them and were seldom valuable as items for scrap. They could be sold off, and as mentioned elsewhere the Great Western did indeed offer old carriages for sale; it delivered them free of charge to stations on its network. The best an old carriage could expect was to be used as a summer cottage, but many simply became storage sheds or hen houses.

It was in 1933 that the London & North Eastern Railway hit upon the idea of converting surplus railway carriages to camping coaches, basically self-catering holiday accommodation, located in disused sidings at stations that were in either tranquil surroundings or close to resorts. The Great Western was much taken with this idea, having a long running rivalry with the LNER over which company served the better holiday destinations, and eventually all of the 'Big Four' offered camping coaches. In 1934, the first GWR 'Camp Coaches' appeared.

The coaches were old compartment six-wheel carriages, usually with about five compartments. In typical Great Western fashion a booklet was commissioned, written and published, to introduce the public to the idea. Each camp coach would have one

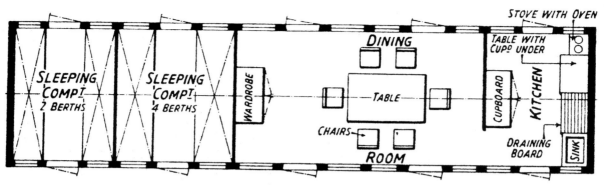

Plan of Great Western camping coach

Redundant railway carriages were sold off to anyone who might want to buy them, but later an initiative by the LNER was adopted, the so-called 'Camp Coach', using withdrawn carriages as self-catering holiday accommodation. This is a plan of the layout. *(Kevin Robertson)*

Not all trains could be crack expresses or have the most modern rolling stock, as this photograph taken at Laira, Plymouth, in 1923 shows. An unidentified 0–6–0ST pilots a 2–6–2T with a passenger train comprised of four-wheel and six-wheel carriages. No doubt some of these would become camp coaches within the next ten years or so. *(HMRS AEQ802)*

compartment fitted out as a kitchen, another two knocked into one as a living room with table, and the remaining two as sleeping cabins.

In the publicity material and the booklet, much was made of the fact that the company provided everything for its campers. The coaches all came with cutlery and crockery, saucepans, a cooking stove, tablecloths, towels, broom, blankets and sheets. A hurricane lamp was provided, with oil lamps for the sleeping cabins and another type of lamp for the living room, while the 'cooking stove' was a primus with an oven, there was a jug for carrying paraffin and a bucket, as well as deck chairs so that the campers could sit outside. This may seem primitive to us today, but this was reasonable comfort. The sleeping cabins could only be reached by stepping outside. Charges were fair at £3 per week for up to six people, and employees of the Great Western could hire the coaches at a discount outside the main holiday season.

For the first season there were just nineteen coaches, with locations including Penryn, Fowey, Blue Anchor and Princetown (handy for Dartmoor Prison), but this was soon extended and by 1939 there were sixty-five scattered throughout Cornwall, Devon, Somerset and rural Wales. Each season, demand exceeded the number of places available.

The venture ended with the outbreak of war. Many of the camp coaches were used as emergency wartime accommodation, some of them being moved to new locations, but almost all seem to have suffered neglect and even misuse during the war years.

Chapter Ten

Riviera and Flyer –
The Named Expresses

Mention the Great Western Railway and most people will think of the famous expresses, most probably the 'Cornish Riviera', redolent of holidays in Cornwall, or the 'Cheltenham Flyer', at one time the world's fastest regular train service. These were only a small part of the GWR, or even of its passenger services, but as on other railways, it was the great expresses that raised the image and were so often part of the public profile for a railway.

The GWR had an advantage over its rival, the Southern Railway, for traffic to Devon and Cornwall in that it had the main line and the large towns and cities, with a number of branch lines coming off this trunk route rather like bones off a spine, while the Southern had a route that fragmented, with a number of places with more or less equal status, but none of them, apart from Exeter and Plymouth, of great potential, especially out of season. Indeed, between Exeter and Plymouth, the Southern's inland route via Okehampton was less direct than that of the GWR from Exeter.

On its other flank, the GWR faced competition from the London, Midland & Scottish Railway for traffic to the Midlands, and especially Birmingham, but once again it had the better route, only slightly shorter, but much more modern and with fewer major intermediate junctions. It was the Great Western in the years between the two world wars

An express is taken towards Toddington by 4–6–0 class No. 2906 *Lady of Lynn* in 1931. *(HMRS/D.H. Haines AEU935)*

The interior of a new first-class carriage for the 'Cornish Riviera' in 1929 looking towards the corridor. This was a time when doors proliferated, as passengers liked easy access to their compartments. (*HMRS/J. Tatchell ADC517*)

for travel between London and Birmingham, and the LMS if you wanted to go further north, to Manchester or Liverpool, or beyond to Glasgow.

On the other hand, the GWR was not a major fan of the Pullman concept, in which heavy and luxurious carriages provided an 'at seat' meal service on payment of a supplement, and which were so favoured by the Southern Railway. The GWR's speciality was the 'limited' express, which ensured a seat for every passenger by requiring a prior reservation.

The GWR had not neglected the Pullman concept entirely, however. Plymouth still had a transatlantic liner traffic during the early days of the grouped railways and before Southampton became the dominant passenger liner port. One company, the French Line, had ships pick up passengers off Plymouth on their way from Le Havre to New York, and the GWR ran boat trains in connection with this service. In May 1929, as an experiment, Pullman carriages were added to the boat trains running between Plymouth and Paddington. This was followed in July by the 'Torquay Pullman', an all-Pullman express. The Down train left Paddington daily at 11a.m., and ran the 194 miles to Newton Abbot non-stop in 3 hours 25 minutes, reaching Torquay at 2.40p.m. and Paignton 10 minutes later. The Up train left Paignton at 4.30p.m. and Torquay at 4.40p.m., reaching Paddington at 8.30p.m. This wasn't a bad performance by the standards of the day, but another express had more convenient timings and was indeed to be the predecessor of another named express, and did not have the Pullman supplementary fare, something never fully understood or appreciated by many travellers on the Great Western or elsewhere.

In 1930 the Pullman cars were removed from the boat trains and the 'Torquay Pullman' was withdrawn, with all of this rolling stock transferred (since it actually belonged to the Pullman Car Company) to the Southern Railway, where it continued to operate on boat trains, but this time between Waterloo and Southampton, and on the all-Pullman 'Bournemouth Belle'.

The Bristolian

In 1935 the GWR main line between Paddington and Bristol celebrated its centenary, and the GWR aimed to accelerate the service. The initial aim was to offer an end-to-end journey time of just 90 minutes, but to avoid excessive speed and ensure acceptable standards of punctuality this ambition was scaled down to 105 minutes, still a quarter of an hour better

More spartan was the third-class compartment as, unlike some other companies, the GWR did not believe in providing three seats a side and armrests for third-class passengers. Again, this is 1929 stock. *(HMRS/J. Tatchell ADC516)*

than the best express of the day. Unusually, the Up and Down trains used different routes. The Down train took the original route, the 118.3 miles through Bath, while the Up train used the Badminton cut-off, opened in 1901, which was slightly shorter at 117.6 miles. The overall average speed was 67.6mph westbound, but 67.2mph eastbound. In practice, despite the tight curve through Bath, the eastbound train had to work even harder than these figures suggest because of the gradients on the Badminton route. On the Up working, the highest speed reached was 77mph between Badminton and Southall. This was the only GWR train to run non-stop throughout its journey.

The usual rake for 'The Bristolian' consisted of just seven carriages, necessary for the high speeds, with two third-class brakes, three composites and a third-class carriage, and in the centre of the train one of the company's newest buffet cars with a full-length counter and pedestal seats. The carriages were of the widest type available, with recessed end doors. The demanding schedule was considered to need a 'King', but in practice it was found that the 'Castle' class was capable of pulling the 221 tons (235 tons with passengers) of the train. The train used the same link of crews and the same well-tended locomotives that were also responsible for the 'Cheltenham Flyer'.

The train left Paddington at 10a.m. and reached Bristol Temple Meads at 11.45a.m., and in the return direction left Bristol at 4.30p.m. and arrived back in London at 6.15p.m. It was withdrawn on the outbreak of war in 1939 and not reinstated until some time after nationalisation.

Cheltenham Spa Express and Cheltenham Flyer

Many maintain that, contrary to folklore, the 'Cheltenham Flyer' was never an official title, no matter how well deserved the appellation. Certainly the name does not appear in the timetable and the train was officially known as the 'Cheltenham Spa Express', which in turn had its origins in a train introduced shortly after the end of the First World War, departing from Cheltenham at 2.30p.m. and reaching Paddington after calls at Gloucester and Swindon at 5.10p.m. The confusion over the title is understandable, as the GWR did indeed refer to the train as the 'Cheltenham Flyer' in its own internal magazine, and also sponsored a book about the train.

In 1923 the GWR decided that rather than simply speed up this service as part of its overall programme of accelerating its longer-distance trains, it would aim instead to

'The Cheltenham Spa Express' is taken out of Paddington in 1930 in the charge of 4–6–0 29XX No. 2950. The clerestory coach on the far left is a slip coach. (HMRS/J. Minnis AAA822)

The famous 'Cheltenham Flyer' made its way onto souvenir baggage labels but never into the timetables, where it remained the 'Cheltenham Spa Express'. Nevertheless, what mattered was that in 1930 (left) one could leave Cheltenham at 8a.m. and be at Paddington at 10.30a.m., while in 1922 the 7.15a.m. departure didn't reach Paddington until 10.45a.m. (Bradshaw)

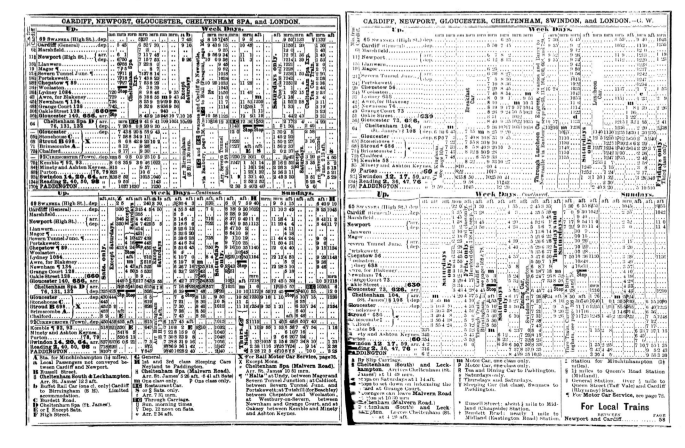

provide the fastest British express. The fastest timings for the day were those on the London & North Eastern Railway over the 44 miles between Darlington and York, against which the GWR could offer the almost level 77.3 miles between Swindon and Paddington. A morning Down and an afternoon Up service was selected and renamed the 'Cheltenham Spa Express' to set the record for a regular scheduled service, initially taking just 75 minutes for the Swindon–Paddington section. The service was never uniformly fast, and indeed the title of express was really earned by the dash between Swindon and Paddington, although by cutting the number of stops between Swindon and Cheltenham the service did maintain a reasonable speed even at the 'country' end.

The period immediately after the First World War saw main-line railway speeds rising rapidly throughout the developed world. The GWR could not afford to sit on its laurels. In July 1929 the schedule between Swindon and Paddington was cut to 70 minutes, giving an average speed for the section of 66.2mph, making it the fastest regular railway service in the world. By 1931 intense competition between the Canadian National Railway and Canadian Pacific Railway between Montreal and Toronto saw the GWR record beaten, so in September the GWR accelerated the 'Cheltenham Spa Express', or 'Cheltenham Flyer', by cutting the Swindon and Paddington timings to 67 minutes, requiring an average speed of 69.2mph. A year later a further cut to 65 minutes gave a start-to-stop average of 71.4mph, allowing the train to remain the world's fastest, but not for long.

As railway speeds continued to rise, by 1939 the 71.4mph average between Swindon and Paddington simply placed the GWR express among the top 200 fastest trains in the world. It was small consolation that it was only narrowly beaten in the UK by the LNER's 71.9mph schedule between King's Cross and York.

Individual trains often offered tighter timings, and the fastest journey for the 'Cheltenham Spa Express' was on 6 June 1932, when with the train being pulled by No. 5006 *Tregenna Castle* the Swindon to Paddington section was covered in 56 minutes 47 seconds, an average speed of 81.7mph, the fastest in Britain for the time and for some

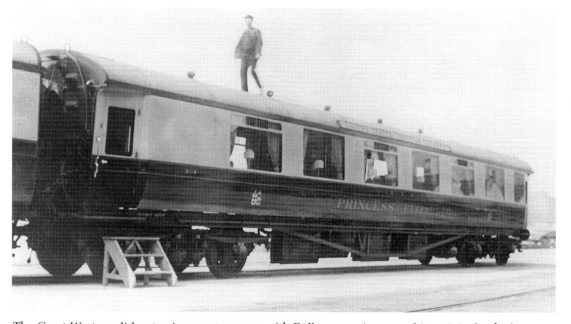

The Great Western did not enjoy great success with Pullman carriages, and its original vehicles were sent to the Southern Railway for the 'Bournemouth Belle'. Later it produced very luxurious carriages with meals served at passenger seats such as these, wide-bodied with the doors recessed at the ends to avoiding loading gauge problems on bends. These were 'Pullman' in all but name, even to the extent of carrying names on the first-class vehicles. This is *Princess Elizabeth* at Plymouth Millbay Docks, after forming part of a boat train for United States Lines. *(HMRS AEL132)*

time afterwards. Between mileposts 2 and 72 the average speed for the 70 miles was 87.5mph, although this was beaten by 70 miles at 91.8mph by the LNER in 1935.

Some accounts maintain that, unusually for a named express, the train ran in one direction only, as the balancing working taking the rolling stock to Cheltenham was a semi-fast. In 1932 the Up 'Cheltenham Spa Express' left St James station at 2.40p.m., calling at Malvern Road, and then running the 7½ miles to Gloucester in 13 minutes. Reversal was necessary at Gloucester and it was at this point that the locomotive, always a 'Castle' class, was attached for the run to London, while at the other end a composite carriage that had come from Hereford was added. The rest of the train usually consisted of six carriages, with two third-class brakes, two corridor composites and a restaurant car as well as another third-class carriage. The train left Gloucester at 2.58p.m., and called at Stroud and Kemble on its way to Swindon, while also tackling the 4-mile climb from Brimscombe to Sapperton Tunnel with gradients between 1 in 90 and 1 in 60, so that it was hardly surprising that the 44¼ miles from Cheltenham to Swindon took 71 minutes. Leaving Swindon at 3.55p.m., arrival at Paddington was at 5p.m.

Nevertheless, in the 1938 timetable the train was shown as the 'Cheltenham Spa Express' in both directions. The Down train left Paddington at 5p.m. and arrived in Cheltenham at 7.27p.m., while the Up working left Cheltenham at 8a.m. and arrived at Paddington at 10.30a.m. Interestingly, the Up train had a restaurant car, but a buffet sufficed in the Down direction. Breakfast has long been the most popular meal served on Britain's railways.

The service was suspended on the outbreak of war in 1939 and the postwar 'Cheltenham Spa Express' never reached the timings of its pre-war counterpart, and certainly could not be said to be a 'Cheltenham Flyer'.

The Cornish Riviera Limited and The Cornishman

As early as July 1904 the GWR was seeking to accelerate its services to Cornwall and introduced a summer-only train that would run non-stop between Paddington and Plymouth, using the Temple Meads avoiding line at Bristol. As the Westbury route had still to be completed it became the world's longest regular non-stop run at 245.7 miles. This was a seven-carriage train, including a dining car, with one carriage for Falmouth and the remainder running through to Penzance. Usually the locomotive was a 'City' class 4-4-0.

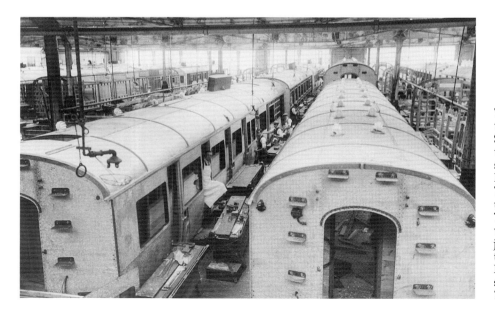

This is the carriage workshops at Swindon in 1929, with new rolling stock for the 'Cornish Riviera' and the Torbay expresses under construction. These carriages would be replaced just six years later by the 'Centenary Riviera' wide-bodied stock. (HMRS/J. Tatchell ADC505)

An exterior view of the 60ft-long bow-ended stock built in 1929 for the 'Cornish Riviera' and Torbay expresses. (*HMRS AEQ927*)

In 1906, the Westbury route came into use and the train became an all-year operation over the 225.7 miles between Paddington and Plymouth.

The new train replaced one of the earliest named trains, 'The Cornishman', which also had the distinction of being the last broad gauge train when it left Paddington on 20 May 1892. In fact, 'The Cornishman' was just two years old when the change of gauge came, having been introduced for the summer of 1890, when it was the fastest train to the West of England and one of the fastest in Britain. It left Paddington daily at 10.15a.m., reaching Bristol at 12.45p.m., Exeter at 2.20p.m., Plymouth at 3.50p.m. and Penzance at 6.57p.m. In the Up direction, the train left Penzance at 11.15a.m. and arrived at Paddington at 7.50p.m. 'The Cornishman' was unusual at the time in that it carried all three classes of passenger, while most of the great expresses of the day only carried first-class and second-class passengers.

The schedule was good for the time, but even better if one bears in mind that the GWR's efforts to run faster trains were crippled by an agreement made with the owners of the hotel and refreshment rooms at Swindon that all trains would stop there for at least 10 minutes to allow passengers to buy refreshments. The GWR finally released itself from this unrealistic burden in 1895 by paying £100,000 in compensation to the owners of the hotel, which was doubtless good value, although it converts into a present-day value of around £8.5 million. The other problem that hampered the longer-distance railways was the need for locomotives to stop to take on water, and around this time the provision of water troughs at Keynsham, near Bristol, and Goring, near Maidenhead, also helped to accelerate trains. Starting in October 1895, 'The Cornishman' made the first regular non-stop runs between Paddington and Bristol, leaving London at 10.30a.m. and still reaching Bristol at 12.45, an average speed of 52.6mph. Later, a further cut gave a two-hour Paddington–Bristol schedule. The train also started to divide with a Newquay section, and at peak times this developed into a Newquay relief train.

The title 'Cornish Riviera Limited' came into use before the First World War. The train developed with slip coaches detaching at Westbury for Weymouth, Taunton and Exeter. Those for Westbury and Taunton then became two carriage 'slips', and eventually it became apparent that there was considerable traffic to be picked up at Exeter for points further west, and so an Exeter call was inserted into the schedule between the wars. The main train with the restaurant cars ran through to Penzance, but there were still the carriages slipped at Westbury for Weymouth, while the two carriages slipped at Taunton were for the Ilfracombe and Minehead branches. In addition, a carriage for Kingsbridge was detached during the Exeter stop, and sometimes a carriage would be detached at Plymouth. On reaching Cornwall, a carriage for Newquay was detached at Par, one for Falmouth was detached at Truro and finally one for St Ives was detached at St Erth. This was the winter working; in summer the number of portions was reduced by the inclusion of additional express workings. In summer, the train operated non-stop between Paddington and Plymouth, but a working timetable stop was inserted at Newton Abbot on the Down service for a banking locomotive to join for the run through to Plymouth.

Such a heavy train with such long distances demanded the best available locomotives, and after the 'City' class the 'Star' class 4–6–0s took over before being displaced by the 'Castle' class in 1923 and then in 1926 by the new 'King' class. The 'Castle' class locomotives held on to the train for the run through Cornwall for many years, however, as these were the heaviest that could run across the bridge at Saltash, until replaced by the 'County' class later. The rake of carriages also changed, with the train usually showing the best that the GWR had to offer, with two different generations of 70ft vehicles followed by 60ft vehicles and then, during the late 1930s, by the 'Centenary Riviera' stock with its wide compartments and recessed end doors. Over the years between 1902 and 1939 the empty weight of the train went from 200 tons to 498 tons, or more than 530 tons with passengers and luggage, while the number of carriages had risen from seven to fourteen. While the gradients on the route made it a demanding working, cut-offs to avoid both Westbury and Frome helped, albeit at the cost of the Westbury for Weymouth slip coaches being slipped a mile or so early and having to be taken to the junction by a shunting engine.

In 1922 in the off season the train would leave Paddington at 10.30a.m., reaching Plymouth at 2.37p.m. and Penzance at 5p.m. The Up working left Penzance at 10a.m. and arrived at Plymouth at 12.30p.m. and Exeter at 1.45p.m., arriving at Paddington at 4.45p.m.

As if to prove that the GWR was not an inward-looking insular institution, for a week in May 1925 the 'Cornish Riviera Limited' was worked turn and turn about by No. 4074 *Caldicot Castle* and the LNER's A1 Pacific No. 4474 *Victor Wild*. Despite it being a 4–6–0 rather than a 4–6–2, the 'Castle' class produced the better timings, and used less fuel.

Only those interested in railways would have noticed the substitute locomotive. Probably of far greater interest to the majority of passengers were the experiments with 'wireless' on the 'Cornish Riviera' in April 1926. Radio was still a novelty, and most homes did not have it at the time. Car radio was still unknown. The experiment did not last long as difficulties were experienced with reception, and it could also have been the case that many passengers resented it as an intrusion.

In 1935 the train was so popular that it operated in several parts and was augmented by a new train, 'The Cornishman', while the main train became the 'Cornish Riviera Limited' and operated with compulsory seat reservations. The 'Cornish Riviera Limited' left Paddington at 10.30 as before, but ran non-stop Monday to Friday over the 279½ miles to Truro. On Saturdays it went even further non-stop, running for 299½ miles from Paddington to St Erth, carrying passengers for St Ives and Penzance. There were no slip carriages Monday to Saturday. Summer Saturdays saw a relief train leave Paddington at 10.25 with carriages for Falmouth and Hayle. At the same time 'The Cornishman' ran on Monday to Saturday, leaving Paddington at 10.35 with portions or slip carriages for Weymouth and Newquay, while also calling at Plymouth and Helston on its way to Penzance.

To celebrate the centenary of the Great Western the train also had new rolling stock, the wide-bodied stock with recessed doors at the end that became popularly known as 'The Centenary Riviera' rolling stock. Each train had ten carriages, consisting of two composite brakes, two brake thirds, three third-class carriages, a composite, and a first-class dining car with kitchen and a third-class dining car. The new carriages were among the first on the GWR to have doors at the ends only, and they also had drop windows for the compartments.

These arrangements continued until the outbreak of war in 1939, with the train departing from Paddington at 10.30, and on those occasions when it stopped at Plymouth it reached the city at 2.30p.m. and continued to Penzance at 4.55p.m., without an Exeter stop during the summer months. Timings were the same in the Up direction in 1939, except that there was no Exeter stop during the summer and Paddington was reached five minutes earlier at 4.40p.m. These timings seemed to have improved little, but the train was much heavier than in 1922, perhaps almost twice the weight.

After initially attempting in the first wave of wartime austerity measures to combine the 'Riviera' with no fewer than three other trains and run once again via Bristol, although on this occasion calling at what was by then a much larger Temple Meads, the service survived. A compromise solution that saw the 'Riviera' and a Torbay train combined also failed to produce the expected benefits, and in the end the 10.30 from Paddington became the 'Cornish Riviera' again, albeit unofficially as although it carried headboards on its carriages, this was a train that made more stops and in wartime could never be limited to those with seat reservations. No doubt it was saved by the immense wartime movement of naval personnel to and from Plymouth, and by the number of RAF Coastal Command and Royal Navy Fleet Air Arm bases in Cornwall. As it was, fourteen carriages became the standard, and the Down train called at Exeter, arriving at Plymouth at 3.25p.m. and Penzance at 6.25p.m. In the Up direction it left Penzance at 9.30a.m., but still managed a 12.30p.m. departure from Plymouth, and reached Paddington at 5.30p.m., again after a call at Exeter. Restaurant cars disappeared at the outbreak of war, but despite being reinstated in November 1939 disappeared again in October 1942, and did not reappear until 31 December 1945. Nevertheless, strenuous efforts were made to improve timings with the return of peace, and in summer 1946 Paddington–Plymouth became non-stop once again, with 4 hours 30 minutes Down and 4 hours 40 minutes Up, and Penzance taking 6 hours 55 minutes Down and 7 hours 15 minutes Up.

The train survived nationalisation, and at one time a second train was added as the 'Golden Hind', with an afternoon departure from Paddington and a morning departure from Plymouth, intended to cater for business rather than holiday traffic. 'The Cornishman' title was also resurrected after nationalisation.

The Irish Mail

One problem in dealing with titled trains is that sometimes the names were unofficial, or semi-official, as a fast express carrying mail would become known as the 'XX Mail'. The situation with the 'Irish Mail' was that there were always two of them, one being the London & North Western train from Euston, and the other being that of the GWR, more usually known as the 'Irish Mail via Fishguard'.

While the GWR in its early days saw itself as the railway for those heading across the Atlantic, and Brunel himself was one of the leading naval architects of the day, the railway did not ignore the potential of the far shorter crossing of the Irish Sea. The route, that between Fishguard in West Wales and Rosslare in the south of Ireland, lacked the obvious potential of those Irish Sea services that went to Dublin or Belfast, but in doing so produced a far more direct route for those wanting the far south of Ireland, and the important towns of Cork, Waterford and Wexford.

The GWR's services into Wales were the key to the new route, but first the company had to create a new port at Fishguard, and the station alone required the removal of a rocky hillside. To ensure that the service would be viable it was not only necessary to ensure a good service to Fishguard and GWR steamers for the crossing of the St George's Channel, but also to encourage good connecting railway services on the other side, with the Great Southern Railway of Ireland introducing restaurant car trains linking Rosslare with Cork

Apart from excursion carriages and some vehicles for the Irish Mail trains, which proved unpopular, the only open rolling stock for main-line services was the dining car. This is the 1929 first-class end, for many years the only preserve of large picture windows. *(HMRS/J. Tatchell ADC520)*

and Waterford, followed by a service between Rosslare and Wexford. The shipping service was operated by the Fishguard & Rosslare Railway & Harbour Company, which itself was a fifty-fifty partnership between the Great Western Railway and the Great Southern Railway of Ireland, as covered more fully in Chapter Twelve.

The GWR's faith in Fishguard seemed to be justified when one of the main transatlantic steamship companies, Cunard, chose to use it as a port of call, so that mail and passengers could disembark or embark and use the GWR line to Paddington, rather than remain aboard and continue to Liverpool, only to have to travel south again. So important was the promise of this traffic to the GWR that it built an avoiding line at Swansea, which while it saved little in terms of distance did avoid the congestion around the Swansea area. Unfortunately, the greater appeal of Southampton, so much closer to London than Fishguard or Liverpool and with the option of calls at Cherbourg or Le Havre to tap traffic to and from the Continent, wooed Cunard away and Fishguard was left solely with the Irish traffic.

As a result, Fishguard never gained the importance for Irish passenger traffic of the other ports in North Wales, the north-west of England and the west of Scotland. This meant that the boat trains also handled a great deal of business for intermediate stops, as Newport and Cardiff were both seen as too important to miss, and a stop was also made at Landore for passengers for Swansea.

The ferry service included day and night sailings, with departures from Paddington at both 8.45a.m. and 8.45p.m., taking 5½ hours for the 261 miles to Fishguard. In addition to the calls in South Wales, the morning train called at Reading and the evening one at Swindon. Both morning and evening services had restaurant cars, but the evening train also included a first-class sleeping car, although this was of doubtful appeal as the occupants were roused at 2.15a.m. from a warm berth and a deep sleep to transfer to the ferry.

The First World War saw the end of the day packet steamer and this was not reinstated when peace returned. The night ferry continued to run on three nights a week at first, until

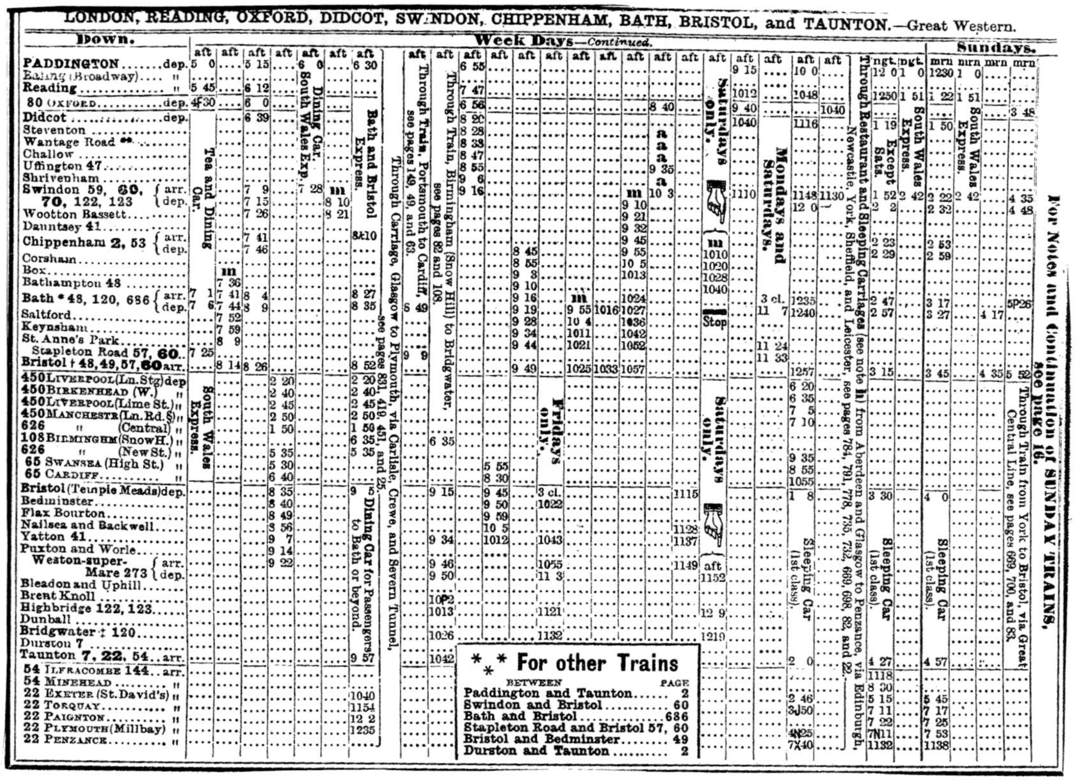

LONDON, READING, OXFORD, DIDCOT, SWINDON, CHIPPENHAM, BATH, BRISTOL, and TAUNTON.—Great Western.

Down. — Week Days—Continued. — Sundays.

PADDINGTON dep.; Ealing (Broadway); Reading; 80 Oxford dep.; Didcot dep.; Steventon; Wantage Road; Challow; Uffington 47; Shrivenham; Swindon 59, 60, 70, 122, 123 arr./dep.; Wootton Bassett; Dauntsey 41; Chippenham 2, 53 arr./dep.; Corsham; Box; Bathampton 48; Bath 48, 120, 686 arr./dep.; Saltford; Keynsham; St. Anne's Park; Stapleton Road 57, 60; Bristol 48, 49, 57, 60 arr.; 450 Liverpool (Ln. Stg) dep; 450 Birkenhead (W.); 450 Liverpool (Lime St.); 450 Manchester (Ln. Rd.); 626 " (Central); 108 Birmingham (Snow H.); 626 " (New St.); 65 Swansea (High St.); 65 Cardiff; Bristol (Temple Meads) dep.; Bedminster; Flax Bourton; Nailsea and Backwell; Yatton 41; Puxton and Worle; Weston-super-Mare 273 arr./dep.; Bleadon and Uphill; Brent Knoll; Highbridge 122, 123; Dunball; Bridgwater 120; Durston 7; Taunton 7, 22, 54 arr.; 54 Ilfracombe 144 arr.; 54 Minehead; 22 Exeter (St. David's); 22 Torquay; 22 Paignton; 22 Plymouth (Millbay); 22 Penzance.

Train notes: Tea and Dining Car. South Wales Express. Dining Car, South Wales Exp. Bath and Bristol Express. Dining Car for Passengers to Bath or beyond. Through Train, Glasgow to Plymouth, via Carlisle, Crewe, and Severn Tunnel, see pages 831, 419, 451, and 25. Through Carriage, Portsmouth to Cardiff, see pages 49, 49, and 63. Through Train, Birmingham (Snow Hill) to Bridgwater, see pages 82 and 108. Fridays only. Saturdays only. Mondays and Saturdays. Through Restaurant and Sleeping Carriages (see note h) from Aberdeen and Glasgow to Penzance, via Edinburgh, Newcastle, York, Sheffield, and Leicester, see pages 784, 791, 778, 735, 732, 689, 698, 82, and 22. Except Sats. Sleeping Car (1st class). South Wales Express. Through Train from York to Bristol, via Great Central Line, see pages 699, 700, and 83. For Notes and Continuation of SUNDAY TRAINS, see page 16.

*** For other Trains BETWEEN	PAGE
Paddington and Taunton	2
Swindon and Bristol	60
Bath and Bristol	686
Stapleton Road and Bristol 57,	60
Bristol and Bedminster	49
Durston and Taunton	2

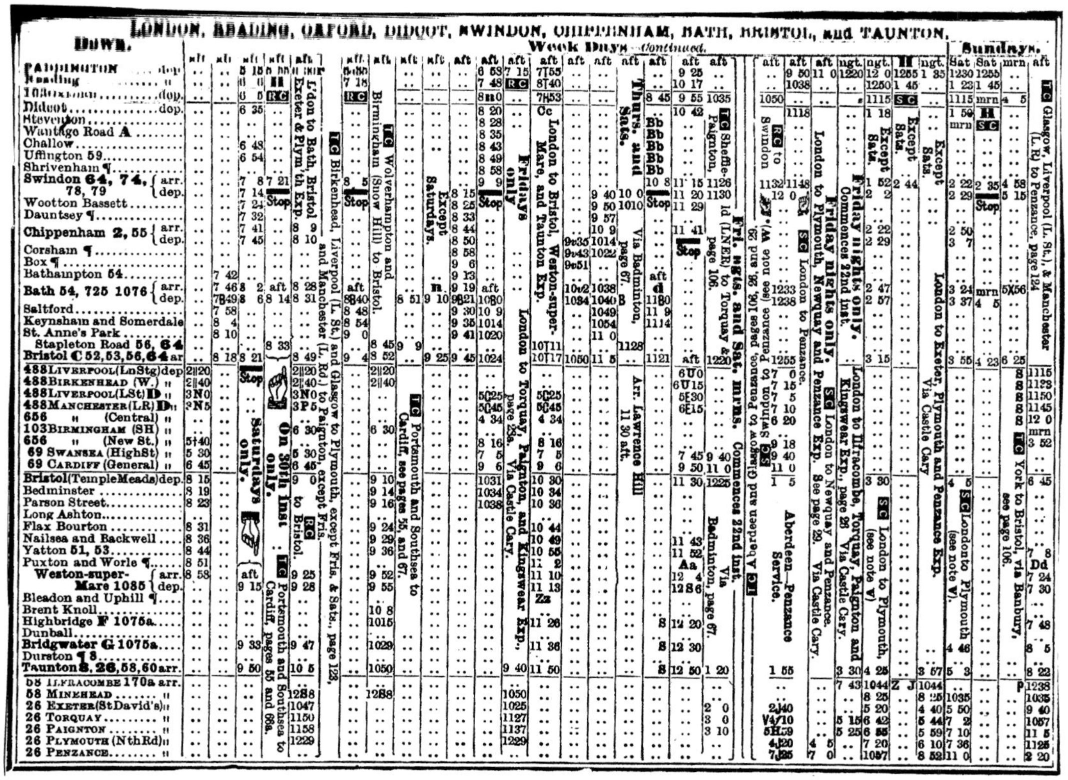

LONDON, READING, OXFORD, DIDCOT, SWINDON, CHIPPENHAM, BATH, BRISTOL, and TAUNTON.

Down. — Week Days—Continued. — Sundays.

Paddington dep.; Reading; 103 Oxford dep.; Didcot dep.; Steventon; Wantage Road A; Challow; Uffington 59; Shrivenham; Swindon 64, 74, 78, 79 arr./dep.; Wootton Bassett; Dauntsey; Chippenham 2, 55 arr./dep.; Corsham; Box; Bathampton 54; Bath 54, 725 1076 arr./dep.; Saltford; Keynsham and Somerdale; St. Anne's Park; Stapleton Road 56, 64; Bristol C 52, 53, 56, 64 arr.; 488 Liverpool (LnStg) dep; 488 Birkenhead (W.); 488 Liverpool (LSt) D; 488 Manchester (LR) D; 656 " (Central); 103 Birmingham (SH); 656 " (New St.); 69 Swansea (HighSt); 69 Cardiff (General); Bristol (Temple Meads) dep.; Bedminster; Parson Street; Long Ashton; Flax Bourton; Nailsea and Backwell; Yatton 51, 53; Puxton and Worle; Weston-super-Mare 1085 arr./dep.; Bleadon and Uphill; Brent Knoll; Highbridge F 1075a; Dunball; Bridgwater G 1075a; Durston; Taunton 8, 26, 58, 60 arr.; 58 Ilfracombe 170a arr.; 58 Minehead; 26 Exeter (St David's); 26 Torquay; 26 Paignton; 26 Plymouth (NthRd); 26 Penzance.

Notes such as 'South Wales Express' were not so much named trains as guidance for the passenger, as was 'Bath & Bristol Express'. The upper timetable is for July 1922, the lower for July 1938. *(Bradshaw)*

this too was suspended for a while. Postwar the move to standardise departure times out of Paddington for main-line trains saw those for South Wales allocated departures at 5 minutes to the hour, so the evening boat train had its departure time advanced to 7.55p.m., and also called at Swansea rather than taking the cut-off. The train included two slip carriages for Bristol. Arrival at Fishguard was also brought forward, to 1.40a.m. The Up train left Fishguard at 3.55a.m. instead of 1.40a.m. as previously, with banking assistance for the long climb out of the harbour station. The arrival at Paddington at 9.47a.m. came after some fairly relaxed running to avoid the morning peak period trains into the station.

Between the wars the train normally included a composite sleeping car, composite restaurant car, corridor first and three corridor thirds and a third-class brake, the Bristol slip coaches and two or three brake vans in the Down direction, while in the Up direction there were no slip coaches. A 'Castle' class locomotive handled the Paddington–Cardiff section, while locomotive power between Cardiff and Fishguard was more varied.

The Fishguard–Rosslare service was withdrawn shortly after the outbreak of the Second World War, and not reinstated until October 1945. Even then the boat train did not run daily. It was not until 1964 that a day ferry service was revived.

The Torbay Express and Torbay Limited

Little distinguishes 'The Torbay Express' other than that it was a train that was both fast and popular, and the latter might simply be a reflection of the popularity of the 'English Riviera' itself. Indeed, its most unusual feature was that at Taunton it slipped a four-carriage portion for Ilfracombe, which was distinguished not only by having four carriages but is believed to be the only slip portion to have included a restaurant car. Slipping even a single carriage always called for great skill on the part of the guard who had to be careful to bring the carriage or carriages to a stop at the station, not too soon and not too late, but any guard who left four carriages awaiting the attentions of a shunter would not have been allowed to forget it.

In its early days before the First World War 'The Torbay Express' left Paddington at 11.50 and took 3 hours to run to Exeter non-stop, slipping the Ilfracombe portion on the way. The departure was put back 10 minutes to 12 noon before the outbreak of war, and when reinstated after the war this became the new departure time, but the Ilfracombe portion was no longer included. Speed increased slightly between the wars, so that by 1939 the train left Paddington at noon and reached Exeter in 169 minutes, requiring an average speed of 61.6mph for the 173½ miles to St David's. The train spent 6 minutes at Exeter and then took another 35 minutes to cover the 26 miles to Torquay, so that end to end the journey took exactly 3½ hours. Still with the same locomotive, in its later days a 'King' class, the train continued to Paignton and Churston, finally descending to Kingswear to arrive at 4.05p.m. By this time the summer Saturday traffic was so busy that the train ran non-stop to Torquay, covering the 199.6 miles in 3 hours 28 minutes, but the timings beyond Torquay remained the same, possibly because of the single-line section from Goodrington Sands. The status of the train improved, with some photographs showing it carrying 'Torbay Limited' headboards, although this title does not appear in the timetables.

Not all railway lines offer the same running conditions in both directions, and the line between Exeter and Kingswear was a prime example. Leaving Kingswear, the line was level for a mile, allowing some frantic acceleration before tackling the climb to Churston, with a 2 mile stretch varying between 1 in 75 and 1 in 66. Departing from Torquay the train immediately encountered a 1 in 55 gradient for ¾ mile, and then the same distance again at 1 in 73. Banking assistance was necessary when the train was heavily laden or the rails were wet. The Up train left Torquay at 12 noon, and despite the gradient was still scheduled to reach Exeter in 35 minutes. Again, the train spent 6 minutes at St David's, but was allowed 174 minutes for the run to Paddington. The big difference by this time was

A 2–6–2T class 44XX locomotive pulls five carriages, with those furthest from the locomotive possibly dropped from an express at Redruth, near Perranporth Beach in 1932. Those closest are elderly clerestory stock in either lake or brown livery and probably cascaded, to use a modern term, onto branch-line duties. *(HMRS/J. Scott-Morgan AAH931)*

that on summer Saturdays the Up train also ran non-stop from Torquay, leaving at 11.50 and being allowed a generous 3¾ hours, while there was another train making the weekday calling pattern that was also given an extra 15 minutes.

After attempting to combine 'The Torbay Express' with 'The Cornish Riviera' shortly after the outbreak of the Second World War, but finding the load too great for a single locomotive, the 'Torbay' resumed its autonomous existence. The departure from Paddington was brought forward to 10.40a.m. and additional stops included at Taunton, Dawlish, Teignmouth and Torre, and it was scheduled to arrive at Torquay at 3.18p.m. and Kingswear at 3.50p.m. In the Up direction, the train left Kingswear at 11.25a.m. and Torquay at 11.55am, linking up with a portion from Penzance at Newton Abbot, after which it called at Exeter, Taunton and Reading to reach Paddington at 4.50p.m. The arrival at Paddington was brought forward by 15 minutes in October 1945.

The summer of 1946 saw the 12 noon departure from Paddington reinstated, but given the wartime neglect of rolling stock and infrastructure, the 'Torbay' was probably doing well to reach Exeter in 183 minutes and Torbay in 3¾ hours. The Up train was allowed an extra 5 minutes for the run from Torquay to Paddington. While the train survived nationalisation, by the mid-sixties it had lost its name.

Chapter Eleven

Go Great Western

It was not until the late nineteenth century that the railway companies began to look beyond advertising cheap day trips or announcing the opening of new lines or stations, and began to fully exploit the potential of advertising. One reason for this broader approach was the growing trend towards paid holidays, even for factory workers in the industrial towns. The holiday market soon became one for the railway companies to aim for, with the pre-grouping GWR proclaiming itself as 'GWR The Nation's Holiday Line' as early as 1914, while post-grouping in 1923, a triangular emblem, similar to a 'no smoking' sign in shape, simply declared 'Go Great Western'.

The Great Western was publicity conscious, and did not simply depend on advertising, but also invited journalists on inaugural runs and to celebrations such as those for the centenary in 1935. It even went further, with its own monthly publication for employees, *The Great Western Railway Magazine*, which first appeared in 1888.

A substantial element in the publicity output was the steady stream of books and booklets aimed at the public, and not just the intending traveller. The annual publication *Holiday Haunts* grew in size each year between the wars, although the price remained steady at 6d, and another publication was devised to promote camp coaches, but there were also books for boys interested in the company's locomotives. Other publications were aimed at those using the company's goods services, doubtless attempting to attract premium traffic rather than the heavily regulated traditional traffic.

There were some self-imposed constraints. As road traffic increased in volume and traffic jams became a reality in the larger conurbations, the railway companies combined to let the public know that it was 'quicker by rail' in those pre-motorway and even pre-arterial-road days. Road accidents were also rising, and someone suggested that the railway companies should also advertise that it was 'safer and quicker by rail'. Such a campaign would certainly not have offended the present-day Advertising Standards Authority, with just one passenger killed on the Great Western between 1916 and 1934, but even the Great Western knew better than to tempt fate. One just has to look at the history of railway accidents to appreciate that in a bad accident a hundred or more people could be killed, and it would just be the misfortune of some railway marketing manager to initiate a campaign boasting of railway safety on the Monday and have many of his customers dead and injured a few days later.

Publicity extended to posters, press advertising, leaflets and handbills, and to what might be variously described as promotional items or 'giveaways'. Some of these would seem strange today, and show just how much life has changed; for example, the 'Go Great Western' slogan was to be found on glass inkwells in the 1920s. The age of the franking machine had already dawned, and 'Go Great Western' appeared on correspondence sent out by the company. Probably one item that was both a souvenir and an aid to the traveller, and to staff such as porters, was the 'Cheltenham Flyer' luggage label introduced in 1932, despite the train's title being unofficial. Publicity was also used to try to change the habits of the travelling public, with an 'Earlier Holidays' campaign in the 1920s and 1930s attempting to spread holiday travel into the late spring and early autumn. At one stage the

GWR allowed its optimism to let it promote holidays in Cornwall in February, which was perhaps a month or two too early in the year. Another campaign adopted by all of the railway companies and promoted jointly tried to encourage passengers to take their dog with them, assuring them that water would be available for their animals at manned railway stations. Sending luggage in advance was another shared campaign.

The 'Big Four' railway companies not only combined on many advertising campaigns, they also undertook a considerable amount of international marketing together. Two good examples were the shared premises in both Paris and New York. The Great Western also undertook to market the continental services offered by the Southern Railway at selected stations on its network.

International tourism is so much associated with the 1960s onwards, that it is worth noting that as early as 1930 the Great Western had joined the Travel Association of Great Britain and Ireland, an organisation formed to promote the British Isles to overseas visitors.

Less happily, the last great joint advertising campaign was launched in 1938 calling for a 'Fair deal for the Railways'. This was an effort to get the government to repeal the regulations governing their freight charges, and in effect also to drop the common carrier obligation which had so blighted the economics of running railways, especially once road transport competition developed in the years following the end of the First World War. Not only did war and government control intervene, but the newly created Mass Observation movement researched public attitudes towards the campaign and found that it had aroused little public sympathy. There was a sense that the man in the street believed that the railways were protesting too much.

While the many short railway lines in South Wales absorbed under the grouping needed little in the way of publicity and had little to offer the potential holiday-maker, the Cambrian Railway did reach the resorts. As early as 1909 it had sponsored a 'Cambrian Resorts Association' to promote the attractions of its operating area, and the GWR wisely adopted and adapted this into its own marketing.

This 55ft-long third-class compartment carriage, still in lake livery, was forty-five years old when photographed at Goodrington Sands in 1947. *(HMRS/P.J. Garland AEL532)*

SWANSEA, CARMARTHEN, TENBY, NEYLAND, and FISHGUARD HARBOUR.

Down. Week Days—*Continued.*

PADDINGTON........dep.
Reading........................dep.
14 Oxford.......................dep.
Swindon.........................dep.
Wootton Bassett.............
Brinkworth.....................
Little Somerford 49........
Hullavington...................
Badminton......................
Chipping Sodbury...........
Coalpit Heath A.............
Winterbourne.................
Filton Junction 57..........
Horfield..........................
Stapleton Road 56..........
Lawrence Hill 53, 54.......
Bristol E 14, 52, arr........
Bristol (Tm. Mds.) dep....
Lawrence Hill.................
Stapleton Hill.................
Horfield.........................
Filton Junction..............
Patchway.......................
Pilning (H.L.) 57.............
Severn Tunnel Jn 75 arr...
76 Chepstow 89............dep.
Magor............................
Llanwern........................
Newport C 77, 80...........
81, 85, 125, 485, 494.....
Cardiff D E 80, 85, 97 arr.
86 Barry Docks...........arr.
Ely (Main Line)..............
St. Fagan's....................
Peterston.......................
Llantrisant 83, 86..........
Llanharan......................
Pencoed........................
Bridgend 88, 90, 97.......
Pyle 97..........................
Port Talbot (General).....
Briton Ferry 91..............
Neath (Gen) 89, 91, 94...
Skewen..........................
Llansamlet.....................
Landore 76.....................
Swansea (High...............
Street) 485, 493............
Cockett..........................
Gowerton 485, 493........
Loughor..........................
Llanelly 149...................
Pembrey & Burry Port....
Ferryside........................
141 Aberystwyth...........arr.
Carmarthen 141, 493...arr.
Carmarthen..................dep.
Sarnau...........................
St. Clears.......................
Whitland 96...................
96 Tenby........................
98 Pembroke Dock.........
Whitland........................
Clynderwen 85...............
Clarbeston Road.............
Haverford West G..........
Johnston (Pem.) 92........
92 Milford Haven..........arr.
Neyland........................arr.
Fishguard & Goodwick....
Fishguard Harbour.......arr.

The service between London and South Wales did not accelerate as much as on some other routes, between 1922 (right) and 1938 (left), but frequency increased. The GWR was highly active in promoting business in South Wales, struggling to overcome the problems of recession and the after-shocks of the miners' strike in 1926. (Bradshaw)

More modern was this 57ft-long third-class carriage with 'toplight' windows, with happy holidaymakers crowding the corridor as it neared Newton Abbot in 1947. *(HMRS/P.J. Garland AEL515)*

Most industries have their own means of handling publicity matters, and on the railways this was largely under the overall control of the superintendent of the line, which in other modes of transport might be termed the traffic manager.

Advertising and Booklets

In common with many railway companies, the Great Western was an early user of newspapers for advertising, although the early advertisements were fairly unexciting announcements. On 2 June 1838 *The Times* carried an announcement that the Great Western Railway would be opening its line from Paddington to Maidenhead. In the years that followed not only the national newspapers but the regional and local press also became important conduits between the company and its customers. There was logic in this, especially as people in, say, Bristol or Plymouth were more likely to read their regional or local paper than a national one than is the case today. Opening a new station or a new branch in the south-west or in Wales would in any case be of scant interest to most of the readers of the national press.

The early advertising was made all the less exciting by the strict embargo in many newspapers on the use of large type in advertisements. Many of them were similar to the small advertisements placed by individuals today, and even the larger ones were similar to that which a highways authority might use to announce a planned road scheme. It was not until 1904 that the pre-grouping Great Western placed an illustrated advertisement in the *Daily Mail*. From then on, much use was made of this type of advertising for the company's holiday books and booklets, with the public invited to send 6*d* in stamps to the superintendent of the line. The small advertisements continued, and were often located in the same place in newspapers so that the public would know where to find details of weekend excursions or other special trains. To put this into context, this was a period when newspapers carried much travel information that would not appear today, including the sailings of ocean liners, and for the modern equivalent one would have to look at the travel information on the teletext pages or on the internet.

Lord Leverhulme famously remarked, 'I know that half of the money I spend on advertising is wasted, but the trouble is I don't know which half!' To the end of its days the GWR had little idea of how well its advertising worked. Market research was in its infancy, and the Mass Observation example mentioned earlier was not concerned with the business of any particular company but with issues, as an early exercise in assessing public opinion and reactions. There were some instances when something was clearly a great success. A newspaper advertising campaign in 1928 urging the public to take 'Earlier Holidays' resulted in 12,000 enquiries by letter, let alone telephone calls or personal visits to railway stations.

The new general manager of the post-grouping Great Western, Felix Pole, built on the earlier work done by Inglis, who had transformed GWR publicity when he took over as general manager in 1904, despite having an engineering background. One feature that may seem strange to us today was that the public were expected to pay for much of the publicity material. On the other hand, jigsaw puzzles for young boys showing magnificent Great Western locomotives steaming through attractive scenery could be said to have their equivalent today in some of the items offered by airlines in their in-flight sales. Books such as the annual *Holiday Haunts*, first published in 1906, were paid for by the public, but also were underpinned by revenue from advertising. No doubt, prudent to the end, the Great Western felt that the public would value something that they had paid for more than something issued free of charge.

Other booklets included *Smiling Somerset* and *The West Country*, both in 1931, and *The Cotswold Country*, which followed in 1936. These all had attractive covers, but the early editions of some gazetteers intended for American visitors were very dull and looked more like government publications.

The Great Western didn't always mean chocolate and cream, even after the grouping saw the reintroduction of this livery after some twenty years. Lake livery persists on this local train at Paignton in 1926, in the charge of 2–6–2T class 45XX No. 4547. (*HMRS/D.H. Haines AEV001*)

Even before the grouping Felix Pole sponsored a competition in *The Great Western Railway Magazine* in 1922 for poster designs, with the then considerable prize of 100 guineas, or £105. This was equal to about £2,000 today using the standard scales for inflation, but these take so much else into account that it is worth remembering that in other terms it also represented about nine months' pay for a typical employee, or equal to some £15,000 today. Sadly, none of the competition entries was ever used.

The way in which publicity developed is best appreciated by comparing the covers of the first and last editions of the *GWR Engine Book*. In 1911 this had a simple cover, without illustration, and looked like an official document. By 1946 it was illustrated with a steam locomotive on a turntable, and instead of simply offering 'names of engines' it also promised 'names, numbers, type and classes'. In the meantime the price had gone up from 5*d* to 2*s* 6*d*.

It was not until the 1930s that GWR posters began to take on an attractive appearance, with the company lagging behind the trend-setting styles established by the newly formed London Passenger Transport Board under Frank Pick, and even behind the other railway companies.

Throughout this period the needs of the industrial customer were not neglected, with a 142-page booklet called *Guide to Economical Freight* first published in 1936 and replacing an earlier publication for the same market, *How to Spend and Save*. The company magazine also had much to say to its employees about selling the Great Western, and especially to its goods agents, who were expected to canvass business customers.

There was much to suggest that the Great Western took a very broad view of everything that it did. It was not enough simply to sell its services, it also sold the destination. In a slightly different way this also applied to freight traffic. In the depths of the recession, when the South Wales economy was still suffering the after-effects of the mine workers' strike and the loss of many of its markets, the company was active in efforts to revive the industries of South Wales and attract new investment to the area.

An express train with a composite restaurant car at Newton Abbot in 1947. *(HMRS/P.J. Garland AEL626)*

The main feature of the GWR's publications throughout the post-grouping period was *Holiday Haunts*. This first appeared in 1906, and its contents consisted of short introductory paragraphs about each county, a line or so about each place of interest, coming in alphabetical order, and then a tabulated directory of accommodation showing the facilities offered and, of course, the distance from the nearest station. A remarks column gave useful additional information, such as 'facing sea' or 'good cooking and homely'. This was before the introduction of hotel grading schemes. Most of the space was taken up by advertisements for hotels and boarding houses. Not surprisingly, the book included a large folding map of the Great Western, and there were also articles and photographs about the company's 'cut-off' routes such as the Badminton and Castle Cary lines, and the new facilities available for passengers to Ireland. Cross-country services such as Cardiff–Newcastle and Birkenhead–Dover were also featured 'without change of carriage'.

Initially, *Holiday Haunts* cost 1d and in 1906 had 538 pages. It was only slightly larger in 1922, by which time the price had risen to 6d. It then started to grow in size, with 624 pages in 1923, and by 1933 it had risen to 1,032 pages, mainly advertising, but at least the price remained the same. The last edition was in 1940, published while the so-called 'Phoney War' allowed people to think that holidays were still a possibility. Even so, as late as 1942, with the war far from won and shortages growing, booklets for ramblers were still on sale, undoubtedly for those who would really like to get away from it all.

Of course, the GWR was not slow in promoting its own range of holiday haunts, the so-called 'Camp Coaches' using redundant passenger carriages. A booklet was published extolling their virtues and the thoughtfulness of the company in providing these fully equipped. There was also advertising that reflected the standards of the day, with male and female holiday-makers in segregated sleeping cabins. It was also clear that the male holiday-makers had nothing better to do than relax while their wives or girlfriends got on with the chores, even on holiday.

The Great Western was always active in promoting Cornwall, one of the many holiday areas served by the railway, with advertising and the publication of guidebooks. *(Kevin Robertson)*

The Great Western showed considerable optimism in promoting 'Bathing in February' in Cornwall, especially in an era when holidays were shorter than today and more likely to take place during the traditional holiday months. *(Kevin Robertson)*

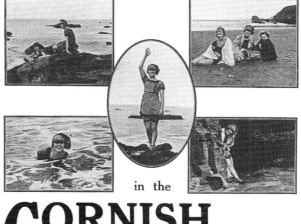

Great Western Railway
BATHING in FEBRUARY
in the
CORNISH RIVIERA

PADDINGTON STATION, W.2.
FEBRUARY, 1923

FELIX J. C. POLE,
General Manager.

Having bought a copy of *Holiday Haunts*, and doubtless having also bought a GWR guidebook or the 'Camp Coach' booklet, and then purchased tickets with a seat reservation, the Great Western publicity machine was still not finished with the passenger. The long journey from Paddington to Penzance, 305 miles, would clearly be so much more enjoyable if one also bought a copy of *Through the Window: Paddington to Penzance*, a book of strip maps with numerals placed on the interesting sights that would be passed and cross-referenced with the text on the facing page.

The Great Western Railway Magazine

The Great Western had been one of the first railway companies to produce a magazine for its employees, starting in 1888. This was published monthly, and it is interesting to note that although some railway company magazines went to alternate months during the Second World War, that of the GWR remained monthly, but it did get much thinner and in 1942 and 1943 the paper used was noticeably poorer in quality.

In some ways, the contents of *The Great Western Railway Magazine* would not surprise anyone picking up a similar publication at their workplace today. There was an element of sermonising in the leading article from the general manager, which post-grouping was Felix Pole, and there were details of staff clubs and sports societies, as well as fairly exhaustive lists of staff movements and details of senior appointments, as well as obituaries. Profiles of different areas of a company's operations are another typical feature of the genre and the magazine was no exception, while the early post-grouping issues contained histories of the 'absorbed' companies.

On the other hand, the magazine provided other features that would surprise many today. There were detailed statistics about the business and time-keeping, and productivity figures as well, much of which would be left for management communications today. There was extensive and often very technical information about new rolling stock, and also lengthy features about major industries served by the Great Western, including a two-part feature on the tobacco industry. Sometimes there would be an extract of a paper read before a professional institution and, ironically given the subsequent history, one of the first in 1922 concerned the advantages of railway electrification.

Book reviews were included, and these could range from a railway subject to those dealing with other matters that might interest staff, including books on the places served. Strangely, there seldom appeared to be any correspondence from staff.

While the magazine had its origins under the control of an unpaid voluntary editor, it became a part-time job when Felix Pole took over as editor in 1903. Pole already had a reputation as a railway enthusiast and writer, and under his control the magazine was also targeted at this element among the company's employees. Indeed, reprints of timed journeys on the Great Western from the railway magazines of the day were one feature that appeared from time to time. Under Pole, the magazine's circulation rose from 2,000 copies per month to more than 20,000. As Pole was steadily promoted towards the top of the company, eventually he had to hand over the editorial chair to the first full-time editor, Edward Hadley, who remained in this post for eighteen years from 1919. Under his editorship, circulation rose to 46,000 copies, while the price remained at a penny.

Avoiding accidents to trains and passengers was just part of the safety problem for railways, and remains so today. The Great Western was anxious to reduce accidents to its employees, and used the in-house magazine to promote 'safe working'. (*Kevin Robertson*)

On a lighter note, there were many special features, such as this cartoon, 'Railway Ribaldry', from the centenary issue of *The Great Western Railway Magazine*. (*Kevin Robertson*)

Hadley's innovation was to write about the different jobs that people on the Great Western did, but this was no quick visit by an editor from head office. Instead, he insisted on trying to do the job himself for a week, perhaps working in the foundry at Swindon or on a permanent way gang, and as expected, his presence was often viewed with suspicion by his temporary workmates, and perhaps by their superiors as well. In addition, in 1937 a new feature, 'Spotlight on My Job', was introduced, in which employees were supposed to write about *their* work, almost a predecessor to the 'Day in the Life of . . .' style of feature.

Campaigning journalism seems to have been the ambition, if not necessarily the forte, of the editor. When the general manager complained about the slow turn-round of goods vehicles, this became the theme in the magazine for a period. The trouble was that it was often the customers rather than the employees who were to blame, especially when private sidings were used. The 'Safety Movement' also dominated the publication at times, with safety crosswords and prizes in competitions for the best 2-minute safety speech for use at social occasions. Hadley also introduced competitions, including the 'All Line Goods Train Competition' and later a similar scheme for passenger trains, with the aim of improving efficiency in timekeeping and shunting. Looking at these competitions, it becomes clear that performance varied considerably throughout the operating divisions of the company.

The need for economy was stressed from the beginning. This included such matters as stationery, but it was also aimed at drivers and firemen. Locomotives entering the shed for cleaning and maintenance were expected to do so with the minimum of coal in the firebox, as this had to be raked out onto the track before work could start.

Wartime saw the magazine cut back in size, having reached a record 104 pages for the centenary issue in September 1935, and at the nadir of the country's fortunes some issues had as little as 16 pages. There were other unexpected difficulties, with Hadley's successor, R.F. Thurtle, collapsing in the office and dying shortly afterwards. Production was also disrupted by a flying bomb landing on Paddington station, but no issue was ever missed during the war.

In common with other employers, the Great Western saw many of its staff volunteer for service with the armed forces during the Second World War, even though many of them were in reserved occupations. So the magazine started a new feature, 'Great Western Men Overseas', and employees in the UK were urged, once they had read it, to send their copy of the magazine to a former colleague who was away with the forces, telling them that this link with home and peacetime would be appreciated. Less happily, later this was to be joined by news from ex-GWR prisoners of war, and worse still, by news of the deaths of some of those in service. Nevertheless, the magazine kept faith with its former readers, and medals and decorations awarded to those serving in the armed forces were also part of the news. It was a happy day when the magazine could start to run 'Liberated Prisoners' Adventures'.

The true Great Western man was expected to be actively involved in his local community, and from time to time there would be illustrated features on 'Great Western People Who Have Become Mayors'. In late 1945 a new twist on this was an illustrated feature on 'Great Western People Who Have Become Members of Parliament'. The company seemed proud of their achievement, but since most of the seven people who had gained seats on the back benches seemed to have had a trade union connection, mainly with the National Union of Railwaymen, one doubts that any of them were likely to be voting against railway nationalisation. Strangely, in all of these political features, the political affiliation of the employee was never mentioned.

While the war had never stopped the magazine, the postwar fuel crisis meant that in 1947 only eleven issues could be produced, with the last in December 1947.

There was often humour, with cartoons at different times. These sometimes poked fun at staff, sometimes even at passengers. One set of cartoons was on 'Things That Are Never

As was its custom, the GWR did not simply advertise holidays but also produced booklets as well. This is the cover page of the booklet on 'Camp-Coach' holidays. *(Kevin Robertson)*

Heard'. It included a cartoon showing a train leaving the station just as a passenger comes running up with his luggage.

TICKET INSPECTOR: I am afraid that you have missed the last train, sir.
PASSENGER: Oh, never mind. At least I am in good time for the 6.15a.m.

Chapter Twelve

Shipping

While the engineer for the Great Western Railway, Isambard Kingdom Brunel, spent the second half of his career building large steamships with the traffic to North America in mind, the company itself had more realistic ambitions for its shipping business, which effectively extended its services to the south of Ireland and to the Channel Islands.

The Great Western was not as well placed for traffic to Europe as the companies in the south, all three of the pre-grouping 'Southern' companies were heavily involved in cross-Channel traffic, or even the Great Eastern for that matter. After the grouping, this meant that traffic with mainland Europe was effectively handled by the Southern Railway and the London & North Eastern Railway. It was also true that the Great Western was not best placed for traffic to Ireland, with services from Holyhead in North Wales, Liverpool and Heysham in Lancashire being more convenient for travellers heading for or coming from Dublin and Belfast, and these ports were all served by the London, Midland & Scottish Railway as successor to the London & North Western Railway and the Midland Railway. The LMS was also able to serve the Scottish ports from which services to Ulster operated.

There was also an element of bad luck in the Great Western's attempts to develop its ports into calling places for transatlantic liners. The GWR saw Fishguard as a calling point for liners heading for Liverpool, so that mail and passengers to London could have an earlier arrival, while Plymouth served the same role for ships heading for Southampton or London. Fishguard never did manage to acquire a share of the transatlantic trade, despite a number of calls by ships of the Cunard Line, possibly because many liners called at Cork and a second call so soon afterwards delayed their passage onwards to Liverpool. An attempt between the wars to attract transatlantic liner traffic to Cardiff met with little success, although there were a few calls by Canadian Pacific liners in the late 1920s. Plymouth did, for many years, attract a considerable transatlantic traffic, so much so that until the Castle Cary route was completed, there was substantial competition between the Great Western and the London & South Western for this traffic. Once the 'cut-off' route was opened, the traffic became largely the preserve of the Great Western. Post-grouping, the Great Western maintained four tenders at Plymouth to bring passengers and mail ashore. Nevertheless, the real competition for the Plymouth traffic came from the port of Southampton, which had been given a new lease of life by the LSWR in the nineteenth century, and then an even greater stimulus through the opening of the new West Docks by the Southern Railway, which persuaded a number of shipping lines to transfer their liner services from Liverpool and London to Southampton.

While there was considerable competition between the LSWR and the GWR for Channel Islands traffic, with the former using Southampton and the latter Weymouth, this eventually was reduced to a joint operation, which given the relatively small size of the market, even in pre-air-travel days, must have made sense. On the other hand, the Great Western route to Ireland, while it missed the two largest and politically most important cities, did offer a faster and more direct service for those heading for the far south and who had started their journeys in London, the West of England and the Midlands or, of course, South Wales.

Channel Islands

Given the small size of the islands and their population, it seems strange that the Great Western Railway accorded a high priority to establishing ferry services between Weymouth and the Channel Islands, and even more so that there was at first intense competition between the GWR and the London & South Western Railway. The LSWR had become involved with the services from Southampton to the Channel Islands and northern France in 1849. Initially, the Great Western involvement had been to provide trains that connected with the Weymouth & Channel Islands Steam Packet Company from 1857, and it was not until 1889 that the company launched its services from Weymouth to the Channel Islands with three ships. The period of intense competition between the two companies came to an end in 1899, when a joint steamer service was agreed and receipts were pooled.

After pooling, it was agreed that both companies would operate three services a week to the islands during the winter, but that during the summer the Great Western would run day services only, while the LSWR would provide overnight sailings to the islands and return during the day. Sailing times were widely spaced to avoid any temptation for the masters of the steamers to race one another.

The joint services to the Channel Islands survived the grouping, with the LSWR services becoming part of the Southern Railway's considerable shipping operations. Despite the lack of competition, between 1889 and 1923 the through railway and sea journey time between London and Jersey fell from 14¼ hours to 10¾ hours.

At the time of the grouping it was clear that the GWR fleet was beginning to show its age, despite some updating of the ships and the facilities on offer. In 1923 the directors of the Great Western inspected all of their shipping services and the ports which they used, and decided to replace all of the vessels serving the islands.

Two new passenger ships were built for the GWR on the Clyde by John Brown, while two cargo ships were built on the Tyne. The first of the new passenger ships, *St Julien*, entered service in May 1925, and was followed in June by her sister, *St Helier*, by which time the two new cargo ships, *Roebuck* and *Sambur*, were already in service. Of the old ships, only the *Reindeer* remained, both as a relief ship and for day excursions, but she was kept in service only until 1928, when she was withdrawn.

The two railway companies continued to operate jointly. After the Southern Railway had improved its facilities for the Channel Islands and cross-Channel services at Southampton, both companies pressed the islands' authorities to improve the facilities at Jersey and Guernsey, while the Great Western did the same with Weymouth Corporation. On Guernsey, a new jetty was built and the harbour dredged between 1926 and 1929, while Jersey carried out similar works between 1928 and 1931. Weymouth followed between 1931 and 1933.

Meanwhile, the GWR was concerned that with the withdrawal of the *Reindeer*, no standby vessel was available, although another ship, *The Great Western*, had been used on a few sailings in the summer. When the Fishguard vessel *St Patrick* was lost to fire in 1929 it was decided to build a replacement that could be used on both the Fishguard and the Weymouth services. The new *St Patrick* was built by Alexander Stephen on the Clyde and entered service in April 1930. Her pattern of working was to spend the summer months on the Channel Islands service and the winter months on the Irish Sea. *St Patrick* was officially owned by the Fishguard & Rosslare Railway & Harbour Company, which itself was a fifty-fifty partnership between the Great Western Railway and the Great Southern Railway of Ireland.

Both the Southern and the Great Western used their ferries for a number of cruises to Channel ports, with the *St Patrick* using her positioning voyages between Weymouth and Fishguard for cruises that took visitors to the Isles of Scilly. There were also day excursions from Weymouth and Torquay to Guernsey, and the ships even visited Cherbourg and Alderney.

In 1932, on Friday 5 August, the *St Patrick* had a narrow escape while sailing in thick fog. As she approached Jersey with 314 passengers aboard, she struck rocks off Corbière, on the west of the island, damaging the port side so badly that water rushed into the boiler room, which flooded and all power was lost, leaving the ship to anchor off the Kaines Reef. The Southern Railway ferry, *Isle of Sark*, managed to get alongside and take off all the passengers, while *St Julien* and a local tug stood by. Nevertheless, the fog made relief work difficult and it was not until 7a.m. on the Sunday that *St Julien* was able to take *St Patrick* in tow to St Aubin's Bay, waiting there until the evening when she was finally towed into St Helier by two tugs. Only temporary repairs could be provided at St Helier, and she was later towed to Plymouth for full repairs.

No fewer than three earlier steamers had been lost in similar circumstances, as the Channel Islands have always been notoriously prone to thick fog, while the waters around them have substantial reefs and there are strong tides with a large difference between high and low water. The Southern Railway was to lose one of its steamers in 1935, again off Corbière, but in this case the reason for the loss was fire.

Despite having operated jointly to the Channel Islands from 1899, it was not until 1932 that the railway companies merged their separate staffs in the Channel Islands.

Within a fortnight of war being declared in 1939, *St Helier*, *St Julien* and *St Patrick*, and many of their Southern Railway counterparts, had been withdrawn from the Channel Islands services and the Weymouth services completely suspended. Two Southern Railway steamers continued the service from Southampton, painted in grey wartime colours. After Dunkirk, the Great Western and the Southern Railway had another problem, being called upon to undertake the evacuation of the civilian population from the Channel Islands after the armed forces had been withdrawn and the islands declared a demilitarised zone following the fall of France. The local people were given the choice of staying or being evacuated to the mainland, but of the islands only Alderney was evacuated completely. Despite the suspension of the Weymouth service, the two railway companies had continued operating services to the Channel Islands jointly, and their staff were asked to stay at their posts while attempts were made to continue sailings to and from the islands as far as possible, given that many ships had been taken up by the Admiralty.

Even once the evacuation was completed, sailings to both Jersey and Guernsey continued, and there were twelve sailings from the islands between Sunday 23 June 1940 and Friday 28 June, when the last sailing was made during an attack on Guernsey by the Luftwaffe. Among the last passengers were thirty-eight out of the forty-nine railway company staff in Guernsey, with three more definitely left behind but another eight unaccounted for at the time. After a German aircraft had landed on Guernsey on 30 June and found that there was no resistance, German forces occupied the islands starting on 1 July. During the war at least one message was received by *The Great Western Railway Magazine* assuring their readers that its railway company employees in Jersey were safe and well.

When the Channel Islands were liberated on 9 May 1945 normal shipping services could not be restored immediately as there was a shortage of vessels. It was not until 26 June that the Southern Railway steamer *Isle of Guernsey* arrived in the islands, flying the house flags of both companies. The GWR cargo steamer *Sambur* arrived on 19 September, while *Roebuck* resumed sailings on 17 October.

The shortage of shipping and the heavy demands of the Allied forces in Europe meant that *St Julien* and *St Helier* were not 'demobbed' until 1946. Both ships needed extensive refitting before they could return to service. *St Helier* eventually resumed services to the islands on Sunday 16 June 1946.

The Great Western ordered two new passenger ferries from Cammell Laird on Merseyside, but in the meantime, returning islanders and members of the armed forces working on mine clearance in the islands and looking after German prisoners were too much for the limited shipping service and naval vessels had to be pressed into service. When the first of the new GWR ships was delivered, she was initially employed on the Fishguard services, but in September 1947 the new *St David* was sent to the Channel Islands to see if she was suitable for the service. She remained for four weeks, and did return to the islands afterwards, but spent the remainder of her time after nationalisation on the Fishguard services.

Ireland

Originally, the Great Western had ventured onto the Irish Sea services with a packet service between Neyland and Waterford, but shortly after the turn of the twentieth century the company developed a new port for its services to Ireland at Fishguard. It was from Fishguard that the newly formed Fishguard & Rosslare Railway & Harbour Company, a fifty-fifty partnership between the Great Western Railway and the Great Southern Railway of Ireland, commenced ferry services in 1906. The Great Southern Railway operated the harbour at Rosslare while the Great Western did the same at Fishguard. The ships were individually registered in the UK or, after 1922, in the newly independent Irish Republic.

Fishguard in West Wales was ideally suited for shipping services to the far south of Ireland, being closer to the open sea than Neyland, which had also required ships to sail past Milford Haven and round the 'Welsh Hook'. The distance from Fishguard to Rosslare was just 54 miles. Although it had less potential than the main routes to Dublin and Belfast, travelling via Fishguard to Rosslare or to Waterford saved a considerable detour via Liverpool and Dublin for those wishing to reach the south. Because of Fishguard's geographical position, the Great Western was optimistic about getting transatlantic liners to call, but while this did happen occasionally, it never became a liner port.

On the other side of the St George's Channel, the Great Southern Railway instigated a number of improvements to its services, including trains with dining cars, so that passengers could easily travel on to Dublin as well as Wexford or even to Waterford and Cork. The Great Southern operated through much sparsely populated countryside, but it was efficiently run and seems to have been the ideal partner for the Great Western. Cooperation between the two was, of course, limited by the differing track gauges, that of Irish railways being 5ft 3ins.

At the opening of the service in 1906 sailings between Fishguard and Rosslare were handled by three new steam packets, *St George*, *St David* and *St Patrick*, while in 1908 a fourth ship, *St Andrew*, joined them, allowing the full service to be maintained when a ship had to be withdrawn for maintenance. Nevertheless, four ships seem to have been too many for the service as, in May 1913, *St George* was sold to the Canadian Pacific Railway Company and the service was operated by the three remaining ships. After the grouping, both *St David* and *St Patrick* were re-engined in 1925 and 1926 respectively, but in 1930 all three ships were replaced. The new *St Patrick* was first, followed shortly afterwards by a new *St Andrew* and a new *St David*. Ferries at the time were much smaller than today, with *St Patrick* and her sisters being just 2,143 gross register tons, but even so, they could carry 1,000 passengers, which must have made them fairly crowded. Accommodation was first class and third class, with the latter often being fairly basic, with cabin accommodation charged as an extra. Nevertheless, had the ships been much larger, they could not have acted as relief vessels on the services to Jersey and Guernsey.

Meanwhile, two other ships, *Great Western* and *Great Southern*, had maintained a service from Pembroke to Waterford, but this had also moved to Fishguard for the 92-mile crossing by 1933, when the ships for the service to Waterford were also replaced, with the new ships continuing the *Great Western* and *Great Southern* names.

As mentioned in Chapter Seventeen, on the outbreak of the Second World War the British-registered ships were called up, or 'taken up from trade' in naval parlance, so that services were soon scaled back, and eventually only the Fishguard–Rosslare service was operated. After the sinking of *St Patrick* (see Chapter Eighteen) services were suspended for a period mainly because of the shortage of shipping, but reinstated temporarily in December 1943 between Fishguard and Waterford to cater for the movement of the many Irish workers employed in Britain's war industries. It was not until after the war in Europe ended that Fishguard–Waterford reopened on 16 July 1945, followed by the service to Cork on 13 August, both three times weekly in each direction. Reinstatement of the Fishguard–Rosslare service had to be deferred until 1947, and the arrival of the new *St David*.

Chapter Thirteen

Road Transport

It was a proud boast of the Great Western Railway that it had operated motor buses even earlier than any operator in London, with a service from the station at Helston in Cornwall to the Lizard inaugurated on 3 August 1903. This was soon followed by a bus service from Penzance to Newlyn.

The railways had been users and providers of road transport almost from the start. Their freight customers often needed goods to be collected from their premises and taken to the railway station or goods depot, and at the other end of the journey, delivered from the railway to their premises, as not every customer had his own transport and even fewer justified their own private branch line or siding. To serve those communities or tourist attractions away from a railway line, and to which building a line would be uneconomic, some form of bus service soon appeared desirable. Nevertheless, these were the limits of railway involvement in road transport for many years. A railway company could collect or deliver goods and passengers to and from its premises, but it could not engage in road transport as a separate part of its operations. The irony of this situation was that the railway companies, who conducted their business by steam, remained for many years major owners of heavy horses for their collection and delivery services for goods customers. Some railway yards even kept a horse for moving single wagons.

By the time of the grouping, 1923, the GWR operated a fleet of ninety-six buses on thirty-seven routes, with the main area of operations being around Kingsbridge and Dartmouth in South Devon. The newest vehicles, introduced that year, were twenty-two single-deck buses on AEC chassis. Dartmouth was the most unusual of Great Western stations, for it had no trains and no tracks! The nearest railway station was at Kingswear on the line from Torquay and Exeter, across the River Dart, and the GWR had acquired the company operating the ferry and established the ferry terminus at Dartmouth as a fully fledged station. Between Dartmouth and the station at Kingsbridge lay an attractive area of South Devon completely without railways.

The bus fleet continued to expand and for this and the replacement of earlier vehicles, eighteen Maudsley 32-seat single-deck buses were obtained in 1926. In addition to operations in the south-west of England, these also provided services at Abergavenny in Wales and, much closer to London, at Slough in Berkshire. The fleet began to standardise on vehicles of around thirty to thirty-two seats capacity, for which conductors were legally required at the time, but for the thinner routes and narrow country lanes, a number of one-man-operated buses with sixteen to eighteen seats were also operated. The following year, forty Guy single-deck buses were bought, with bodywork by three different builders, with some models having roll-back canvas roofs while others had fixed roofs with roof-racks for luggage. By this time the Great Western had substantial bus depots at Kingsbridge, St Austell and Penzance, and smaller depots at Bovey Tracey, Paignton and Callington, near Saltash, and was busily developing services in and around Falmouth and Redruth in addition to its existing services at Helston and Penzance. Whole districts were being served by GWR buses, such as the villages around Calne in Wiltshire and Reading in Berkshire. The company made much of the fact that it was replacing older buses that still had solid tyres with new vehicles with

Road haulage was confined to collection and delivery work until 1929. All the railway companies had large fleets of motor vehicles and, even up to the outbreak of the Second World War, horses. While the three-wheeled 'mechanical horse' was to be the popular mainstay of much of this work by the late 1930s, these two tractors were at the heavier end of the scale in 1936. The middle vehicle seems to be a Scammell, and the one on the right might be as well. *(HMRS/J.E. Cull AEQ333)*

pneumatic tyres. A much less conventional vehicle, looking very much like an army lorry, was pressed into service as a 'bus' carrying holiday-makers to the summit of Plynlimmon from Aberystwyth. This vehicle was without any protection from the elements as, it was explained by the company, the high winds would simply tear away any canvas structure.

There was another change taking place at this time, however. The GWR had finally woken up to the advantages of road transport and was including buses in its timetables. The next step was what would now be known as 'bustitution', substituting buses for trains, saving train mileage and freeing up space on the lines for goods trains. This was inevitable, but the company seemed to keep quiet about the other advantage that accrued from this, which was that buses were far cheaper to operate than trains, and services that might not be viable by train were profitable by bus.

Buses and trains were brought together in much of the GWR's planning. When a series of land cruises was introduced in 1928, passengers in effect enjoyed tours, mainly by train but buses played a part. That same year saw the introduction of combined bus and railway tickets.

On 3 August 1928 the railway companies were granted powers to involve themselves in road transport when the enabling Act received the Royal Assent. Equipped with its new powers, the Great Western, in common with the other railway companies, began to invest in bus companies and eventually in road haulage as well. The earlier heavy investment in its own buses meant that the GWR was well placed to make lucrative deals that would create strong local bus companies in many areas. The first of these came in January 1929 and was an agreement with the National Omnibus and Transport Company to create a Western National Omnibus Company, which saw the GWR's bus services in Cornwall and the western part of Devon transferred to the new company on which both the GWR and the National company had equal representation on the board.

In May 1929 the Western National example was followed by another venture into bus operation when the new Western Welsh Omnibus Company was formed out of the railway bus services and those of a number of existing independent local companies, South Wales Commercial Motors, Lewis & Davies and Western Valleys Motor Services. The Great Western again had half the board representation with four of the eight directors. That same year, horror of horrors, the Great Western even bought a luxury motor coach built by the small concern of Gilford, based at High Wycombe. An integrated road and rail service was also initiated between Marlborough and Newbury, Reading and Paddington with the Marlborough to Newbury section worked by bus, with the company explaining that Marlborough was far better suited to a combined bus and railway service than one entirely by train. Despite this development the GWR's inventiveness did not extend to road-railers, that is buses that could run on roads or railway lines, probably because such hybrid vehicles would have been unable to perform well at main-line railway speeds and would have been too heavy for economical service on the roads.

The Great Western's Western National venture with the National Omnibus and Transport Company had its equivalent on the Southern Railway, which established Southern National. In 1930 the two railway companies purchased the Devon General Omnibus and Touring Company, each having equal shares. Further north, further acquisitions saw the Great Western emerge as the owner of another bus company, Wrexham & District, and again the railway bus services and their vehicles and personnel were transferred to the bus company. After the takeover, Wrexham & District changed its name to the Western Transport Company. This was clearly a company undergoing a period of metamorphosis, as in 1932 it became part of Crosville Motor Services, with the GWR and London, Midland & Scottish Railway having equal shares in this company, which operated bus services in North Wales and on Merseyside.

In 1931 the Great Western became associated with both the Birmingham & Midland Motor Omnibus Company, better known as 'Midland Red', and City of Oxford Motor Services, as well as London Coastal Coaches, which owned, among other things, Victoria coach station. The Great Western also became associated with two long-distance coach operators, Black & White and Greyhound, the latter being owned by Bristol Tramways. All in all, the GWR had associations of one kind or another with eight bus companies operating a total of 3,500 vehicles. 'Bustitution' was still being practised, and a good example occurred in 1932, when the passenger services of the Wantage Tramway were transferred to City of Oxford Motor Services.

The involvement with bus companies represented both a growing active interest in road transport and a general 'tidying up' of the company's operations. Operating buses as an extension of its railway services may well have been very convenient for the traveller, but it did mean that there were many small bus depots with just a few buses that were a nuisance for the management of a large transport undertaking. Logic meant that when new and substantial bus operators emerged in an area, the railway buses should be absorbed. This thinking explains why a number of Great Western buses and services passed to Southern National, in which the Southern Railway had a half-share with the National Omnibus and Transport Company. As well as the Devon General, the GWR and SR were also jointly involved in Thames Valley. Having the National shareholding meant that relations between the Southern and Western National companies were close, and they combined to acquire the 'Royal Blue' coach operations of Elliott Brothers of Bournemouth in 1935, while the main local bus company, Hants & Dorset, in which the Southern Railway was involved, took over the 'Royal Blue' bus services.

The paradox here was that for all the GWR's complaints about unfair road competition, it was competing with itself by running express coaches under the 'Royal Blue', Black & White and Greyhound names.

While the railway companies kept their own collection and delivery services for their goods, parcels and 'luggage in advance' services until they were nationalised, and these remained for many years with British Railways, the moves into road passenger transport were matched to some extent by those into road freight. The big difference was that the 'Big Four' railway companies acted in unison when they bought Pickfords and Carter Paterson in 1933. The reason for this was in itself logical, as they saw these businesses as being national rather than local or regional, and as an adjunct to their combined operations. After all, as mentioned in an earlier chapter, the GWR, LMS and LNER had been working hard to reduce conflict between themselves wherever their goods services overlapped.

By contrast, the bus companies were always confined to a specific area. Even the coach operators with their express services linked their home area with London and other major cities. It was to be some time before a truly national coach network emerged through Associated Motorways, the predecessor of National Express.

The goods vehicles operated by the railways suffered considerably from the shortages brought about by wartime. Many of the collection and delivery vehicles were still petrol-engined, which meant that a substantial number of these were converted to run on gas, with large gas bags carried on the roof. This was not the most successful wartime expediency, but petrol and diesel were at a premium. More effective in saving fuel and manpower was the pooling of the collection and delivery services of the different railway companies, which had originated in London before the war and was extended to provincial centres within the first couple of years of conflict. It says much for the overlap between the different companies, even after the grouping, that there were more than a hundred places throughout Great Britain where this type of pooling was found to be worthwhile.

Chapter Fourteen

Air
Services

For a railway company to become involved with air services might seem strange to modern eyes, when train and aeroplane are seen as rivals. Yet, not just in the British Isles but also in a number of other countries, such as Canada and South Africa, the railways made a significant contribution to the development of domestic air services. The attraction of air travel to the railways had much in common with the appeal of road transport – flexibility. It needed a much smaller market to justify a bus service than a railway service, and needed much less expenditure on infrastructure, and much the same applied to aviation. Geography also dictated that the journey by railway between two points on the British mainland could sometimes be very lengthy and circuitous, and on the Great Western's network the journey between Cardiff and Plymouth was one of the most obvious examples.

With the Southern Railway, the Great Western was among the pioneers of domestic air services in the 1930s.

It was during 1933 that the Great Western first ventured into air transport, with a twice-daily service linking Cardiff with Torquay and Plymouth. Aircraft, aircrew and ground crew were all supplied by Imperial Airways, but the aircraft, three Westland Wessex six-seat trimotor monoplanes, were painted in GWR colours. The airport for Torquay and the surrounding district was Haldon, while that for Plymouth was Roborough.

Inaugurated on Wednesday 12 April 1933, the timetable was:

Cardiff, dep:	9.15 a.m.	1.45 p.m.
Haldon, arr:	10.05 a.m.	2.35 p.m.
dep:	10.10 a.m.	2.40 p.m.
Plymouth, arr:	10.35 a.m.	3.05 p.m.
Plymouth, dep:	11.25 a.m.	3.55 p.m.
Haldon, arr:	11.50 a.m.	4.20 p.m.
dep:	12.00 noon	4.30 p.m.
Cardiff, arr:	12.50 p.m.	5.20 p.m.

A flight of 1 hour and 20 minutes was far better than spending much of the day travelling via Bristol and Exeter by train. No doubt the stop at Haldon was considered necessary to extend the market as much as possible – on such a short flight, even by 1933 standards, it certainly would not have been necessary as a refuelling stop. The service was far from cheap, with a single fare from Cardiff to Plymouth of £3 10s (about £210 by today's values) and a return of £6, while luggage was limited to 35lb. To put this into perspective, a skilled worker would have earned around £3 per week in 1933. If these figures seem somewhat distorted in any comparison of travel costs and wages today, it is because not every element in pricing rises at the same rate, and in the intervening period wages in the UK have risen far faster than airline ticket prices. At the time of writing an average wage for a week would be around £400.

Despite the novelty value and excitement that flying enjoyed during the pre-war days, that the fares were not regarded as a bargain by the travelling public can be judged by the

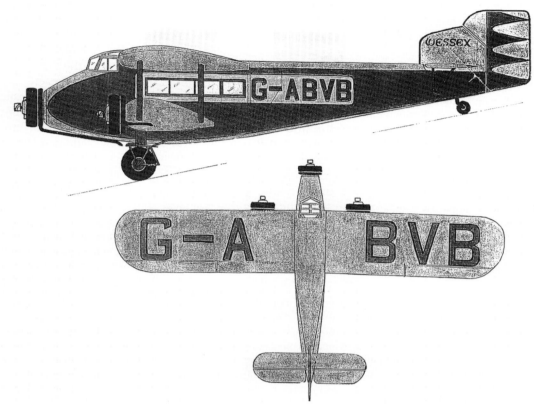

Great Western Air services started with the Westland Wessex trimotor, operated on the company's behalf by Imperial Airways. It carried just six passengers. *(Westland Aircraft)*

fact that for the summer, fares were cut to £2 5s single and £4 return. Operating an aeroplane with at least two crew and three engines and just six passengers would have been expensive, so it is not surprising that the service lost money, but the GWR was one of the more 'air-minded' railways and realised that it needed the experience.

That same year the 'Big Four' also formed their own airline, Railway Air Services, with a capital of £50,000. In May 1934 the Plymouth-Cardiff route was extended to Liverpool by RAS, with connections at Cardiff with Western Airways and with the Dutch airline, KLM Royal Dutch Airlines, at Liverpool, where passengers could change onto a flight to Amsterdam via Hull. There were further extensions to the route network in 1935. As far as the GWR network was concerned, these included air services from Liverpool to Birmingham, Bristol, Southampton, Portsmouth and Brighton, which must have made the through Liverpool to Brighton journey rather long. There was also a service from Plymouth to Denbay, near Newton Abbot, and on to Cardiff, Birmingham and Nottingham. Fares were kept to the minimum, but were still beyond the reach of the man in the street at £3 15s for the through Liverpool to Plymouth single fare.

The aircraft became much more suited to the service being provided, with elegant de Havilland Dragon Rapide twin-engined biplanes carrying names such as *City of Birmingham*, *City of Bristol*, *City of Cardiff* and *City of Plymouth*. These could still only carry six passengers, and had a crew of two.

Nevertheless, not all was well with Railway Air Services, as the LMS and LNER seemed far less interested in aviation than the Great Western and the Southern, which didn't like the heavy losses being incurred on routes outside their own areas of operation. This could have been a case of differences in route structures and opportunities for air transport to develop, or it could simply have been that the two laggards were the companies with the poorest financial situation. In 1938 a new airline was formed from Great Western Air Services and Southern Air Services – Great Western and Southern Air Services – which also operated in conjunction with the Cunliffe-Owen and Olley business, Channel Air Ferries, on services to Jersey and Guernsey to eliminate competition. A new airline, Channel Islands Airways, was formed in the late 1930s, and in 1942, at the height of the war, the GWR and the Southern Railway increased their shareholdings in the company to 50 per cent each.

The involvement with air transport was not confined to the operations of an embryonic airline. The Great Western came to an agreement with Imperial Airways for the movement of parcels to the airport at Croydon and the flying-boat terminus near Southampton. Incoming parcels were distributed on the GWR network, and consignors could send their parcels from a GWR station to the airline.

While the outbreak of war saw the suspension of domestic air services, Railway Air Services did provide a number of domestic services for the use of members of the government and their officials, while a limited service was available across the Irish Sea to Dublin and the Isle of Man.

By 1944 many believed that the end of the war was in sight, at least in Europe, and started to plan postwar air services. Part of this sense of optimism was based on the mistaken optimism that the German commander in the Channel Islands would surrender soon after the invasion of France, or at least after the liberation, but unknown to the planners, the man in question was a fanatic, determined not to surrender. In the end, Jersey and Guernsey were not liberated until 9 May 1945.

Not all of the planning was in vain. On 13 November 1944 Railway Air Services was able to reintroduce scheduled air services between London and Liverpool and Liverpool and Belfast, while there was a connection from Liverpool's airport at Speke to the Isle of Man with Isle of Man Airways. New aircraft were planned for these services postwar, with ex-RAF Douglas C-47 Dakotas, as well as the 32-seat Bristol Wayfarer, a passenger development of the Bristol 170 Freighter.

Far less fruitful were the plans being laid for a new airline, British & Foreign Air Services, formed during the war years and owned jointly by the 'Big Four' railway companies. This was to be overtaken by events once the Labour Party won the 1945 general election.

Postwar, Channel Islands Airways resumed operations, with air services to and from Jersey and Guernsey reinstated even before the full reinstatement of shipping services, and the Dragon Rapides were soon joined by the Wayfarers. Nationalisation of air transport was, nevertheless, even higher up the new Labour government's wish list than railway

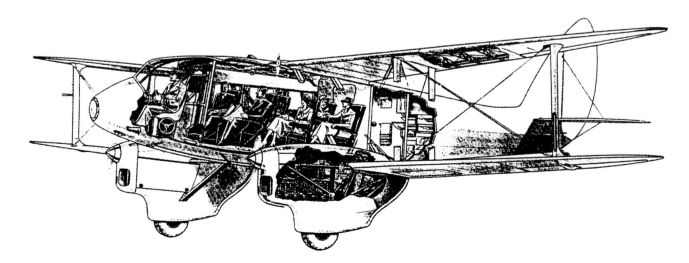

The next aircraft, actually operated by Great Western & Southern Air Lines, was the de Havilland Dragon Rapide, also a six-seat aircraft but with just two engines. This is a cutaway. *(BAe Systems)*

A Rapide of Railway Air Services loads cargo. *(NRM 494/93)*

A common scene at Croydon Airport during the 1930s. As well as their luggage, passengers also had to be weighed, as weight was a critical factor on such light aircraft. *(NRM LMS 7143)*

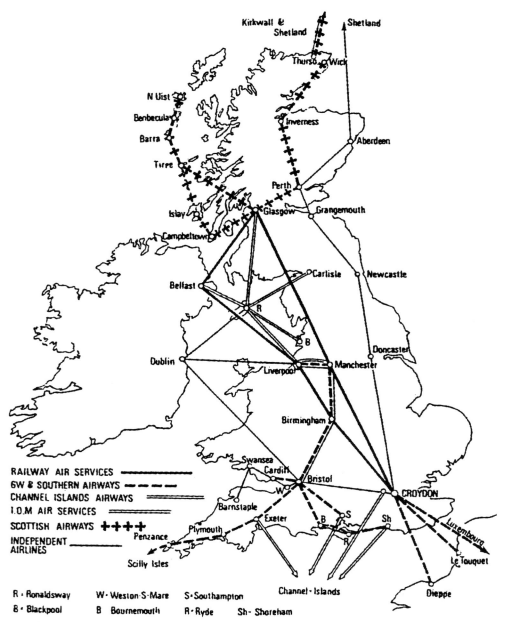

RAILWAY AIR SERVICES ━━━━━━
GW & SOUTHERN AIRWAYS ━ ━ ━ ━
CHANNEL ISLANDS AIRWAYS ═══════
I.O.M AIR SERVICES ═══════
SCOTTISH AIRWAYS ✚✚✚✚✚
INDEPENDENT _____
AIRLINES

R · Ronaldsway   W · Weston-S-Mare   S · Southampton
B · Blackpool   B · Bournemouth   R · Ryde   Sh · Shoreham

This was the route network for Railway Air Services in 1939. There was no operational connection between the GWR and Southern on the one hand and Scottish on the other, but they used the same type of line for the convenience of the cartographer working in black and white.

nationalisation. This may have been partly because the state already owned one airline, the British Overseas Airways Corporation, BOAC, formed in 1940 from a merger of Imperial Airways and its main competitor on European routes, British Airways. BOAC had continued limited operations during the war years, but postwar it was decided that it should lose its European services to a new nationalised airline, British European Airways, BEA. BEA also took over the air transport operations of two RAF squadrons, and on 1 April 1947 these were joined by the services of Channel Islands Airways and Railway Air Services. For many years after this privately owned British airlines could only exist by confining themselves to charter flights or as 'associates' of BEA or BOAC.

Chapter Fifteen

Accidents and the 'Safety Movement'

From grouping to nationalisation, the Great Western had one of the best safety records of any of the main railway companies. A number of factors contributed to this, including the company's growing involvement with automatic warning systems, in which a raised ramp between the lines would catch a device under the locomotive as it approached a distant signal and sounded a horn for 'caution' or a bell for 'clear'. The driver had to acknowledge the 'caution' warning by operating a lever to cancel it, otherwise the locomotive's brakes would be applied automatically. The GWR also lacked the traffic density of many of the other companies on its main lines into London, where it also had a smaller and less dense suburban network.

Nevertheless, the company's management must have had to work hard to bring the standards of the grouped companies up to its own, with the Cambrian having suffered a major accident as recently as 1921 at Abermule.

It was perhaps not too surprising that of the two major accidents, that at Norton Fitzwarren was in wartime and that wartime conditions were contributing factors.

There was another side to the question of safety, however. Of major concern to the GWR's management was the number of accidents involving its own personnel. This is a problem, even today, on most railways. Before the First World War the 'old' GWR had instigated a 'Safety Movement' to make staff more aware of the dangers on the railway, and its work continued after the grouping, while the company actively encouraged its staff to participate in the St John Ambulance movement.

Shrivenham

Even without automatic train protection, railway lines were guarded by track circuits, which coordinated the workings of home and distant signals, and of signals and points. The result was that a train could not enter a block section until the train in front had passed the distant signal, actuated the track circuit and then passed clear of the following home signal. Further interlocking meant that a signalman could not lower a starting signal to allow a train to run to the next signal-box along the line until the signalman in that box had accepted the train and pegged his instrument to 'line clear'. Nevertheless, there were weaknesses in the system, especially if a starting signal was not linked to the following distant signal by a track circuit. The system was complicated by a railway that had to accommodate slow and heavy coal trains among fast-running expresses, as on the main line between South Wales and London, necessitating many passing loops.

Shrivenham was at the eastern end of a section of double track and at the western end of a 2½-mile-long loop that ran as far as Knighton Crossing, but which also had a further entry at Ashbury Crossing, almost ¾ mile east of Shrivenham. Both the Shrivenham and Ashbury Crossing signal-boxes were on the Down side of the line.

At around 5 a.m. on 15 January 1936 a goods train with fifty-three wagons was running from Aberdare to London, and the signalmen controlling the section of line had agreed to keep the train on the main line as far as Ashbury Crossing, where it would be turned into

Westbury Depot when new in 1915. The use of a redundant locomotive boiler for the boiler house, seen protruding beyond the wall with a heightened chimney, gives an almost surreal appearance. *(Kevin Robertson)*

Westbury Depot again, but in 1947, with work in hand to supply fuel oil so that the depot could refuel oil-burning locomotives. Despite government encouragement for this work, the programme had to be cancelled after the country ran into a foreign exchange crisis and could no longer afford to import oil. *(Kevin Robertson)*

the loop to allow the Up Penzance sleeper express, which ran via Bristol rather than on the GWR cut-off to Exeter. The signalman at Shrivenham had only just given 'train out of section' for the coal train when he was offered and accepted the sleeper express. In fact, because his view had been obstructed by a Down train of empty milk wagons, the coal train was not actually out of section as a coupling had broken and five coal wagons and the brake van had been left behind. The next signalman at Ashbury Crossing then failed to realise that the coal train had no tail lamp, which should have alerted him to the fact that some of its wagons were left behind on the line. Incredibly, the guard of the coal train, by this time sitting on his own with five goods wagons, did not realise immediately that this was not the goods train stopping normally. In the event of an unscheduled stop, it was his duty to walk back along the track and protect his train, and by implication any train following, by laying detonators on the track at a set distance from his train. By the time he realised what had happened and the implications dawned on him, it was too late for him to protect the detached portion of the goods train.

This combination of factors meant that the Penzance sleeper express running at 55mph and hauled by a heavy 'King' class locomotive headed straight into the guard's van and coal wagons. Despite the best efforts of the driver of the express, who was cut fatally injured from the wreckage with his hand still grasping the brake, a number of people aboard the sleeper were injured, and one of the passengers was killed.

The two signalmen and the guard of the goods train were all dismissed as a result of their action, or inaction.

Norton Fitzwarren

In common with most automatic safety systems, the GWR's automatic train control warning system allowed the locomotive driver to cancel a warning, retaining full control of the train if he decided that an emergency brake application was unnecessary.

On the night of 4 November 1940 the driver of an overnight passenger train from Paddington to the West of England was routed onto the Down relief line as the service was running late. On the GWR, drivers sat on the right-hand side of the cab, unlike the other railway companies, and the driver of this train thought that the signals on the main line, set at 'clear' for a Down newspaper train, were for his train, while the signals for the relief line were set at danger. When the alarm sounded in his cab, he cancelled the warning and continued towards the station. As he approached Norton Fitzwarren station, 2 miles west of Taunton, the newspaper train began to overhaul his train as they passed alongside through the station. Only then did the driver of the passenger train realise his mistake and apply the brakes. The main line and the relief line converged at points on the west side of the station, where the main line was protected by a trap point that took the relief line into a dead end with soft ground on the other side. With the relief line signals set at danger, the trap point took the passenger train towards the end of the line. While the driver was braking hard, there was not enough room for him to stop and his 'King' class locomotive, No. 6028 *King George VI*, ploughed into the soft ground and six of the carriages behind it were derailed, scattering over the tracks.

As with most wartime trains, there was severe overcrowding, with an estimated 900 passengers on the train, of whom 27 were killed and another 25 injured, 56 of them seriously.

The newspaper train escaped, but only just, and probably only by virtue of its much higher speed. The paintwork of the last coach was scraped and bits of wreckage from the passenger train flew into the guard's van.

While the driver of the passenger train was at fault, the accident was caused in part by the difficulties of working in the blackout. The driver's house had been damaged in bombing only two days earlier, so in this case criticism by the accident inspector was far less severe than would have been the case otherwise.

The 'Safety Movement'

On most railways the vast majority of accidents are confined to railwaymen themselves, and it is perfectly possible for a railway to have what appears to be an exemplary safety record and yet suffer a number of fatalities and serious injuries to its own employees. Most at risk are workers on the track, but shunting is another area full of hazards, especially with goods wagons running on their own noiselessly on a gravity working, while employees at depots and workshops will often take a short cut across the track as the quickest route.

The GWR was no exception to this situation and, recognising the risk of accident inherent in their daily work, set about a campaign that endeavoured to alert employees to the dangers. This included competitions in which employees had to prepare short 2-minute speeches on safety for use at social gatherings and other functions, as well as photographs of the right way and the wrong way to conduct themselves while at work.

Employees were also strongly encouraged to take first-aid training with the St John Ambulance Service. This was viewed as almost part of the job, as passengers might be taken ill or suffer an accident themselves, and the attention they received while waiting for an ambulance could affect the outcome. Again, competitions were held, and there were annual prizes for those judged to have handled the most serious incidents successfully.

A regular feature in *The Great Western Railway Magazine* was a photograph of railwaymen exposing themselves to danger. Not all of the dangers were due to their own carelessness: it was an unfortunate porter who hastened to turn the handle of a carriage door to the closed position as a train accelerated out of a station, just at the same time as the passenger on the other side turned the latch, catching the porter's jacket sleeve, with the result that the unfortunate man was dragged to his death.

Other reminders included the occasional 'safety' crossword puzzle.

All this effort was not in vain. In 1926 the magazine was able to tell its readers that accidents in 1925 had been down by 4.39 per cent compared with 1924 on the Great Western, but on the other 'Big Four' railway companies, accidents to employees had risen by 0.67 per cent, 1.18 per cent and 21.11 per cent – perhaps it was fortunate that the companies were not identified. On the other hand, railwaymen, especially footplate men and guards, but also travelling ticket inspectors and catering staff, did find themselves on other companies' lines from time to time, or had other companies' locomotives and trains on their line.

Chapter Sixteen

Developing the Infrastructure

The grouping enabled the Great Western to manage its entire territory for the first time, and the railways in the Welsh valleys could be considered as a whole rather than as small individual and individualistic companies. The poor financial position of many of its absorbed companies and the pressures of the First World War had also meant that much of the system was out of date and overburdened. Indeed, even many of the GWR's own stations were beginning to look tired and were inadequate for the volume of traffic that they were expected to handle. These problems extended over many miles of route as well, as the lines had often been laid over wooden trestle viaducts on some of the branches, usually to save money, and many of these were coming to the end of their lives.

New Stations

One of the first acts was to rebuild the railway station at Newton Abbot in South Devon. This was a station built for the broad gauge, and while this normally guaranteed generous dimensions, the station building at Newton Abbot was the exception to the rule. The station layout was cramped and completely inadequate for the heavy trains working through it, especially when trains had to be divided or joined together with portions to or from Torbay and Plymouth. The work was not easy, as the original station had an all-over roof, and the only way forward was complete demolition. Giving Newton Abbot a station worthy not just of the town but of the traffic that passed through it took most of 1924 and 1925. The disruption must have caused considerable inconvenience to the people using the station, which had to be kept open during the work, but despite this, on completion of the new station the people of the town subscribed for a plaque to express their gratitude to the company for their new station.

The next task was to ensure that the running sheds in South Wales were rebuilt to the Great Western standard. Between 1926 and 1930 new 'straight' sheds were built at Abercynon, Barry, Cardiff East Dock, Radyr and Treherbert. Other depots to receive this attention included Landore, Duffryn Yard at Port Talbot and Pantyffynnon.

Newton Abbot apart, most of this modernisation was out of sight and irrelevant to the ordinary railway passenger. To some extent, having ownership of several major ports cast upon it, the Great Western was distracted for a while from the real needs of the railway as the main priority on grouping had been to modernise the ports of South Wales for both general traffic and coal. This was important, as until 1926 South Wales steam coal enjoyed a worldwide export market because of its quality. The miners' strike of 1926 finished most of the export traffic, as customers were forced to look elsewhere for their coal. In the age of steam, coal was, as some have put it, 'king', and the lack of it meant a complete breakdown of an economy. As with the 20-ton steel coal wagons that the GWR believed would transform its coal traffic, most of the money invested in the ports was wasted as first the coal traffic disappeared and then the remaining traffics were hit by the worldwide slump of the depression years. The problem was that this left the Great Western with relatively little money to spend on other major infrastructure projects.

TRURO and FALMOUTH.—Great Western.

Miles	Down.	Week Days.																Sundays.			
		mrn	mrn		3 cl.	mrn	mrn	aft	aft	aft	aft	aft	aft	aft	aft			mrn	aft	aft	
—	Truro ... dep.	6 15	6 45	Sats.	7 12	9 30	1020	1215	2 25	3 20	4 20	5 30	7 0	8 28	9 27	....	....	1040	2 12	4 52	....
4¼	Perranwell ...	6 28	6 57		7 27	9 43	1035	1228	2 38	3 33	4 32	5 43	7 12	8 41	9 40	....	....	1053	2 30	5 4	....
8¾	Penryn ...	6 43	7 13		7 41	9 57	1049	1247	2 53	3 47	4 47	5 57	7 27	8 55	10 0	....	....	11 7	3 0	5 19	....
11¾	Falmouth, for St. Mawes .. arr.	6 53	7 23		7 51	10 7	1059	1257	3 6	3 57	4 57	6 7	7 37	9 5	1010	....	....	1117	3 20	5 29	....

Miles	Up.	Week Days.																Sundays.			
		mrn	mrn	mrn	mrn	mrn	aft	aft	aft	aft	aft		3 cl.	aft	aft	aft		mrn	aft	aft	
—	Falmouth ... dep.	7 0	8 30	1010	1035	1120	1235	1 35	4 5	5 15	6 8	Fris.	6 55	7 15	8 15	9 15	....	9 45	1230	4 0	...
3½	Penryn ...	7 12	8 45	1022	1048	1132	1250	1 47	4 17	5 28	6 20		7 8	7 27	8 27	9 27	....	9 57	1242	4 12	...
7½	Perranwell ...	7 26	9 2	1037	11 1	1146	1 6	2 1	4 31	5 42	6 34		7 26	7 41	8 42	9 41	....	1011	1256	4 26	...
11¾	Truro 22, 27, 50 ... arr.	7 37	9 13	1048	1112	1157	1 17	2 12	4 42	5 53	6 45		7 38	7 52	8 53	9 52	...	1022	1 7	4 37	...

TRURO and FALMOUTH

Miles	Down	Week Days																								Sundays											
	HOUR ☞	6	6	7	8	9	10	11	S 11		12	1	2	E 3	S 3	S 4	E 4	S 4	5	E 5	E 6	S 6	6	7	8	S 10	E 10 R	6	9	11		1	3	4	6	7	8	10	
—	Truro ... dep.	5	40	0	4	23	0	15	30	.	40	48	43	20	45	10	18	37	20	45	10	28	52	55	48	12	30	50	55	55	.	35	0	45	10	30	50	5	.
4¼	Perranwell ...	15	50	12	14	36	10	26	**42**	.	50	**1**	55	30	58	20	28	48	32	55	20	38	**2**	**6**	58	22	.	**0**	**6**	**6**	.	46	11	56	21	41	**1**	17	.
8¾	Penryn ...	25	**10**	21	24	44	20	35	53	.	**2**	10	**4**	40	**9**	29	37	57	41	**4**	29	48	13	15	**7**	31	**20**	10	15	15	.	55	20	**5**	30	50	10	26	.
10½	Penmere Platform ...	30	16	26	30	50	27	41	59	.	7	15	9	45	15	35	43	**5**	46	10	35	55	19	20	13	37	.	15	20	20	.	**0**	25	10	35	55	15	32	.
11¾	Falmouth F ... arr.	35	20	30	35	55	32	45	**5**	.	12	20	15	50	20	40	48	10	50	15	40	**0**	24	25	18	42	30	20	25	25	.	5	30	15	40	**0**	20	37	.

Miles	Up	Week Days																												Sundays											
	HOUR ☞	6	7	8	9		10	10	11		S 12	12		1		2	S 4	E 4	E 5	S 5	6	7	7	7	9	9		S 10		9	11		12	2	4	5	6	8	9	10	
—	Falmouth ... dep.	50	35	14	15	.	10	40	25	.	10	50	.	40	.	35	0	27	10	30	20	5	25	45	20	45	.	50	.	15	5	.	50	15	5	30	50	10	30	45	
1½	Penmere Platform ...	54	40	18	19	.	15	44	29	.	14	54	.	44	.	39	4	31	14	34	24	8	30	49	24	49	.	54	.	19	9	.	54	19	9	34	54	14	34	49	.
3½	Penryn ...	**1**	47	24	25	.	20	50	35	.	20	**0**	.	50	.	45	10	37	20	40	30	14	36	56	31	56	.	**1**	.	26	16	.	**1**	26	16	41	**1**	21	41	54	.
7½	Perranwell ...	11	56	33	35	.	30	**0**	44	.	30	10	.	**0**	.	55	20	48	31	50	40	24	48	**6**	40	**5**	.	10	.	35	25	.	10	35	25	49	10	30	50	**3**	.
11¾	Truro **26, 31, 59** ... arr.	22	**7**	45	46	.	41	10	55	.	40	20	.	10	.	**5**	30	**2**	41	**0**	50	35	58	20	50	15	.	20	.	45	35	.	20	40	35	**0**	20	40	**0**	15	.

A St David's **D** Sta for Porthleven (2¼ miles), Mullion (6 miles), The Lizard (10 miles), Kynance Cove (10 miles), Housel Bay (10½ miles), Cadgwith (9½ miles), and Coverack and St. Keverne (10½ miles)
E Except Sats **F** Sta for St. Mawes **H** Dep Exeter 3 34 aft. on Sats **K** 20 mins later on Sats
R Road Motor (Rail Tickets not available). Runs to Falmouth (Moor). **S** Sats only. **T** 5 mins. later on Sats.
X One class only (limited accommodation).

Where the MINUTES under the Hours change to a LOWER figure and DARKER type it indicates the NEXT HOUR

The Falmouth branch benefited from the rebuilding of its wooden viaducts, and also with a new halt at Penmere. This service became faster and more frequent between 1922 (upper) and 1938 (lower). *(Bradshaw)*

The situation changed almost overnight with the decision by the then Chancellor of the Exchequer, Winston Churchill, in his 1929 Budget to end the Railway Passenger Duty on condition that the railway companies spent the money on modernisation. Churchill was not thinking of the passenger or the freight customer, but of finding a way to reduce unemployment by means of substantial works programmes. In addition to the funds thus released to the railway companies, the Treasury also offered what would be today described as 'soft' loans, again for major works, using the Government Grants (Development Loans, Guarantees and Grants) Act 1929. The railways were not the only beneficiaries of this programme, which also saw road building and the construction of reservoirs for hydroelectric schemes, but they were the main recipients. The schemes might have transformed the business of all of the railways had it not been that they were accompanied by falling traffic.

The modernisation of the terminus at Paddington has already been covered in Chapter Two. It also included resignalling of the approach lines using colour light signalling, but unlike the four-aspect colour light signalling favoured by the Southern Railway, which had been developed by the Institution of Railway Signal Engineers, the GWR insisted that the signals should only show those aspects that semaphore signals displayed at night. This may have been a reflection of the need to match the automatic train control system being extended throughout the system, but it was a limiting factor. The GWR 'searchlight' signals could only display two aspects. On home or starting signals, the colours were red and green, while on the distant signals, amber or green. This had the advantage that drivers had nothing new to learn, but it meant that a major step forward in modernising the signalling system was missed. Colour light signals of this kind were also included in the resignalling at Bristol Temple Meads and at Cardiff General, and when the main line was resignalled between Paddington and Southall.

At Temple Meads, once again reconstruction took place on a substantial scale. The 'through' platforms were under an all-over roof and were inadequate for the traffic handled. To get round this, new platforms were built east and south of the station, while under the roof the centre platforms were removed and the outside platforms widened. There was also work on the approaches from the west. Trains had to continue to run while the work was carried out, and it is perhaps not surprising that demolition and the rebuilding, including work on track and signals, took no less than 7½ years.

Cardiff General was another important reconstruction, but here the problem was not so much one of the through trains but of coordinating and combining the services of the former Barry, Rhymney and Taff Vale with those of the Great Western in one large station. Only the Barry Railway had run its trains into Cardiff General, while the Rhymney and the Taff Vale had each had their own station. The Taff Vale had a connecting line to Cardiff General, but there was no physical connection between the Rhymney and the GWR until 1928, and even then this was through a connection to the Taff Vale. The reconstruction did not simply bring all four companies into one station, it showed commitment to operating the railways in South Wales as a single integrated system, and was in marked contrast to developments within other members of the 'Big Four'.

New Lines

During the early years of the twentieth century the Great Western had spent considerable sums on building more direct routes and shortening journey times. During the 1930s attention turned to easing some of the bottlenecks on the system as well as improving

The permanent way and the emergency crews needed their own rolling stock, such as this six-wheel breakdown stores van seen in the yard at Newton Abbot in 1947, with a breakdown crane on an adjoining track. *(HMRS/P.J. Garland AEL230)*

stations. Owing in no small part to the Great Western's own efforts, traffic during the summer holiday period to the resorts in Devon and Cornwall had reached embarrassing proportions, with delays at peak times. Part of the problem was that the traffic did not simply all flow from London, but was augmented by considerable traffic flows from the Midlands and beyond. Trains from all over the country heading south-west converged on Cogload Junction, 5 miles north of Taunton, where peak-period delays could last as long as two hours. Worse still, most trains called at Taunton itself, and some of them had to detach carriages for Ilfracombe and Minehead, which took time. The line through Taunton was only double track, again contributing to the pressure on this vital part of the system. Earlier, as a means of providing relief, the goods lines to the east of Taunton station had been upgraded for passenger running, and at peak periods expresses not scheduled to stop at Taunton could bypass the station by taking the goods line. However, this was an unsatisfactory solution as the sharp turnouts onto the goods lines and the severe curves on the lines themselves meant that speeds were low. One observer recalled that an express that passed Cogload at more than 60mph, and afterwards took the avoiding line at Taunton without stopping, took 10 minutes to cover the 4.4 miles between Creech Junction and Norton Fitzwarren.

The line from Cogload Junction through Taunton to Norton Fitzwarren, where the Minehead and Barnstaple branches diverged, was quadrupled, which meant that Taunton station had to be rebuilt, while at Cogload Junction, the Down line from Bristol and the Midlands was carried over the tracks on a flyover to avoid conflicting movements. The Minehead branch was converted from single line with passing loops to double track for part of its length.

Services to the south-west were also accelerated and reliability much improved by the construction of bypass lines at both Frome and Westbury stations. These not only saved the delays caused by slowing down to pass these stations at just 30mph, but also ensured that trains were travelling at a more suitable speed to tackle the rising gradients that followed the speed restrictions. The Great Western estimated that avoiding the speed restrictions, or 'slacks' in railway terminology, saved a ton of coal a day and also saved each express running non-stop around 5 minutes. Nevertheless, express trains not stopping at Westbury but which had previously detached a slip carriage there, now had to drop the slip carriage at Heywood Road Junction, a mile to the east of Westbury.

Not all of the new lines were on holiday routes, with a new line opened in 1925 between Dunstall Park and Brettell, a 12-mile route that allowed not only passenger and parcels trains but goods trains as well to bypass Walsall and Wolverhampton. For the local passenger traffic that the Great Western was anxious to encourage, a steam railmotor service was introduced. Later, as a benefit of the funds released under the 1929 Act, quadrupling also took place at Birmingham.

Further west, many of the branch lines had been built as cheaply as possible, and wooden viaducts were much in evidence. Many of these were replaced, including those on the Falmouth branch, which had given more than seventy years of good service. There was also a new viaduct over the River Thames at Littlemore. In Cornwall, double line was installed between Bugle and Goonbarrow, and between Scorrier and Redruth. In Wales, the viaduct over the River Usk at Newport had to be rebuilt and widened.

Marshalling Yards

Once money became available for modernisation, the Great Western started on a steady programme of improvements. While many of the more obvious were for passengers, with rebuilt stations and improvements that accelerated their trains, or at least increased reliability and time-keeping at peak periods, goods traffic was also important to the company. The ports in South Wales had been an early priority for redevelopment, but in the 1930s attention was paid to the marshalling yards at Acton and South Lambeth. A new marshalling yard was built at Banbury, while that at Severn Tunnel Junction was enlarged.

The new idea in handling goods wagons at marshalling yards was 'gravitation shunting', which required humps to be installed at the yards so that wagons could be shunted to the top and then allowed to roll downhill, being switched into the appropriate siding as they rolled. A new hump was built at Bristol East, among others.

Less extensive but also for goods traffic was the new goods depot at Paignton, while Cardiff Cathays received a new carriage and wagon repair shop. The repair shop at Swindon was also modernised and a carriage disinfectant facility opened, so that rolling stock infested by vermin or by a contagious disease could be treated.

Wartime

Some of the infrastructure work brought about by the Second World War is mentioned in Chapter Seventeen, but the war was more notable for what it didn't allow. Plans for a bypass or cut-off at Dawlish on the South Devon coast would have added considerably to the reliability of services, especially in bad weather when the sea wall proved vulnerable to stormy seas, and would have been welcomed by travellers on the line, even today.

Wartime was also responsible for another innovation, concrete sleepers, which at the time were used so that the superior wooden sleepers could be reserved for the main lines. Concrete sleepers were seen as being less durable and were also more prone to damaging the ballasting. At the time, concrete sleepers were regarded as being only good enough for branch lines and shunting yards.

Mention is made in the next chapter of conversion of a 6-mile length of line from Lansdown Junction at Cheltenham to Engine Shed Junction at Gloucester from double to quadruple track to ease congestion in moving coal from South Wales to the Midlands. This was only one of the improvements needed as a result of increased wartime traffic, with no fewer than fifty-one new passing loops built in 1942 and 1943.

Postwar, while the plans for many new or improved stretches of line were dusted off, the civil engineers had bigger problems attempting to repair wartime damage and overcome arrears of maintenance, despite shortfalls in the supply of necessary materials, while the management at head office found the certainty of nationalisation inhibiting their freedom of action. Work was started on converting locomotive depots to support oil-fired engines, with the installation of fuel tanks, but despite this being encouraged by the new government, work came to an abrupt end when the same government found that the country did not have enough dollars to pay for imported oil.

Chapter Seventeen

Railways at War

There were two aspects to the story of Britain's railways in wartime. On the one hand, there is the story of the railways struggling to meet their increased wartime commitments and the relationship between the railways and the state, which became both their biggest customer and also their controller, imposing restrictions and effectively taking their revenue and using them as subcontractors. On the other hand, there was the way in which the railways and railway personnel, both men and women, coped with enemy aerial attack.

Government interest in the potential of the railways dated from as early as 1871 and the Regulation of the Forces Act of that year, which allowed the government to take control of the railways in a national emergency. The real interest at the time seems to have been more a concern with internal unrest than an external threat. The first major use of the railways for military purposes came later, with the Boer War, but that did not require control of the railways, and indeed it really only affected one company, the London & South Western

The railways were not only expected to play their part in the war, they also had to look after themselves as far as possible, as with this mobile fire-fighting unit based at Reading in 1941. (*Kevin Robertson*)

Railway, one of the Southern Railway's ancestors. In common with the other companies, the Great Western Railway did not have the benefit of what amounted to a practice run during the Boer War, when the LSWR was the prime mover of men and horses from London and the military training grounds across the south of England to Southampton. The LSWR experience had been unique. When the First World War came, in common with every other railway in Great Britain, the 'old' pre-grouping Great Western found itself under state control between 1914 and 1918.

The actual basis for state control had occurred in 1912, with the formation of the Railways Executive Committee consisting of the general managers of ten leading railway companies, including the GWR. The role of the REC was to run the railways as a single entity in the case of war. When war came, the main pressure fell upon the companies in the south, especially those serving the Channel ports closest to France. Initially, only the railways in Great Britain were administered by the REC, but those in Ireland, at this time undivided and all of it within the United Kingdom, were added in 1917, although this was due more to the unrest in parts of Ireland than to the war in Europe.

The railway companies not only had to adapt to centralised control, they also lost some 200,000 of their employees, who numbered around 600,000 in total, to the armed forces. Passenger services were cut back to allow paths for troop trains and to save fuel as well as wear and tear on track and rolling stock. Some minor branch lines were closed to save fuel and manpower, and some of them never reopened. Nevertheless, it was not until 1917 that cheap fares were abolished and ordinary fares increased by 50 per cent, with even greater restrictions on the number of trains available for civilian passengers. On the other hand, in contrast to the practice during the Second World War, while the availability of restaurant cars was reduced considerably, the facility did not disappear completely.

Fortunately, the railways had, for the most part, enjoyed a period of great prosperity during the years leading up to the First World War, and so the problems encountered in assessing fair payment for the use of their facilities in the later conflict were not so serious. One or two companies encountered delay in receiving the grants due for abnormal maintenance costs, and there were some disputes that had to go to law. Overall, for the First World War, the government paid the railways £60 million to be shared between the companies.

The attitude of the government towards the railways during the First World War was still remembered by many of those running the railways at the beginning of the Second World War. After all, the period between the two wars amounted to slightly less than twenty-one years. Directors and senior managers were also painfully aware that the years between the two world wars had not been good ones for the railways, and the GWR had been the exception in being able to pay a dividend every year, although for the first time in almost seventy years, for 1938 the dividend fell below 3 per cent and just $\frac{1}{2}$ per cent was paid. By contrast, in 1912, before the outbreak of the First World War, the 'old' GWR had paid $5\frac{5}{8}$ per cent and this prosperity continued into the following year. As any government compensation would be based on average turnover for the years immediately preceding the war, it was with considerable foreboding that the new conflict was anticipated. Added to which everyone realised that the growing potential of the bomber, a nuisance to the railways during the First World War rather than a serious threat, meant they would be in the front line. There were also problems of administration, with key personnel evacuated to areas where it was hoped that they could continue with their work uninterrupted by heavy bombing.

Preparing for War

Preparation for the wartime operation of the railways was put in hand as early as 1937. In September 1938 the Ministry of Transport warned that as soon as the danger of enemy aggression was imminent, a Defence of the Realm Act would be passed, and that one of its provisions would be for the government to take control of the railways and the railway

Given the vast extent of their networks, the railways were highly vulnerable to bombing, and a prime target. This derailment on the Falmouth branch in 1941 was the direct consequence of a bomb. *(Kevin Robertson)*

operations of the London Passenger Transport Board. It was realised that bombing would be a threat, and in 1937 a technical committee laid plans for dealing with the effects. Prominent among those involved in the preparations was Gilbert Matthews of the GWR, engaged in dealing with operational matters, while F.H.D. Page represented the company on matters of signalling and communications. As expected, in late September 1938 once again a Railway Executive Committee was formed, with the Great Western represented by its general manager, James Milne. Initially the REC was chaired by Gilbert Szlumper of the Southern Railway, but he later became Director-General of Transportation at the War Office.

One of the early tasks for the committee was to draw up a list of measures, including protection of employees and their administrative centres, as well as locating material for emergency repairs and any additional equipment needed. For the railway companies and London Transport, the total estimate came to £5,226,400, and a foretaste of things to come followed when the government decided at the end of 1938 to provide a grant of just £4 million, of which £750,000 was to go to the LPTB, with the companies left to fund the balance themselves. The GWR share of this reduced sum was £472,000, the lowest for any railway company.

Part of the money was spent on relocating the headquarters, as it was vital that the railway continued to function no matter what happened. The main centre for the GWR became Beenham Grange, close to the station at Aldermaston in Berkshire. This was really not quite big enough, but additional buildings were found for some of the departments at Brimpton, Thatcham, Cholsey and Reading. Despite the disruption caused by a serious signal-box fire at Paddington, arrangements continued, and a trial blackout was tried at Paddington with a major air-raid precautions, ARP, exercise between 1a.m. and 4a.m. on 29 January 1939.

Meanwhile, many employees enrolled in the civil defence and air-raid precautions services, while others were already in the Territorial Army, many of them in the Railway Supplementary Reserve of the Royal Engineers, or were planning to join.

State Control

On the eve of war, as threatened, the Minister of Transport moved quickly to seize control of the railways on 1 September 1939, using powers granted to him under the Defence Regulations Act. There was considerable delay in fixing the basis on which the railways would be paid, with the state taking all of the receipts and allocating what it regarded as a suitable sum to each of the four main-line railway companies and London Transport on a predetermined basis. There was little real negotiation, with the government hinting at acceptance or nationalisation. The inclusion of the London Passenger Transport Board in the scheme was opposed by the 'Big Four' railway companies, who believed that passenger traffic would slump in wartime, and that as the only all-passenger operator, London Transport would become a liability for the others. It certainly meant that the allocated funds would have to be spread around more thinly.

The state also decided what resources could be made available in terms of raw materials and manufacturing capacity to keep the railways running. This was not nationalisation in the true sense of the word, but it was a bureaucratic straitjacket, although it must be borne in mind that the control of labour, raw materials and manufacturing capacity applied to the entire economy and not just the railways.

Despite the haste to grab control of the railways, there was considerable delay in finalising the means of working. The system of state control meant that the railways effectively became contractors to the government, with all revenue passing to the government, which then allocated a share-out of a pool set at a guaranteed £40 million. The GWR share of the pool was fixed at 16 per cent, the same as for the Southern Railway, while the LPTB received 11 per cent, the LMS 34 per cent and the LNER 23 per cent. These percentages were based on the average net revenues for the companies and LPTB in the three years 1935–7, which the government regarded as the standard revenue for each company. Once the guaranteed £40 million had been paid, any balance was allocated to the five train operators on the same percentage terms up to a maximum of £3.5 million. After this the arrangements became complicated, since if there was a further balance, the revenue over a total of £43.5 million would be divided equally between the government and the pool until the pool total reached £56 million. At this stage, if the revenue share allocated to any of the companies then exceeded its standard revenue – the figure the companies had been expected to earn annually at the time of the grouping – the excess would be shared out proportionately among the other companies.

Costs of maintenance and renewals had to be standardised, while the cost of restoring war damage would be met up to a total of £10 million in a full year. Privately owned wagons were also requisitioned by the Ministry, and the individual companies had to meet the costs and revenue attributed to the wagon owners out of their share of the revenue pool.

This was a 'take it or leave it' type of agreement, with the government leaking threats of nationalisation if the companies failed to agree, although these were officially denied. The years in question had not been good ones for the British economy, although 1938 had been worse and the railways had had to work hard to get the government to recognise this. The difficult economic conditions that had prevailed for almost all of the interwar period had meant that none of the railway companies had ever achieved the standard revenues anticipated by the Railways Act 1921, the measure that authorised the grouping. The best that can be said for the deal was that the government was anxious to avoid inflationary pay claims from railway employees, and no doubt anxious to ensure that it did not play a part in war profiteering since it was likely to be its own single biggest customer, but the inescapable fact was that the railways were having their revenues more or less fixed while costs were bound to rise as they struggled to meet the increased demands that wartime placed upon them. Establishing an upper limit on the cost of making good war damage was another instance of either political expediency to keep the unions quiet and the Labour Party within the wartime coalition government, or simple naivety since normal insurance measures were not available in wartime.

Nevertheless, within little more than a year, what had become the Ministry of War Transport reneged on the original agreement and left the railway companies to pay for war damage out of revenue. The fixed annual payments were also changed, with the provision for extra payments dropped, so that any surplus would be taken by the government, which generously also offered to meet any deficit, which was an unlikely event given the demands placed on the railways. The new deal provided for the following annual payments:

Great Western Railway	£6,670,603
London & North Eastern Railway	£10,136,355
London, Midland & Scottish Railway	£14,749,698
Southern Railway	£6,607,639
London Passenger Transport Board	£4,835,705

The railway companies were once again left with little option but to accept. The mood of the times was that any argument was unseemly, as it seemed that invasion was a very real danger.

Bus services were not included in the scheme and neither was road haulage. The reasons for this were ones of practicality, as there were so many operators, including a number of owner-driver operations, especially in road haulage and coach private hire, that it would have been extremely difficult. In any case, the state had other means of regulating these modes of transport, by tight controls on the allocation of fuel and vehicles, with the armed forces free to requisition vehicles as necessary, and the Ministry of War Transport able to allocate vehicles from one operator to another if it thought fit. The irony was that many bus operators in the provinces, and especially in what in peacetime would have been resort areas, found wartime demand heavier as new bases for the armed forces were often established in these areas, especially along the south and east coasts of England. Areas in which transport had been heavily affected by the blitz, such as London and Coventry, often had their vehicles replaced by vehicles from other operators before the limited production of utility vehicles was finally authorised.

Ferry services were badly disrupted, as ships were taken over by the Ministry of Transport, with many needed to help move the British Expeditionary Force to France and then to keep it supplied. Other small ships were taken up by the Admiralty as they were needed for the many tasks around the main naval bases.

Railways During the Second World War

There had been much rehearsal of wartime operating conditions on the railways from 1938 onwards. Railwaymen had practised working in blackout conditions, which meant that no lights could be shown externally, with all windows screened, while station platforms could only be lit by blue lights or, as there were still many lit by gas, specially shaded gas lamps, and drivers and motormen had to pull up their trains beside oil lamps placed on the

Inevitably, it took some time for nationalisation to extinguish the identity of the old companies, and the Great Western was no exception. This is 'County' class No. 1011 *County of Chester* still in GWR livery. (*Kevin Robertson*)

platform as markers. Steam locomotives had canvas draped between the engine cab and tender to hide the light of their fires, while the side windows that had appeared on the more modern locomotives were blanked out.

None of this, of course, can truly give a real impression of what it must have been like operating a railway in the blackout, or of the problems of individual railwaymen and women having to report for work after a broken night's sleep in a crowded air-raid shelter, or of coming off a night shift to find that their home no longer existed, and perhaps face the loss of family members and neighbours. The efficient working of a railway required skill and experience, but under wartime conditions most adults had to be available for either the armed forces or prepared to be directed to essential war work, and as skilled men volunteered or were conscripted into the armed forces, many of their places were taken by women. This may have been a factor in the eventual Allied victory, as many historians believe that one factor in the defeat of Germany was that the Germans were reluctant to mobilise the civilian population and instead relied too heavily on slave labour and people conscripted from the occupied territories or Vichy France.

Wartime acted as a spur to extending loudspeaker announcements to stations, and while initially station name signs were no longer lit, those under station canopies were allowed to be illuminated later provided that they were swung round at right angles to the platform. Those stations that had had their names painted on the canopies to help airmen with their navigation had them blanked out. A final safety measure at stations was the removal of glass from roofs and canopies, essential since even a small bomb could create so many shards of broken glass as to be an effective anti-personnel weapon.

As a fuller understanding of the implications of working a railway in wartime dawned on those involved, many were thankful that the main Great Western express locomotives had been fitted with speedometers, as in the blackout picking up those points of reference that would give an experienced driver an idea of his speed was to become so difficult as to be almost impossible. Indeed, in the accident at Norton Fitzwarren, all the evidence suggests that the driver had either become completely disorientated or was exhausted and stressed for understandable personal reasons, and quite possibly both.

Evacuation and Emergency Measures

After the false hopes raised by the resolution of the Munich Crisis of 1938, it soon became clear that war was more of a probability than a possibility. Preparations were made by the railway companies, although these were not helped by threatened industrial action by their employees, which was only averted at the last moment. Anticipating a possible surprise attack, on virtually the eve of war, evacuation of children and many others, including their teachers and expectant and nursing mothers, started to get them away from London and other major cities, especially those such as Birmingham judged to be likely targets. The pressure on the GWR and other railways was such that during the four days of the operation, from 1 to 4 September 1939, only a skeleton service could be provided for the public outside the rush hours. In fact, while the Great Western ran a train from its evacuation station at Ealing Broadway every 10 minutes, its main-line services were reduced to just eighteen trains from Paddington between 8.40a.m. and 6.35p.m., with those to the West Country all being routed the 'long way round' via Bristol. Many goods trains were stopped during the period of the evacuation, with few, if any, run on 1 and 2 September.

On 31 August the order to begin the evacuation was given. Evacuation from London was shared by all four railway companies, while that from Birmingham was shared by the Great Western and the London, Midland & Scottish. Children assembled at their schools and from there either walked or were taken by bus or Underground train to the station allocated to them, with many having to use suburban stations either because of convenience or because the London termini could not handle all of them.

For the London evacuees being taken away by the Great Western, Ealing Broadway became the main station, being closed to the public between 8a.m. and 5.30p.m. each day, while the GWR was ordered to run the special evacuation trains between 8.30a.m. and 5.30p.m. The GWR suffered from having just one London pick-up point, doubtless selected for easy transfer from the London Underground trains, while much of its area, such as the West Country and Wales, was seen as ideal for evacuees, almost as far away from the threat of German air attack as it was possible to be. In London alone, 5,895 buses, more than half the London Transport fleet, were required to move 345,812 passengers to the stations. While the Great Western was not unique in handling this traffic, the company did account for a substantial proportion of it, being told to expect more than 138,000 passengers, although not every parent sent their child away, and some had made their own arrangements with relatives living away from the threatened areas rather than leaving the evacuation to chance and officialdom. The GWR also carried a substantial number of the 46,934 people evacuated from Birmingham and provided many of the 170 trains needed.

Drastic Cuts

On the outbreak of war, excursion and cheap-day tickets were withdrawn, but day tickets were reintroduced on 9 October, although with tighter conditions that meant they were not available before 10.00a.m. and could not be used on trains departing from London between 4p.m. and 7p.m. Monday to Friday.

After the evacuation was over, services returned to normal briefly, for on 11 September drastic cuts were imposed, meaning great hardship for passengers since, although the late holiday and day-tripper traffic had virtually disappeared, normal business travel was still almost at pre-war levels, especially with large numbers of people commuting to their offices in the City. Some large companies had dispersed, especially those with strategic importance such as the shipping lines, but it was not possible for everyone to do so, for apart from business considerations, the number of suitable venues outside London and other major cities was limited.

Not only did this lead to unacceptable levels of overcrowding, with many passengers left behind, it also meant that station dwell times were extended as passengers struggled to alight from trains or to climb aboard. After the uproar that followed, normal services were reinstated on weekdays from 18 September.

Nevertheless, this was simply a temporary reinstatement and indicated nothing more than that the blanket reductions of 11 September had not been properly thought out in the short time available to the timetable planners. Wartime conditions meant that services had to be reduced, both to save personnel, fuel and wear and tear and to make trains and paths available for the military. New timetables imposing reductions in passenger services followed on 25 September, with the GWR being one of the first companies to introduce its new timetable, although on this occasion better allowances were made for peak period travel. Off-peak, most main-line services lost their usual trains with the service halved, often running to extended timings.

Some idea of the impact of the cuts on the travelling public can be gathered from the fact that the service from Paddington to Birmingham was cut from fourteen trains in 1938 to eight in 1939. The average journey time was increased from 125 minutes to 171 minutes, but the fastest in October 1938 had been just 2 hours for the 110.6 miles. Other destinations suffered similar cuts, but despite its importance to the Royal Navy, Plymouth suffered a double blow. Not only did it see its trains cut from twelve to nine daily, but they were all sent via Bristol, increasing the journey time dramatically from an average of 284 minutes in 1938 to 386 minutes a year later, while the best 1938 time had been just 245 minutes for the 225½ miles of the direct route through Castle Cary. There was considerable debate over whether sleeping-car services could continue, but a number did, although for the ordinary traveller the reprieve was short-lived.

Meanwhile, carriages were converted for use on ambulance trains for the military and others converted for the evacuation of civilian casualties in anticipation of widespread disruption by heavy bombing, although the latter were never needed. Locomotives were also modified, with a number fitted with condensing gear and pipes for obtaining water from streams, anticipating widespread disruption to water supplies following bombing. The major stations and depots formed their own volunteer fire-fighting forces, while there were also fire-fighting trains, able to rush to wherever they might be needed, not only because of the greater speed of the railway than road transport, but also because many fires might be more easily accessible from the railway than from the road.

The 'Castle' class provided the power for the great expresses until the arrival of the 'Kings', and even then had better route availability, which meant they continued to handle the named trains on many routes, including west of the Tamar Bridge. This is No. 5029 *Nunney Castle*. (*Kevin Robertson*)

Security considerations also meant that the regular monthly diet of statistics fed to the readers of *The Great Western Railway Magazine* had to be suspended. In the event, while this was doubtless a necessary precaution, it is now known that there were few German spies during the war, and those who did arrive were soon detected. There may have been fewer statistics, but rather more than the odd figure did leak out, especially at the Great Western's Annual General Meeting, possibly because it was felt that by the time these were announced their intelligence value was much diminished.

The spread of rationing, introduced in early 1940, and the difficulty that many had in shopping with so many women working, and many of them working very long hours, led to a growth in the number of staff canteens on the Great Western. Rolling stock was also modified and equipped as 'mobile canteen' trains, able to be sent to wherever such facilities were needed, either because the station canteen had been bombed or because large numbers were involved in dealing with the after-effects of an 'incident'.

Despite many railway jobs being classified as 'reserved occupations', the Great Western Railway saw a growing number of its personnel leaving to join the armed forces for the duration of the war. By February 1941 no fewer than 8,401 men had left their jobs on the railway, about 7.5 per cent of the total number of employees, and rather higher in terms of male employees as much office work was carried out by women. Their work on the railway and in the workshops was taken over by women, who even undertook some of the heavier jobs, including those of porters. At first the new recruits did not have uniforms, but this was quickly remedied. Uniforms were important on a railway, not only because much of the work was dirty, but also for security and so that passengers knew who to turn to for advice and help.

Almost coinciding with the growing number of women employees was the introduction of small platform tractors to handle parcels and baggage. These improved productivity as one tractor with a driver could handle a number of trolleys, saving manpower as well as moving parcels much more quickly. Inevitably, these became known on the GWR as 'trolley-trains'. The major stations were first to receive these, including Paddington, Birmingham, Cardiff, Newport, Swansea and also Taunton and Torquay.

The 'Star' class were really the founders of the GWR locomotive dynasty, with most of what followed being developments and improvements of this successful design. This is 'Star' class No. 4040 *Queen Boadicaea*. *(Kevin Robertson)*

Despite the cut in the number of trains, passenger traffic was 3 per cent higher in December 1939 than for the previous December. As industry got into its stride and was placed on a war footing, general goods traffic rose by 51 per cent, while that for coal rose by 41 per cent. Goods train mileage increased by 18 per cent. In the docks, traffic was up by 31 per cent. All of this happened on a railway which had already lost many skilled personnel for service with the armed forces, as well as losing almost forty locomotives that had been requisitioned and sent overseas. Employees were given the first of a series of wartime advances on their pay in recognition that the cost of living was increasing.

The New Year started badly, with many trains cancelled in what the company magazine proclaimed as the 'Worst Winter Ever', as heavy falls of snow blocked lines and trapped trains.

Nevertheless, a sense of normality seemed to be in the air when the Great Western launched its new edition of *Holiday Haunts* early in 1940. The bright posters extolling the virtues of the many resorts on the Great Western, and on other railways, were soon to be replaced by stern messages from the Ministry of War Transport, demanding to know 'Is your journey really necessary?' The Railways Executive Committee did its bit to discourage travel, raising fares in May 1940 by 10 per cent, both to urge against travel and to cover the mounting costs of the railways. There was to be a constant conflict between the authorities and the public at Christmas and the New Year, and in the summer months during the war years. A war-weary and bomb-battered population would do all it could to get away for a summer holiday, while the authorities made it as difficult for them as possible. At Christmas, people working away from home were anxious to get back for a day or two. To try to help, the armed forces eventually refused to issue forces leave passes at peak periods, which was harsh if the individuals concerned were about to be posted abroad. It must have been a considerable delight to the government that later in the war travel to resorts on the south coast was banned due to the preparations for the Normandy landings.

Dunkirk and The Channel Islands

In 1940 the Whitsun holiday was cancelled by the government since the Germans were sweeping through the Low Countries and into France. This ultimately led to the evacuation of the British Expeditionary Force from Dunkirk, along with many French troops and some from Belgium as well.

At Dunkirk four large GWR steamers were employed in bringing troops back across the Channel. These were *St Helier* and *St Julien* from the Channel Island service, accompanied by *St Andrew* and *St David* from the Fishguard–Rosslare service. *St Andrew* and *St Julien* had already been operating as hospital ships. *St Helier* alone carried no fewer than 10,000 troops across the Channel. These were at the smart end of the operation, as the less fortunate troops found themselves on two of the Channel Island cargo steamers, *Roebuck* and the *Sambur*. Their smaller size meant that these ships could go closer in at Dunkirk, and afterwards were sent to St Valéry to rescue troops from there. However, by the time they arrived it was too late, as the port had fallen to the Germans. When the ships arrived, the Germans had shore batteries ready and a number of those aboard were killed as the ships came under fire. Too late for the Dunkirk evacuation, but a sign of the desperation felt at the time was *Mew*, the Dartmouth–Kingswear ferry that also answered the call. However, by the time she reached Dover the evacuation was ending.

Three of the ships, *St Andrew*, *St David* and *St Julien*, were later sent to the Mediterranean, and instead of taking troops off beaches, played an important part in the invasion of Sicily and later at the Salerno landings, taking the Allies on to the mainland of Italy. *St David* was lost, along with many of her crew, including her master, on 24 January 1944 off the beaches at Anzio on the coast of Italy, after being bombed by the Luftwaffe.

Meanwhile, ashore in England, the railways were hard at work handling special trains, many of them heading south to get the soldiers away from the Channel ports. At 5p.m. on 26 May 1940 the code-word 'Dynamo' was sent to the railways, warning them that the evacuation from Dunkirk was due to start. The railway companies provided a 'pool' of 186 trains, of which the GWR share was forty. A problem arose with finding sufficient locomotives capable of running over Southern metals, especially since the route from Reading to the Channel ports was far from being a masterpiece of railway engineering. Most of the locomotives used were 2–6–0s and the 'Manor' class 4–6–0s. At the outset the railways did not know how many journeys would need to be made by these trains and just where the troops would land. While the entire operation ran from 27 May to 4 June, the busiest days were 1 June and 4 June, when the entire operation was achieved by having holding points for empty trains at Faversham, Margate, Queenborough and Ramsgate. Possibly the railways managed so well because they were used to the demand for special trains caused by major sporting events.

Added to the difficulties of organising the railway end of the Dunkirk evacuation was the sudden realisation on the part of the authorities that a second evacuation was needed of many children moved from London to the south coast, but who were now too close for comfort to German airfields.

Neither the railways nor the military knew how many men to expect from Dunkirk. In the end more than 338,000 were carried. This of necessity meant massive disruption to ordinary services, with even the slimmed-down wartime timetable suspended in many cases. The trains with the troops from Dunkirk joined the Great Western Railway at Reading, having taken the all-important cross-country Southern Railway North Downs line bypassing the London area for those being taken to Wales, the West Country and the Midlands. All of the usual passenger trains along the Tonbridge–Reading lines had been suspended and replacement bus services provided, which must have resulted in greatly extended journey times given the meandering nature of the A25.

While in many ways the whole exercise has been seen since as a masterpiece of organisation and improvisation, it took place in an atmosphere of chaos. No one knew how many troops would arrive or when, and certainly they had no idea of how many were fit and how many were wounded, and still less of where to send them when they did arrive. The chaos was such that trains were turned round at Dover and sent off before the authorities had any idea where they could send the rescued troops, so often drivers were instructed to 'Stop at Guildford and ask where you are going to.'

Volunteers tried to ensure that the arriving troops were given tea and something to eat, as well as a card so that they could write home to let their families know that they were safe. A collection at one station to provide food and drink for the troops, organised by the stationmaster's wife, raised more than £1,000 from passengers and from people who had been drawn to the station by the continuous flood of the heavily laden troop trains. Inevitably, everything was under unforeseen pressure. One example was that at some stations used as refreshment stops there weren't enough cups: tins had to be used as improvised cups, and just before a train left from a refreshment stop the order was given for these to be thrown out so that the volunteers could wash them ready for the next train.

Restrictions

Throughout the war years there was an almost constant trimming of services to reduce fuel consumption and eliminate underused train miles. The trains themselves were lengthened, often requiring a call at a station to require two stops as passengers alighted from the front of the train, which then had to be moved forward to allow those in the back of the train to alight or for others to board. On one occasion, in the blackout, an army private, not realising that this method of working was in force, stepped out of one of the rear carriages of a sixteen-coach train at Bath and had an unexpected ducking in the River Avon. Nevertheless, the Great Western did not operate the very long trains found on other railways, where twenty-four or twenty-five carriages were not unusual, and usually limited itself to around sixteen carriages. The very long trains used elsewhere did have the disadvantage that time had to be spent dividing a train on arrival, so that its carriages could be put into

In the early stages of the war, with the British Expeditionary Force in France, railway packet ships were ideal as troop ships and hospital ships. This is the Channel Island steamer *St Julien*, painted as an ambulance ship. *(NRM BTC1155/70/63)*

two platforms, and then the reverse would happen on departure, with the front half being drawn clear of the station and then reversed onto the back half.

Often journeys were delayed by the need for heavy trains to be given banking assistance, usually requiring stops while the banker was coupled and then later uncoupled.

At first, the instruction was given on all railways that on an air-raid warning being given, passenger trains were to stop and passengers allowed to alight and seek shelter if they wished, after which the train would continue at a maximum speed of just 15mph. As the full impact of the blitz took effect and air raids became so frequent, this slowed traffic down to an unacceptable extent, and the instruction was revised with trains allowed to proceed at 25mph from early November 1940. The danger of a derailment to a train running onto bomb-damaged track at high speed during an air raid was obvious, but away from the most heavily blitzed towns, many drivers took a chance and often ignored the speed limit, guessing that the risk of bomb damage was relatively light.

Shipping services did not escape the cuts. After helping in the evacuation of those civilians who wished to leave the Channel Islands, services to the islands were abandoned once the Germans invaded. Nevertheless, on the Irish Sea, just one ship was left to work the Fishguard and Rosslare route, so that the service was reduced to a frequency of three times a week in each direction. The Fishguard–Waterford service was maintained by the *Great Western*, again initially at a frequency of three times a week in each direction, but this was cut back to twice weekly in August 1940 after a large minefield was sown off the south coast of the Irish Republic. As a further security measure, since many in the UK and in Ireland believed that Southern Ireland could be used as a stepping stone for an invasion of Great Britain, the harbour at Waterford was closed during the hours of darkness. The Waterford service was suspended from April 1944, so that the *Great Western* could be taken up from trade for the Normandy landings. As we will see in the next chapter, the remaining Irish Sea steam packet, *St Patrick*, was to meet an unfortunate end.

One other absence from the railways during the Second World War was the travelling post office trains, probably both to free the lines for other more essential traffic and also release manpower for the war effort.

In addition to trimming services, as the war progressed other restrictions were applied. On 6 October 1941, under the directions of the Minister of War Transport, all London suburban trains became third class only, with the definition being that this applied to any train starting and ending its journey within the London Passenger Transport Board's area. The reasons for the move were practical, the idea being not only to make the best use of all accommodation on the reduced number of trains, but also to recognise the difficulty in finding the right class of accommodation in a hurry during the blackout. To drive the point home, carpets were removed from first-class compartments and the first-class indications on the compartment doors painted out, while timetables and departure indicators described trains as 'Third Class Only'. After the withdrawal of first-class accommodation, blackout or not, regular travellers still seemed able to find their way to the most comfortable part of the train with the superior legroom and elbow room, and plusher upholstery, of the former first-class compartments, so that these soon became shabby with intensive use.

There was constant debate over whether sleeping cars should or should not be withdrawn. Many felt that passengers needed this facility, which was once again restricted to first class only, but others argued that extra day carriages provided better use of the limited number of trains being run. In one sense, this was a small matter as the sleeping cars had been available on just eight daily trains pre-war, using a small fleet of just twenty-seven cars. From December 1942 these ceased to be available for civilian passengers, but a skeleton service was maintained for those travelling on government business, using ten sleeping cars and providing services to Plymouth, Penzance, Neyland and Newquay.

While main-line trains retained first-class accommodation, after a period of reduced catering facilities with only a limited number of trains allowed to offer this facility, on 22 May 1942 all catering facilities were withdrawn from trains on the Great Western.

It then became important to discourage unnecessary travel. The lack of sporting events and the fact that the coastal resorts had their beaches wrapped in barbed wire meant that normal leisure pursuits were not available. Again on the instructions of the Minister of War Transport, on 5 October 1942 off-peak cheap returns were scrapped, leaving seasons as the only 'cheap', or discounted, tickets. This gives little idea of the impact of the service on the traveller, since the 'reduced' wartime service included a substantial number of troop trains.

In an attempt to economise, heating was another area in which fuel could be saved, so the pre-war system of switching on full heat on main-line trains between October and April when the temperature fell below 48°F at any one of a number of monitoring points, and half-heat when the temperature fell below 55°F, had been reduced to having full heat when the temperature fell below 45°F and half-heat when it fell below 50°F between November and March.

Shortages of skilled staff in the workshops and the conversion of many of these to war production, as well as shortages of materials, meant that the intervals between routine overhauls were extended. Economy measures on the Great Western included a new colour scheme for passenger carriages of reddish-brown with a bronze waistline and black roof, while locomotives were painted plain green without any lining out on being sent for overhaul or repair. The colour of the locomotives soon became immaterial as standards of cleanliness dropped.

Another aspect of railway operation in which standards dropped, aided by poor lighting and encouraged by wartime shortages, was honesty. There was much concern about the rising level of what was described as 'pilferage' on the Great Western system, and no doubt this was matched or even exceeded on other railways.

Nevertheless, some wartime pressures had to be accommodated by investment in improved facilities. With the Port of London crippled by enemy bombing and because of the unacceptable risks from attack for shipping in the Straits of Dover and the Thames Estuary, other ports became more important, including those on the Bristol Channel. South Wales was also a major area for the production of coal, steel and iron. This put pressure on the railway system as new traffic flows had to be accommodated. In 1941 the Ministry of

A 1923 photograph of 4–6–0 'Star' class or class 40XX No. 4001 *Dog Star. (HMRS/D.A. Bayliss AEP504)*

War Transport gave authority for the conversion of a 6-mile length of line from Lansdown Junction at Cheltenham to Engine Shed Junction at Gloucester from double to quadruple track. This stretch of line was owned fifty-fifty by the GWR and the LMS, and it was agreed that the latter would do the construction work and the GWR would lay the track and provide the signalling. Starting in September, the work required considerable land drainage because of the low-lying ground before the embankments could be built.

Meanwhile, the new chief mechanical engineer, Frederick Hawksworth, had broken with past GWR tradition and increased the degree of superheating on the latest batch of 'Hall' class locomotives, obtaining a vastly improved performance. The significance of this during wartime was that superheating became even more important when the railways could no longer choose the best South Wales coal. Before this, however, the ministry had decreed that all locomotive production from December 1941 onwards would be of the LMS Stanier 2–8–0 design, and the GWR at Swindon built eighty of these. The choice of design was influenced by War Office requirements for locomotives capable of handling heavy goods trains.

Nevertheless, when the War Office demanded locomotives for service overseas, instead of the new austerity 2–8–0 locomotives, troops in North Africa were surprised to see six ex-GWR 0–6–0 Dean goods engines, including one that had served with the War Office in France and Germany a quarter of a century earlier in the previous conflict. The result was that instead of handling heavy military trains during the North African campaign, the former GWR locomotives spent most of their time either shunting or on banking and pilot duties. Unofficially, all six locomotives gained girls' names, although whether these were those of sweethearts left at home, nurses at the nearby military hospital, or, as one account would have it, ladies of the night at another establishment, has never been confirmed.

Swindon, like the other railway company workshops, had to produce and repair locomotives while also playing its part in war work. Guns and gun mountings were produced at Swindon, as well as shells, ball-bearings, bridges and landing craft. Possibly Swindon was more adaptable than the workshops for other companies, as even before the war its 'product range' had not simply included almost everything that a railway company might want, but the production of artificial limbs as well.

Chapter Eighteen

Railways Under Attack

The railways had to continue to serve the nation during the Second World War and also provide numerous special trains of one kind and another amid heavy aerial bombardment. In any modern war, the transport system is one of the most important targets, for it not only allows the swift reinforcement of the front line, but also conveys essential supplies, raw materials and, of course, fuel.

At the height of the blitz there was a near miss at Paddington, but Praed Street station on the Circle Line received a direct hit from a high-explosive bomb and the air-raid precaution services at Paddington were sent down to help. On another night a bomb fell among lorries parked outside Paddington goods station, wrecking eighteen lorries and sending a handcart flying out of the station to land in the Grand Union Canal.

The V1 missile attack on Paddington has already been covered in Chapter Two, but there were many other incidents, although with a network that lay to the West of England and in Wales, the GWR was probably the least badly hit by aerial attack of any of the 'Big Four'. Nevertheless, the so-called Baedeker raids of April to June 1942 had as their objective the destruction of many cities without significant strategic importance, and as far as the GWR was concerned, these included Bath and Exeter.

Bath was treated not to a single night of bombing but to two successive nights. West of the city centre, the line to Bristol was hit in no fewer than nine places. The most serious of these was to the 30ft-high retaining wall carrying the line above and alongside the Lower Bristol Road, which was demolished for a distance of 100ft, leaving the Up railway line hanging in

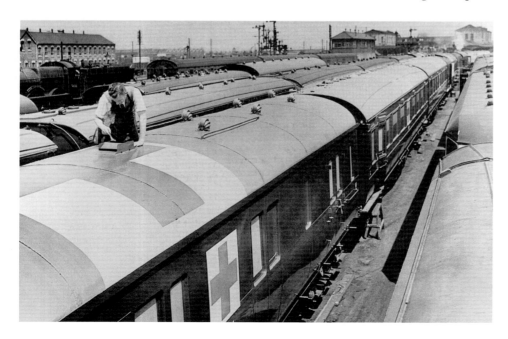

Putting the finishing touches to an ambulance train at Swindon in 1943. This one may have followed the US forces to France after the Normandy landings in 1944. *(NRM 1307/87)*

midair. The Down line was also damaged, but it was decided that this could be made safe by inserting longitudinal timbers, and with cross-over points at each side of the breach, the line could be worked as a single-track section past the damage. Repairs to the Up line meant building a temporary bridge to carry the line over the breach in the wall.

At Exeter the new GWR divisional superintendent maintained that the night of bombing there was more intense than anything he had experienced during the London blitz. This was part of the problem for those facing the Baedeker raids. The towns chosen were far smaller in size than London and the damage tended to be more concentrated. Even the seaside resorts were not immune, and Weston-super-Mare was subjected to a raid using incendiaries in early summer, doubtless aimed at those taking an early summer break, something all too rare and brief in wartime.

While the GWR had its share of bombs on its tracks, in its marshalling yards, works and stations, one of the attacks that stands out was the bombing of the Falmouth branch in 1941. The bomb cratered the track before the driver of locomotive No. 4510 had a chance to stop, and the train of three carriages was derailed. Unlike Weston-super-Mare or Bath, Falmouth was an obvious target area, with extensive ship repair facilities and one of the world's largest and best anchorages, as well as being on the Western Approaches. Ships disabled on transatlantic convoy duty could be saved if they reached Falmouth.

At Plymouth No. 4911 *Bowden Hall* was destroyed by a direct hit from a bomb. Worse could have happened in the marshalling yard at Birkenhead when an incendiary bomb fell into a train carrying bombs for the RAF. The yard was saved by a shunter who scrambled into the railway wagon and managed to prise the incendiary out of it and then threw it clear. This brave man received the George Cross.

The ability of the railways to keep the country moving at the height of the blitz was due in part to their own extensive engineering facilities and the accepted standard that, whenever there had been a peacetime accident, the priority was to clear the wreckage as soon as possible, repair any damage to track and signals and get trains moving again. Those who have experienced the time taken for the recovery of services after accidents in recent years would find this hard to comprehend. These capabilities had been enhanced by the funds made available before the war by the companies and the government to prepare for hostilities.

One example of what could be achieved on the Great Western was when a high-explosive bomb fell on a steel viaduct at midnight, damaging the main lines, a major supporting girder and some of the cross-girders. Within a few hours one line was reopened. Even when a bomb fell on track away from bridges and viaducts, damage was severe, as when a stick of three high-explosive bombs hit a section of main line and damaged all four lines, leaving large craters. Within two hours the craters had been filled with earth and rubble, while another two hours saw the two least-damaged lines restored to traffic, and all four lines were opened four hours after that.

In extreme cases the Royal Engineers could be called upon to help the railway company personnel, which was a fair exchange given that many employees had been members of special territorial units of the RE in peacetime and were no doubt doing sterling work in army uniform.

The Great Western invited its staff to hit back after the Battle of Britain by establishing its own 'Spitfire Fund', to raise £5,000 to pay for an aircraft. To get the fund off to a good start, the directors donated the first £500.

Paddington was hit several times during the war, but the event that caused most disruption to services was early in the morning on a Wednesday in March 1944, when two 1,100lb high-explosive bombs and an incendiary bomb hit the station. The first of the high explosive bombs pierced the road by platform 11, while the second exploded on platforms 6 and 7, creating a crater 40ft in diameter. Debris damaged platforms 3, 4 and 8, while 5, 6 and 7 were out of use. Nevertheless, by 5p.m. platform 5 was back in use, and twenty-four hours later so too was platform 8.

While the Normandy landings had persuaded many that the war was all but over, the flying-bomb campaign with first the V1s and then the V2s meant that peace seemed all too far away for those in London and the south-east. Nevertheless, in 1944 restrictions on lighting on trains and at stations were eased from October, with an interim level known as the 'dim out', and station name-boards started to be returned to their normal positions. The blackout ended on 23 April 1945. Germany surrendered on 8 May.

Overall, the GWR had not had a bad war, although it had lost a number of locomotives to the war effort with these being 'posted' overseas. Its thirty-three incidents per 100 route miles compared very well with the Southern Railway's record of 170, but it was higher than the twenty-nine on the LMS and just twenty-eight on the LNER, despite the latter's lines in Essex and East Anglia and up the east coast being that much closer to the bases for German bombers. The Southern record was boosted by part of its system around Dover being within range of enemy heavy artillery.

Tragedy At Sea

Many feared that the Irish Sea service was vulnerable to attack by U-boats, although the steam packet remaining on the service did attempt to steam fast enough to make herself a difficult target. Nevertheless, despite the considerable distance from enemy airfields, it was in fact the Luftwaffe that was to account for *St Patrick*.

Attack by the Luftwaffe was nothing new for *St Patrick*, as she had been bombed and machine-gunned twice early in the war. However, on the morning of 13 June 1941 *St Patrick* was heading for Fishguard and was only 25 miles from the port when she was surprised by a solitary German bomber and attacked. The first many of those aboard knew of the attack was the sound of an explosion and the lights going out. The ensuing fire soon went out of control and destroyed a number of the ship's lifeboats. One of the stewardesses, Miss May Owen, was in charge of the after-cabin in the third-class section of the ship, where she was responsible for ten women and two children. Six of the women and a child were in the upper section of the cabin while four women and the other child were in the lower section. As soon as she heard the explosion May Owen shepherded the passengers in the upper section of the cabin on deck, and then went to find those in the lower section, but as the ship was already listing heavily, the cabin door was jammed. It took several attempts before she could force the cabin door open, and inside in the darkness she found one of the passengers having hysterics while the others were searching for their luggage. She somehow managed to get them out of the cabin and up to the boat deck, despite the listing of the ship.

There was more chaos on the boat deck, but another steward took charge of three of the women and the child, putting them in the one undamaged lifeboat, while May Owen attempted to calm the hysterical passenger. Nevertheless, time was running out and as the ship began to slide under the waves, it was essential not to be caught too close to it and be sucked under. The hysterical woman passenger had lost her lifebelt in the escape from the cabin, but May Owen managed to get her over the rail and both women jumped into the sea. After trying to grab her rescuer by the neck, the passenger lost consciousness, and May Owen then had to keep her afloat for two hours before they could be hauled aboard a liferaft. For her courage, May Owen was awarded the George Medal and the Lloyds War Medal.

The radio operator had also done his duty, finding his way in the dark to his wireless room and using an emergency transmitter to send an SOS and position before the room itself was flooded. The destroyer HMS *Wolsey* and a minesweeper picked up the signal. They arrived to find many of the survivors covered with oil from the ship's bunkers.

The human cost was heavy. *St Patrick* had been carrying a crew of forty-five and the same number of passengers, and of the total just sixty survived. The master and seventeen crew members perished, as well as twelve passengers.

Later, the steam packet *St David* was to be sunk with her master and many members of her crew in the Mediterranean off Anzio in Italy, again by the Luftwaffe.

Chapter Nineteen

Peace and Nationalisation

For many railwaymen the euphoria at the end of hostilities was short-lived. It would be some time before those serving in the armed forces could be released, and while the war had ended in Europe with German surrender on 8 May 1945, it was still raging in the Far East, and at the time no one knew when a Japanese surrender would come. Indeed, a massive build-up of forces for an invasion was regarded as the most likely next step.

Those departments of the Great Western's head offices that had been evacuated started to move back, and most were safely installed at Paddington before the end of 1946. An earlier return was impossible for some of the departments because of the damage to the station offices and also because of a shortage of transport.

For the railways, peace meant that many of the wartime problems still lingered on. The railways were all in a far worse state than in 1939. They were not only war-battered, but there were massive arrears in maintenance and renewal of track, signalling and rolling stock of all kinds. Unfortunately, the Great Western's management was soon to discover that the

The end was nigh for the Great Western itself when this photograph was taken of 4–6–0 class 10XX No. 1004 *County of Somerset* in 1947. *(HRMS AAC803)*

company would not receive even the normal peacetime allocation of materials, let alone that regarded as essential to make good war damage and catch up on maintenance and renewals. A good example was that in 1938 the permanent way teams had used around 19,000 cast-iron rail chairs, yet in 1946 the Great Western was allocated just 12,500 rail chairs by the Ministry of Supply. This was despite the GWR estimating that 25,000 rail chairs a year would be needed for three years to bring the track back to the pre-war standard. The rolling stock situation was also grim. In 1938 the Great Western had a total stock of 6,168 carriages, and of these 5,819 were available for service every day, but by 1946 the total stock had dropped to 5,738 carriages, and of these just 4,441 were available for service due to the backlog of repairs. This meant that the company had gone from 94.3 per cent passenger rolling stock availability to just 77.4 per cent of a much lower total. The carriages that were left were also much older, as the average age had risen from eighteen years to twenty-two years. On the locomotive front the picture was equally bleak. In 1938 the GWR had suffered a locomotive failure every 126,000 miles, while in 1946 there was a failure every 40,000 miles.

Despite these problems, delays at Paddington in 1946 were 46.8 per cent less than those suffered the previous year, even though the pressures on the railway were such that in 1946, summer traffic was up 70 per cent over 1939. It was clear that getting the railway back to its pre-war condition, let alone developing it for the future, was going to be an uphill struggle. Despite the importance of faster trains, in 1945 the 8a.m. from Cardiff still reached Paddington at 11a.m., 15 minutes later than in 1939.

In fact, all of the railway companies were struggling to cope. The armed forces were still major users of the railways, with more than four times as many men and women in uniform as is the case today. Meanwhile, the general public was attempting to get back to business and was also fully intent on catching up on the holidays that it had missed during the war. In the case of the Great Western, the figures say it all. In the last complete year of peace, 1938, the company had carried 104,595 passengers on its long-distance trains leaving Paddington during the third week of August. In 1941 the figures were inflated by forces' leave travel and reached 178,421 passengers, but despite travel restrictions the figures continued to rise in 1945, to reach 255,756 passengers, and while the total fell back in the first full year of peace, 1946, to 202,270 passengers, this still has to be compared with the 1938 figure. In short, the Great Western was expected to carry almost double the number of passengers in a much reduced number of railway carriages.

Amid these difficulties, the railways were now faced with a new battle. While war still raged in the Far East, there was a general election that produced a landslide victory for the Labour Party in July. The new government was fully committed to the nationalisation of transport and enjoyed a Commons majority that meant that it was unstoppable.

The end of the war with Japan was not announced until midnight on 14 August, and as a result, many people did not hear the broadcast that 15 and 16 August would be public holidays. The result for the railways was that on the morning of 15 August, most people travelled to work as usual, and then almost immediately went home again, by which time an off-peak service was operating. Nevertheless, the Great Western managed to run some extra trains, including a number on its main-line services.

Starting in January 1947, a spell of exceptionally severe weather swept across the country. This was worse than even the wartime winters, themselves exceptionally harsh. Heavy snowfalls were accompanied by strong gales, and in between the periods of calm were marked by freezing fog.

It was inevitable that services were affected both by the bad weather and by the looming shortage of coal. Bad weather kept miners away from work, and the coal that was brought to the surface was often frozen at the pithead and difficult to load. For those railways operating steam locomotives, water was also a problem, as the water troughs were rendered useless by the low temperatures, forcing longer-distance trains to make additional calls to take on water, itself a hazardous task requiring locomotive firemen to climb on top of tenders in freezing conditions and in strong winds. In early February the government introduced curbs on the use of electricity by industry, and this extended to the railways, so that starting on 5 February cuts were enforced on many suburban services, followed within a week, on 11 February, by a further round of cuts, while still more followed on 15 February. The massive freeze continued until 8 March, when a thaw started, augmented by heavy rain on 10 March, which resulted in flooding of many low-lying stretches of line.

Nationalisation

Nationalisation was not a new concept, and in fact consideration of it had been mooted as far as the railways were concerned since the early days. In part, this was because of the continental model, where railways were already owned by the state or had a state interest, while as early as 1838 the Duke of Wellington had argued for state intervention to prevent the railway companies exploiting their monopoly power. A plan for state purchase was published as early as 1843 in William Galt's book *Railway Reform*, which led to Gladstone's Regulation Act of 1844, giving the government the option, from 1865 onwards, to purchase any railway company authorised thereafter. A later edition of Galt's book published in 1865 continued to press for nationalisation, not on doctrinaire grounds as with the Labour Party and the trade unions, but in the interests of the country. A Royal Commission considered the matter in 1865, but decided that nothing needed to be done.

The first British experience of nationalisation was in 1868, with the nationalisation of the hitherto privately owned and fragmented telegraph system. This was successful and when the benefits of an integrated telegraph system became apparent, it fuelled the pressure for nationalisation of the railways. There were many doubters, but even so there were those who attempted to see how it could work. Politics entered the debate, with the trade unions favouring state ownership as early as 1894, while early in the new century nationalisation became official Labour Party policy. A Liberal government appointed a Royal Commission to consider the question in 1913, but the First World War intervened before it could conclude its work.

Wartime government control of the railways, nevertheless, pointed the way to greater state intervention, if not outright control, and this was reflected in the postwar plans to group the railways into four large companies, each with what amounted to a regional monopoly, and with few opportunities for competition. The mainly Conservative governments of the interwar years managed to bury the question, although the London Passenger Transport Board was a further step towards state control of public transport in 1933, as in some ways had been the restrictions on the road transport sector first introduced in the Transport Act of 1930. It could be argued that it would have been better to have removed many of the conditions imposed by Parliament on the railways, and this had been behind the 'Fair Deal for the Railways' campaign of the immediate pre-war years.

The Railway Companies Association mounted a fierce defence of its members' interests, but to no avail. Labour had an overwhelming majority in 1945 and was committed to nationalisation. The fiercest critics of nationalisation were the Great Western Railway and the Southern Railway, the two that had done most to transform their services between the two wars.

Labour in 1945 was determined to nationalise almost all transport, including bus companies, canals, road haulage and airlines, although shipping companies seemed to slip the net, and, as with the ports, shipping was only at risk if owned by the railways. Coal mining and the steel industry were other candidates, along with gas and electricity supply and generation.

Railway shareholders were granted British Transport Stock in return for their shares, with the value of the latter being assessed as the average value of railway shares over the six months prior to the general election or the price immediately before the publication of the Transport Bill, whichever was the higher, with the value of the shares and interest at 3 per cent guaranteed by the Treasury. The interest was to be a charge on the revenues of the new British Transport Commission, which would operate the railways through a management team known as the Railways Executive. Wagons belonging to private owners were simply purchased on the basis of a simple valuation formula, but this was often unnecessary since the main owners were the coal mines, which were also on Labour's shopping list.

Ignoring the evidence of the extensive pre-war modernisation and the heavy investment in rolling stock and marshalling yards, station improvements and automatic train control, among other things, the Chancellor of the Exchequer had the nerve to describe the railways as a 'very poor bag of physical assets'. This hurtful insult was disproved in debate. The railways were war-battered, but so too was the rest of the country.

The final issue of *The Great Western Railway Magazine* was full of a melancholy list of retirements among the directors and senior management. Sir James Milne was offered the chairmanship of the Railways Executive, but declined it. This move was primarily because of his dislike of nationalisation, but it was also to prove to be a wise move, as it soon became clear that the Railways Executive was subject to the whims of the British Transport Commission, itself at the mercy of the Ministry of Transport, and over all of these the Treasury kept a tight grip on the purse strings and the Ministry of Supply kept as tight a grip on materials. No longer were railwaymen allowed to run the railways.

While the management of what became the Western Region of British Railways showed a strong sense of independence, inevitably, in stages, the region began to seem almost like any other. The old Great Western locomotive classes survived to the end of steam in dwindling numbers, but inevitably BR standard classes began to appear, and the Mk I carriage in all its forms began to take over. There was some resistance to the 'Britannia' class express locomotives at first, and the Western Region took just fifteen of these, but they eventually gained acceptance with the crews at Cardiff. Some of the GWR railcars survived until 1960, but gradually the standard diesel multiple units began to appear, including some of the cross-country sets on services such as Bristol to Weymouth. Great Western chocolate and cream was replaced, for a while, by the original BR carmine and cream, variously referred to as 'strawberries and cream' or 'blood and custard'. Still, especially when drawn by a former Great Western locomotive, in monochrome photographs it still looked as if it might be chocolate and cream, except that carriage roofs were now black. This illusion started to be dispelled when the Great Western headcodes were replaced by those of British Railways, with their mix of numerals and letters. Later, as a concession, the chocolate and cream, but still with a black roof, was allowed to be reintroduced for the main expresses.

The Western Region of British Railways started life as being almost pure Great Western, just as the Southern Region initially reflected the Southern Railway, while the LMS and LNER areas were carved up. Nevertheless, neat and tidy bureaucratic minds had to interfere, and the idea that there still might be some vestiges of competition remaining post-nationalisation was taboo. Birmingham was no longer to be served by trains from both Paddington and Euston, but from Euston alone. By the same logic, Plymouth was no longer to be served by trains from both Waterloo and Paddington, but from Paddington alone. In a sense, this seems to have been almost a politically inspired 'deal', with Paddington losing the Midlands but gaining absolute control over the south-west. In fact, it made little sense, with the Waterloo to Exeter line continuing to stay open because of the places served on the way and because of the needs of the British Army, while Paddington was, in the pre-Heathrow Express days, somewhat underused and there was already growing congestion on the lines out of Euston. These were part of the cuts and reforms of the railways implemented by the then Dr Richard Beeching, and sounded the death-knell for any real hope of Western Region electrification.

A degree of independence was evident when large-scale conversion to diesel got under way. The gas-turbine locomotives had not been a great success, with high fuel consumption and the problems of maintaining two highly individual locomotives. Nevertheless, the Western Region did not follow the crowd and opt for the diesel-electric traction favoured elsewhere, but opted instead for diesel-hydraulic traction, arguing that a diesel-hydraulic locomotive of 2,000hp weighed 30 tons less than its diesel-electric counterpart. When the Railway Executive's Traction Committee argued back, the Western Region pointed out that the system worked well in what was then West Germany. That the Western Region got its way with its 'Warship' and 'Western' classes is now history.

Nevertheless, the diesel-hydraulics were not quite as successful as hoped, partly because the British Transport Commission rejected the entirety of the original German designs and insisted on a conventional heavy underframe, so that the early models were almost as heavy as the diesel-electric alternative. Later models followed the German pattern and the weight dropped, which meant that each locomotive was effectively capable of hauling an extra carriage for nothing. Yet still, both classes of diesel-hydraulic suffered from many technical defects, such as problems with bearings and camshaft and transmission problems.

The end result was that the Western Region's chief mechanical engineer sought diesel-electric locomotives 'out of turn', and when these arrived they enabled the Western to become the first region of British Railways to abolish steam traction altogether shortly after the last regular steam working on 3 January 1966. Nevertheless, it also added to the loss of identity as the locomotives, including many Type 47s, were the same as those on every other part of the system. When the new 'British Rail' blue livery and logo came, even the narrow gauge Vale of Rheidol Railway with its steam locomotives was included.

Chapter Twenty

What Might
Have Been

Looking at the history of the Great Western Railway is one thing, but one is on far more dangerous ground when one tries to consider what could have happened had nationalisation not taken place. Considering just what might have happened more than fifty years after nationalisation is paramount to tempting fate, but given what is known about the Great Western Railway and its people, one can certainly look at the first twenty or even thirty years and take a guess.

Very conveniently, the Great Western thought that people would be sufficiently interested in what it could do, or might do, to have published its thoughts in a book, which appeared in 1947. This was entitled *Next Station*, and in 1972 it was reissued as *The Great Western Railway's Last Look Forward* with an introduction by Christian Barman.

Unfortunately, it was clear long before the book had been published that the end was in sight, and that the book would be more in the way of a wish list or recommendations than a programme for action. This is made clear in the introduction, which points out that the management of the company was trying to do three things at once. The big priority was to attempt to repair the damage of a major war while also addressing the backlog of maintenance and renewals that were the legacy of wartime shortages and pressures on the railways. Even while this Herculean task was in progress, the management team was trying to raise its eyes above the day-to-day priorities and take a longer-term view and set achievable targets. If this wasn't enough, the third task was to try to see how its objectives would be affected by nationalisation.

No government had ever been elected on a prospectus promising such wholesale nationalisation as the Labour government of 1945. Even as *Next Station* was being published, air services were being nationalised. The book was realistic and did not attempt to change the political landscape, and not surprisingly, despite the Great Western's involvement with aviation in the 1930s, the future for air transport was omitted from the company's thinking and planning. The book included chapters on each and every aspect of running a railway, of which shipping services appeared to be one, but there was nothing on aviation.

As mentioned in the previous chapter, the Great Western directors were opposed to nationalisation in principle. This view was shared by many in the management team because they realised that nationalisation had nothing to do with running a better railway, but was inspired by people who knew nothing about railways but did want to change the ownership of a number of key sectors of the economy, largely in response to trade union pressures.

The Great Western Pedigree

It would have been hard for anyone preparing a book such as *Next Station* to resist the temptation to remind readers of just what the Great Western Railway had achieved. This can be excused as it would have given the reader not especially interested in railways an idea of the company's background and standing. So, in the original introduction, the GWR reminded its readers that the old Great Western had been the first railway in the world to build eight-wheeled passenger coaches in 1881 and followed this with the first modern full-length passenger coaches in 1905, while in between it had been the first to connect all carriages by corridor in 1892. It was also the first to run a regular service non-stop for 240 miles in 1904, the same year that it became the first to run a steam engine at more than 100mph. It was also the first in the United Kingdom to introduce superheating of steam in 1906 and, in 1908, the first to build a modern 4–6–2 Pacific locomotive, although these last two achievements were somewhat undermined by the extent of superheating on the GWR until the Second World War and by the conversion of *The Great Bear* to a 'Castle' class 4–6–0 locomotive in the early 1920s. The authors of the book were on much firmer ground when they reminded their readers that the company had been the first to study performance scientifically by using a specially built dynamometer car in 1848 and the first to test locomotives under laboratory conditions in 1904. It also pointed out that the Great Western had been among the pioneers of the motor bus as early as 1903.

Perhaps much of this was also necessary because the company felt that it had some explaining to do. It was stating its case for itself after the railways had come in for harsh and undeserved criticism in the debates on nationalisation. Much of what was said about the railways being 'a poor bag of assets' was untrue, but there must have been the feeling that many less aware and less thoughtful members of the public might have taken the criticism as being the truth. People soon lost patience if their daily journey was a misery because their train was overcrowded or late, or more usually overcrowded *and* late, while stations and carriages seemed to be rundown.

Coming up to date, readers were told that the company had made clear its thoughts on the importance of an integrated transport system embracing road and rail, but its scheme for the coordination of road and rail freight transport was rejected by the new government.

On the other hand, without giving a thought to the economic situation, the government did act on the proposal for oil-firing of steam locomotives with support for a scheme to convert 1,200 locomotives as part of a plan to save a million tons of coal a year. When this programme had to be thrown into reverse after the country's dollar reserves proved insufficient to buy the fuel, much of the effort and the materials devoted to converting steam locomotives and their depots for oil-firing was wasted. This at a time when the Great Western was receiving just two-thirds of its normal peacetime requirements of materials for repairs and renewals to its 3,800 route miles, made up of 9,100 track miles, while the company had estimated that it needed twice the materials it was receiving for three years to get the track back into its pre-war condition.

It is easy to be critical of the government for rejecting the proposals for an integrated transport system for freight, but much of what was proposed was integration on railway terms, with the railways effectively providing the trunk services and leaving the haulage industry to act almost as an extension of itself. Even with a large proportion of the UK's road haulage nationalised for part of the post-Second World War period, integration of this kind was hard to find. On a similar note, in later years even when bus services outside the main cities, and even then within a few of those, were mainly provided by the state-owned National Bus Company and Scottish Transport Group, integrated services and through ticketing were seldom on offer.

Why didn't integration work? One reason was that different modes of transport have their own strengths and weaknesses, while another was that the cost base of each mode also differs. Trains are more expensive to run than buses, and until recently with the advent of the low-cost airlines, air transport has been more expensive than travel by train. Shipping tends to be the most expensive of all. There must also have been a sneaking suspicion that a completely integrated transport system could be at the mercy of militant trade unionism, with the country and the public liable to be held to ransom. Perhaps most important of all, the balance of what is a natural traffic for road transport and what is better handled by the railways changes all the time. Even the Great Western saw some places in its area better served by bus than by train.

Passenger Services

Passenger services and their future received prominent attention in *Next Station*, possibly because it was aimed so much at the general public. Readers were reminded that one drawback that a railway had compared to other modes of transport was that it could not close for an overhaul. Ships, aircraft and road vehicles can be taken out of service and a replacement substituted when attention is needed. This meant that the company's planning to remedy the arrears of work that developed during wartime had to take into account that services would have to continue while lines were being relaid and stations and bridges rebuilt. The pressures on the railway were such that in 1946 summer traffic was up 70 per cent over that for 1939. Yet there was a 68 per cent increase in the locomotive failure rate in 1946 compared with 1938. The knock-on effect on punctuality of this diminished reliability was clear for all to see.

The first priority for the postwar Great Western was to be punctuality, with the company giving this a higher priority than running extra trains. This meant improving the reliability of locomotives and also bringing the track back up to an acceptable standard. This made sense, as running extra trains when punctuality was already bad only compounded the problems.

Frequency was important too, despite the shortage of locomotives and carriages, and in 1946 the summer timetable was introduced on 6 May, two months earlier than before the war, which meant that daily train mileage increased by 21,000 miles as the number of trains in the timetable increased by 948. Slip carriages were also reintroduced. All of this must have given welcome relief to those accustomed to overcrowded trains and, although the situation would have been bad again at weekends and in high summer, those travelling in spring and autumn, the so-called 'shoulder months', would have found travel much less arduous.

Even though overcrowding on the railways was falling fast from its wartime peaks, looking ahead the Great Western was concerned at the impact of paid annual holidays on its services, pointing out that in 1946 the number of workers enjoying paid annual holidays was some 15 million, four times the pre-war figure. The company felt that if holidays with pay were to become the accepted standard, then some form of staggering of holidays would be needed. It pointed out that otherwise, thousands of locomotives and tens of thousands of carriages would need to be built that would lie idle for ten months of the year. Even if holidays were spread over twice the peak period, the volume of traffic would still be double that of pre-war days, although presumably the locomotives and carriages would then only have to lie idle for eight months of the year. In this and in the proposals for an integrated freight transport system, there comes through more than a hint of 1940s-style bureaucracy and even bossiness, in effect telling people what was good for them.

On a more customer-friendly note, the Great Western regretted that seat reservations could only be offered on a few trains in the immediate postwar period, and that it was also having difficulty returning to its pre-war provision of catering on its longer-distance trains. Noting that the buffet cars introduced between the wars had been popular, it was proposing a new-style mini-buffet occupying half a carriage length, at which refreshments could be bought and taken to the passengers' seats. As an extension of this experiment, an automatic buffet car was being developed in which customers could purchase refreshments from slot machines.

The government proved extremely slow at releasing sleeping cars postwar so that these could be used by the paying public rather than officials, but by 1946 the situation was beginning to improve, slowly.

Meanwhile, the Great Western was planning its next generation of rolling stock, with bodies built directly onto the chassis or underframe and an increasing use of prefabrication in construction. For the passenger, the most obvious differences would be greater use of fluorescent lighting.

Freight Services

In the immediate postwar period goods trains accounted for 56 per cent of the mileage run by the Great Western's locomotives, while passenger trains accounted for just 44 per cent. This figure becomes even more amazing if one remembers that most of the goods trains were slow, with the express freight trains with fully fitted rolling stock being the exception.

After the war the restoration of the express freight trains was hampered by a shortage of suitable wagons. Priority was given to resuming the services between London and South Wales, then to trains between London and Bristol, followed by those to the Midlands and the south-west, then those between the Midlands and the south-west. By the end of 1945 sixty-eight express goods trains were running daily, and this figure had risen to seventy-five a year later. The seasonal traffics were also handled as early as summer 1945, but the trains bringing early spring flowers from Cornwall were not reintroduced until 1946. Shipping also played a part in the restoration of freight traffic, with spring and early summer 1946 seeing more than 4.5 million packages handled at Weymouth from Jersey and Guernsey.

The travelling post office, withdrawn in 1940, was reintroduced between Paddington and Penzance on 1 October 1945, with three sorting carriages and seven vans travelling via Bristol, Exeter and Plymouth, with most of the mail handled at these stations using the vans.

Partly owing to the reduced size of its motor vehicle fleet which had not seen replacement vehicles added during the war years, the Great Western found itself having difficulty handling the collection and delivery of its goods traffic, and especially small consignments. As an experiment, in Birmingham a zonal system was introduced. Instead of using twenty stations and three subsidiary depots, the traffic was handled through five stations with improved facilities. The question which was not answered, but which with hindsight those of us interested in the railways must ponder, was whether the future viability of parcels and sundries traffic was ever considered?

Motive Power

Despite some wartime locomotive construction, at the end of 1946 the GWR had 546 locomotives over forty years old, compared to 450 in 1938. To remedy this, in 1945 the GWR planned to build ninety locomotives, and in 1946 and 1947 this was intended to rise to 110 locomotives in each year. Nevertheless, shortages of materials meant that only eighty were built in 1945, and again in 1946, while 700 new locomotives were planned between 1946 and 1950.

According to *Next Station*, a rolling programme of conversion of locomotives to oil-burning was in hand, and this included eighteen heavy goods locomotives, of which ten were in service in South Wales by summer 1946. This particular forecast was to be overtaken by events almost before the first copies of the book were off the shelves.

The GWR was not forgetting its diesel railcars, and the sets built for the Birmingham–Cardiff service had been cascaded onto a new Monday to Friday service between Swansea, Cardiff, Newport and Gloucester. Nevertheless, the GWR was not planning any additional railcars in the period immediately after the war. Instead it was planning a substantial increase in its diesel shunter fleet.

After considering steam turbines and rejecting them as not being suitable for railway use, the Great Western announced its plans to experiment with gas-turbine-powered locomotives. The company claimed that it saw 'the possibility of a brilliant future for the new method of propulsion'. In this the railwaymen were to be disappointed.

Had the Great Western Survived

Inevitably, it is tempting to wonder just how much of the Great Western's forward thinking would have made it to reality had the company not been nationalised.

Already, in 1947, one can see some rationalisation of part of its freight traffic with the Birmingham experiment in mind. Would this have become the pattern for the longer term? Almost certainly the company would have been forced to implement this. What is open to question is whether or not in the changed postwar climate it would finally have been able to convince the, presumably also still private enterprise, mine owners to improve their sidings and surface lines to accommodate the larger coal wagons that the Great Western had been offering since the early 1920s. Indeed, having used 40-ton wagons for its own coal in wartime, the company may well have decided that even 20-ton wagons were not good enough.

There would have been a massive push to increase the average speed of freight trains with more expresses. Given the nature of the GWR's freight business even between the wars, there can be little doubt that the company would have been anxious to play a part in the so-called container revolution when it came in the 1960s and 1970s, and that might even have meant the Great Western operating container ships for the Irish Sea and Channel Islands traffic, as well as through inter-company container trains.

Would railways have continued to ply the valley lines carrying coal, or would this have been handed over to some form of conveyor-belt system or automated trains, rather like the Post Office railway, while passenger traffic on these lines was transferred to bus? Given the eventual run-down and spate of mine closures, one doubts whether the valley lines would have survived without drastic cuts, and the railway network in South Wales would probably have differed little from that of today. Indeed, without a healthy market for coal and a steady output from the mines, the lines in the Welsh valleys could well have become a serious liability for the company.

It is doubtful if the fully automated buffet cars would ever have arrived and, if they did, that they would have lasted long. Nevertheless, the company would have found itself following the pattern towards less formal eating, and buffets, including 'mini-buffets', would doubtless have become more commonplace and restaurant car service perhaps scaled back to first-class only and then confined to the busier business expresses. Just as accelerated passenger services have undermined the market for overnight sleeping cars, they have also reduced the demand for full meal service aboard trains.

As costs rose, would separate excursion train rolling stock still have been built, or would a generation of rolling stock suitable for both commuter trains and excursion work have emerged from Swindon?

It seems doubtful that the Great Western would have continued to build steam locomotives for as long as its successor, British Railways, but it does seem that it would have continued to build them into the early 1950s while it awaited the results of its tests with gas-turbine locomotives. Once the economy revived, many steam locomotives would have been converted to oil-firing for their final years.

The gas-turbine experiment would soon have been recognised as a failure, forcing the Great Western to consider diesels. It may have tried to improve steam locomotive performance as well, but it seems unlikely that it would have gone against the trend for dieselisation. No one really knows if in introducing diesels, the Great Western would have done as the Western Region of British Railways did and adopted diesel-hydraulic traction. If it was worried about diesel-electric traction on some of its lines, diesel-mechanical propulsion seems another possibility. It also seems probable that the Great Western would have favoured main-line diesel multiple units given its railcar experience, perhaps even having these for expresses and retaining a stud of diesel locomotives for mixed traffic work and another for freight.

Shunting activities would have been converted to diesel very quickly, and after the initial delay postwar, many more diesel railcars would have been introduced, replacing the last of the steam auto-trains.

The big question mark lies over whether the Great Western would have considered electrification worthwhile, especially on the holiday lines, as it lacked the density of traffic year-round to make this viable. It would also have been wasted on most of its branch lines.

Yet, before the outbreak of the Second World War, the Great Western had commissioned a report from the consultants Merz and McLellan on electrification. Electrification could have been a possibility, as a private enterprise Great Western would have retained its services to the West Midlands, where electrification could have made sense, and with electric trains running between Paddington and Birmingham and Wolverhampton, the case for electrifying to Bristol and Cardiff could have become stronger. In fact, a hybrid system, as originally used on the Waterloo and Bournemouth electrification, could have been viable. Trains could have been electrically powered as far as Bristol and Cardiff, and then taken on by diesel to Plymouth, Penzance, Swansea and West Wales.

While the Western Region of British Railways did look at electrification, the management was told that the electrical equipment industry could not support more than one major scheme at a time, and it was fully committed with the London, Midland electrification. Even the east coast main-line electrification had to be delayed. Paddington accepted this and instead looked forward to the diesel-electric high speed train.

Doubtless, the Great Western would have remained with air transport, and perhaps the railway-owned British and Foreign Airways would have become the so-called 'second force' airline that was much talked about as airline liberalisation began to take place in the UK. Possibly British European Airways would have been happy to leave its loss-making domestic air services to the railways? A commercially minded Great Western free of Treasury interference might have introduced the Heathrow Express earlier, operated by the Great Western itself, and no doubt extended the concept with services from the Midlands, South Wales and the West Country into the airport.

The ferry services would have continued, although on the St George's Channel routes the GWR would have found itself not in partnership with the Great Southern, but with CIE, the nationalised Irish transport undertaking, once transport services within the Irish Republic were nationalised. The days of ships being able to operate on both the Irish Sea and to the Channel Islands would have ended, however, with much bigger ships on the St George's Channel than could fit the ports in Jersey and Guernsey. The company might have been forced to consider rationalising its docks in South Wales, while transatlantic liner traffic would have ebbed away over the years.

There are other tempting thoughts. Would the Great Western have tried to merge with another railway company, perhaps the Southern Railway, to realise rationalisation and savings on their services to the south-west? It might have done the same with the LMS with operations in the Midlands in mind, or both companies could have come to some form of pooling agreement. A pooling agreement couldn't survive today as the Office of Fair Trading would almost certainly object, but it could have worked in the 1950s and 1960s.

So much for a crystal ball.

No. 4079 *Pendennis Castle* at King's Cross on exchange with the LNER, where the locomotive not only proved capable of handling heavy trains, but showed considerable economy in coal consumption compared to the LNER locomotives. *(Kevin Robertson)*

Appendix I

Locomotive Headcodes and Destination Codes

The Great Western Railway used the standard headcodes agreed with the Railway Clearing House as shown in the figures A to L. These merely told signalmen and others what kind of train was coming, and nothing about where it was going to, unlike the system in use on the Southern Railway's steam locomotives. The Southern also used destination codes on its electric trains so that passengers had an idea of the destination of an arriving train.

During the mid-1930s, the GWR decided that its busy peak summer services to and from the West of England on Saturdays could be worked far more efficiently if the trains were numbered. The workshops at Swindon produced metal frames and plates bearing numbers for the express locomotives. These were of necessity quite large, with the three-figure numbers chosen filling the entire width of the front of a locomotive boiler, so that they could be read easily at a distance of more than a quarter of a mile.

The system was intended to allow railwaymen to tell at a glance the starting place of an express, as well as its destination and – a reflection of the popularity of the main expresses – if the train was the second, third, fourth or even the fifth part of a train that was in fact as many as five trains – the original and up to four reliefs.

On every number, the first figure provided the 'key' to the starting place and the remaining two figures identified the particular train. All expresses from Paddington bore the numbers 100–99, while those from Shrewsbury bore 200–99, from Wolverhampton and Birmingham the numbers were 300–99, and from Bristol 400–99, with 500–99 from Exeter and 600–99 from Plymouth, while those from South Wales bore the numbers 700–99. Each train then had a number ending in either 0 or 5, with the terminal numbers 1, 2, 3, 4, 6, 7, 8 and 9 being reserved for use when a train ran in more than one part. This meant that the 'Cornish Riviera' express from Paddington would be known to inspectors, signalmen and porters as 125, and the divisions of the train on the busiest weekends would carry the numbers 126 to 129 inclusive. In the other direction, the Up 'Cornish Riviera' carried the number 615. The 'Torbay Express' was numbered 150 on the Down run from Paddington, and 515 for the Up journey back. In other words, while both trains carried a Paddington number for the Down journey, on the way back to London the 'Cornish Riviera' carried a Plymouth number and the 'Torbay Express' an Exeter number.

The number 100 was reserved for a new 8.30a.m. Channel Islands Boat Express, as it was the first long-distance holiday train to leave Paddington on a summer Saturday.

The system also allowed for special trains, which were always to carry a number with 0 as their first figure. In these cases, the second figure gave the starting point, so that 010 meant a special train from Paddington to the West of England. This was far from an academic exercise, as before 'The Bristolian' was accelerated to its new schedule of 1 hour 45 minutes, a special train was worked to Bristol in connection with the GWR's centenary celebrations carrying just this number.

Introduced on 14 July 1935, the numbers remained in use until 29 September. This pattern of use from mid-July to the end of September became the standard until war intervened, and was resurrected postwar to survive nationalisation.

Train Classification, Head Lamps and Corresponding Bell Signals
GWR 1936

Class of Train	Headcode (white lights)	Description of Train (Bell signal beats)
A		Express passenger train. (4) Breakdown van train going to clear the line, or light engine going to assist disabled train. (4) Empty coaching stock timed at express speed. (4) Express streamline railcar. (4)
B		Ordinary passenger or mixed train. (3–1) Branch passenger train [Notes A, B]. (1–3) Breakdown train not going to clear the line. (1–3) Railmotor car, auto-train or streamline railcar. (3–1–3)
C		Parcels, newspapers, meat, fish, fruit, milk, horse, cattle, or perishable train composed entirely of vacuum-fitted stock with vacuum pipe connected to the engine. (5) Express freight, livestock perishable or ballast train with not less than one-third of the vehicles vacuum fitted and pipe connected to the engine. (4–4)
D		Express freight, or ballast train conveying a stipulated number of vacuum-braked vehicles connected by the vacuum pipe to the engine and authorised to run at a maximum speed of 35mph. (1–2–2) Empty coach stock train (not specially authorised to carry 'A' headcode). (2–2–1)
E		Express freight, fish, fruit, meat, cattle or ballast train. (3–2) Breakdown train not proceeding to an accident. (3–2)
F		Through fast freight conveying through load. (1–4)
G		Light engine or light engines coupled. (2–3) Engine with not more than two brake vans. (2–3)
H		Freight, mineral or ballast train or empty train carrying through load to destination. (3–4–1)

J		Freight, mineral or ballast train stopping at intermediate stations. (3)
K		Branch freight trains (1–2) Freight or ballast train or officers' special train requiring to stop in section. (2–2–3)
L		Royal Train. (4–4–4)

The GWR did not return the compliment by adopting the LNER's penchant for streamlining, but instead contented itself with more modest efforts, as seen here on No. 6014 *King Henry VII. (Kevin Robertson)*

Appendix II

Station Name Changes Post-Grouping

Given the number of companies involved and their often overlapping networks, there was some confusion and duplication over station names, especially in Cardiff with no fewer than seven stations or sidings needing to be renamed. Given the way that the railways had developed in the Cardiff area and in the valleys, that might not have been too surprising, but Hengoed and Maesycwmmer between them had three stations. The Great Western was in fact slower to respond to name duplication than, for example, the Southern Railway, which had announced its station name changes as early as April 1923. There were more names to change in the GWR's case, and possibly because of this and the prolonged negotiations over the absorption of the Midland & South Western, the GWR did not announce its station name changes until July 1924, when they appeared in that month's *Great Western Railway Magazine*.

In many of the places listed below, there would have been other stations that did not need to have their names changed or which were allowed to continue with the original name. At Troedyrhiew, the matter seems to have come down to a change in spelling – perhaps this had been a bone of contention pre-grouping. At Whitchurch, the problem was different: which Whitchurch, Hampshire or Glamorgan? The Southern had the same problem with two places called Hythe. It would even have been desirable to distinguish between Nelson in Glamorgan and Nelson in Lancashire.

Key

AD&R	–	Alexandra (Newport & South Wales) Docks & Railway
Barry	–	Barry Railway
B&M	–	Brecon & Merthyr Tydfil Junction Railway
BP&GV	–	Burry Port & Gwendraeth Valley Railway
Cam	–	Cambrian Railway
CR	–	Cardiff Railway
GWR	–	Great Western Railway
GWR & Rhy Jt	–	Great Western & Rhymney Junction Railway
M&SW	–	Midland & South Western Junction Railway
PT	–	Port Talbot Railway & Docks
Rhymney	–	Rhymney Railway
R&SB	–	Rhondda & Swansea Bay Railway
TVR	–	Taff Vale Railway

Pre-grouping Name	Old Company	New Name
Abercanaid & Pentrebach	GWR & Rhy Jt	Abercanaid
Aberdare	GWR	Aberdare (High Level)
Aberdare	TVR	Aberdare (Low Level)
Aberfan (for Merthyr Vale)	GWR & Rhy Jt	Aberfan

Pre-grouping Name	Old Company	New Name
Aberthaw	Barry	Aberthaw (High Level)
Aberthaw	TVR	Aberthaw (Low Level)
Bargoed & Aberbargoed	B&M	Aberbargoed
Bargoed & Aberbargoed	Rhymney	Bargoed
Bassaleg	GWR	Bassaleg Junction Station
Bassaleg	B&M	Bassaleg
Briton Ferry	GWR	Briton Ferry (West)
Briton Ferry	R&SB	Briton Ferry (East)
Caerphilly	Rhymney	Caerphilly
Caerphilly	Barry	Caerphilly-Energlyn
Cardiff Passenger	GWR	Cardiff General
Cardiff Passenger	Rhymney	Cardiff Parade
Cardiff Docks	TVR	Cardiff Bute Road
Cardiff Docks	Rhymney	Cardiff East Dock
Cardiff Roath Depot	TVR	Cardiff Newport Road
Cardiff Canton Sidings	GWR	Cardiff Canton Sidings (Eldon Road)
Cardiff Canton Sidings	TVR	Cardiff Canton Sidings (Leckwith Road)
Cerney & Ashton Keynes	M&SW	South Cerney
Cirencester	GWR	Cirencester Town
Cirencester	M&SW	Cirencester Watermoor
Cross Hands	GWR	Cross Hands for Penygroes
Cwmsyfiog & Brithdir	B&M	Cwmsyfiog
Cymmer	GWR	Cymmer for Glyncorrwg
Cymmer	R&SB	Cwm Cymmer
Dowlais	B&M	Dowlais Central
Dowlais Cae Harris	GWR & Rhy Jt	Dowlais Caeharris
Dyffryn	Cam	Dyffryn-on-Sea
Ely (for Llandaff)	GWR	Ely (Main Line)
Ely	TVR	Ely (Fairwater Road)
Hengoed & Maesycwmmer	GWR	Hengoed (High Level)
Hengoed & Maesycwmmer	Rhymney	Hengoed (Low Level)
Maesteg	GWR	Maesteg Castle Street
Maesteg	PT	Maesteg Neath Road
Maesycwmmer & Hengoed	B&M	Maesycwmmer
Marlborough	GWR	Marlborough (High Level)
Marlborough	M&SW	Marlborough (Low Level)
Merthyr	TVR	Merthyr (Passenger)
Merthyr Goods	GWR	Merthyr High Street Goods
Merthyr Goods	TVR	Merthyr Plymouth Street Goods
Mountain Ash	GWR	Mountain Ash (Cardiff Road)
Mountain Ash	TVR	Mountain Ash (Oxford Street)
Neath	GWR	Neath General
Neath Low Level	GWR	Neath Bridge Street
Neath	R&SB	Neath Canal Bridge
Nelson	TVR	Nelson (Glam)
New Tredegar & Typhil	B&M	New Tredegar
Pant	Cam	Pant (Salop)
Pengam & Fleur-de-Lis	Rhymney	Pengam
Pengam & Fleur-de-Lis	B&M	Fleur-de-Lis
Penrhiwceiber	GWR	Penrhiwceiber (High Level)
Penrhiwceiber	TVR	Penrhiwceiber (Low Level)
Pontypridd	TVR	Pontypridd Central

Pre-grouping Name	Old Company	New Name
Pontypridd Passenger	Barry	Pontypridd Craig
Pontypridd Goods	Barry	Pontypridd Maesycoed
Port Talbot & Aberavon	GWR	Port Talbot Central
Port Talbot (Aberavon)	R&SB	Aberavon Town
Quakers Yard	TVR	Quakers Yard (Low Level)
Rhymney & Pontlottyn	B&M	Rhymney (Pwll Uchaf)
Savernake	GWR	Savernake (Low Level)
Savernake	M&SW	Savernake (High Level)
Swansea	R&SB	Swansea Docks
Tirphil & New Tredegar	Rhymney	Tirphil
Treforest	TVR	Treforest (Low Level)
Treforest	Barry	Treforest (High Level)
Troedyrhiew	TVR	Troedyrhiw
Whitchurch	GWR	Whitchurch (Hants)
Whitchurch	CR	Whitchurch (Glam)
Whittington	GWR	Whittington (Low Level)
Whittington	Cam	Whittington (High Level)
Withington	M&SW	Withington (Glos)

Halts

Coryton	CR	Coryton Halt
Dynea	AD&R	Dynea Halt
Groeswen	CR	Goeswen Halt
Heath Halt	Rhymney	Heath Halt (High Level)
Heath Halt	CR	Heath Halt (Low Level)
Nantgarw	CR	Nantgarw Halt (Low Level)
Nantgarw	AD&R	Nantgarw Halt (High Level)
Pembrey	BP&GV	Pembrey Halt
Rhiwbina	CR	Rhiwbina Halt
Rhydyfelin	AD&R	Rhydyfelin Halt (High Level)
Rhydyfelin	CR	Rhydyfelin Halt (Low Level)
Treforest	AD&R	Treforest Halt
Troedyrhiw	GWR	Troedyrhiw Halt
Upper Boat	AD&R	Upper Boat Halt

Source: *The Great Western Railway Magazine*, July 1924.

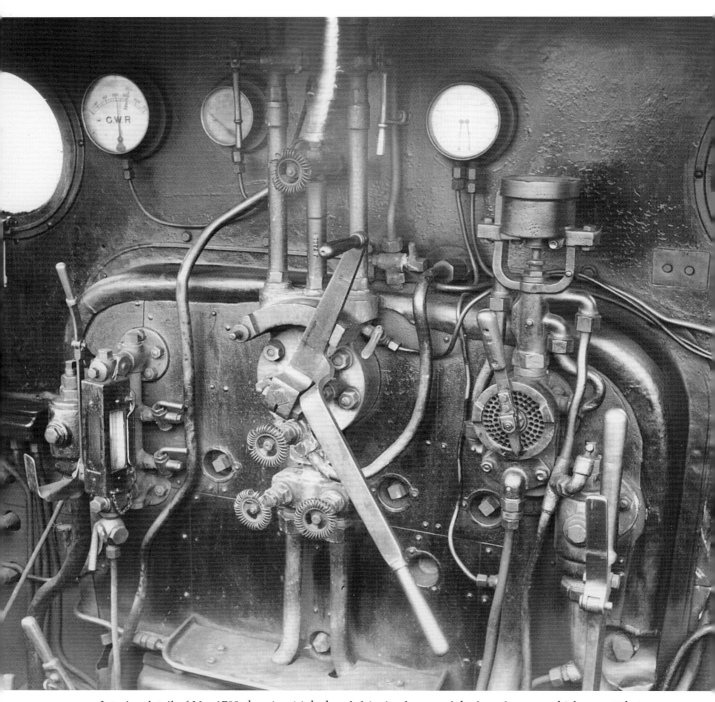

Interior detail of No. 1780 showing 'right-hand drive', a legacy of the broad gauge which meant that signals could be sited between the lines. *(HMRS/J.P. Richards ACC607)*

Locomotive Shed Codes

London Division

DID   Didcot
OXF   Oxford
PDN   Old Oak Common
RDG   Reading
SHL   Southall
SLO   Slough

Bristol Division

BRD   Bristol, Bath Road
SDN   Swindon
SPM   Bristol, St Philip's Marsh
WES   Westbury
WEY   Weymouth
YEO   Yeovil

Newton Abbot Division

EXE   Exeter
LA   Laira (Plymouth)
NA   Newton Abbot
PZ   Penzance
SBZ   St Blazey
TN   Taunton
TR   Truro

Newport Division

ABDR   Aberdare
ABEEG   Aberbeeg
CDF   Cardiff
LTS   Llantrisant
NPT   Newport, Ebbw Junction
PILL   Newport, Pill
PPRD   Pontypool Road
STJ   Severn Tunnel Junction
TDU   Tondu

Neath Division

CARM   Carmarthen
DG   Danygraig
DYD   Port Talbot, Duffryn Yard
FGD   Fishguard, Goodwick
LDR   Landore (Swansea)

LLY   Llanelly
NEA   Neath
NEY   Neyland
SED   Swansea East Dock
WTD   Whitland

Wolverhampton Division

BAN   Banbury
BHD   Birkenhead
CHR   Chester
CNYD   Croes Newydd
LMTN   Leamington Spa
OXY   Wolverhampton, Oxley
SALOP   Shrewsbury
SRD   Wolverhampton, Stafford Road
STB   Stourbridge
TVS   Tyseley
WLN   Wellington

Worcester Division

CHEL   Cheltenham
GLO   Gloucester
HFD   Hereford
KDR   Kidderminster
LYD   Lydney
WOS   Worcester

Cardiff Valleys Division

CED   Cardiff East Dock
CH   Dowlais, Cae Harris
CHYS   Cardiff Cathays
CV.AYN   Abercynon
CV.BRY   Barry
CV.FDL   Ferndale
MTHR   Merthyr
RHY   Rhymney
RYR   Radyr
THT   Treherbert

Central Wales Division

BCN   Brecon
MCH   Machynlleth
OSW   Oswestry

The title of this photograph was 'Cleaning Every Corner'. The amount of maintenance needed by the steam locomotive was one of its great drawbacks. *(Kevin Robertson)*

Appendix IV

GWR Locomotives

These are the locomotives built by the Great Western Railway, with the locomotives absorbed at the grouping being listed in Appendix VI. In each case, locomotives are dealt with in order of wheel arrangement, and the named classes are dealt with in alphabetical order within the appropriate wheel arrangement.

0–4–2T
1400 Class tank engines

Nos 1400–74 built between 1932 and 1936.
Nos 5800–19 built 1933.

0–6–0T
1361 Class saddle tank engines

Built for use in the docks at Plymouth and Weymouth.
Nos 1361–5 built 1910.

1366 Class pannier tank engines

Built for dock work and whose duties included pulling the Channel Island expresses through the streets of Weymouth between the docks and the railway terminus.
Nos 1366–71 built 1934.

0–6–0
2251 Class tender locomotives

Originally built as goods locomotives but often worked on passenger branch and short- distance main-line services.

Nos 2251–70 built 1930. Nos 2271–80 built 1934.
Nos 2281–90 built 1936.
Nos 2291–9, 2200–30 built 1938–40.
Nos 2231–50, 3200–19 built 1944–8.

5400 Class tank engines

Nos 5400–24 built 1930–5.
Two locomotives held the number 5400, as the original was withdrawn in 1932.

Above: The locomotive element of this steam railmotor is well hidden by the carriage bodywork. This is 0–4–0 No. 74 at Barmouth in 1924 in lake colour scheme. *(HMRS/D.H. Haines AEV 024)*

Below: 0–4–2T Class 48XX No. 4851 seen in 1935. These small locomotives were ideal for the tight curves on many of the lines in the South Wales valleys, as well as in the docks and in colliery sidings. *(HMRS/Dr N.R. Ferguson AEP112)*

A mixed goods behind 0–6–0 class 22XX No. 2227 in 1927. *(HMRS/J.P. Richards ACC805)*

A cab detail of 0–6–0PT No. 1780 in 1947. *(HMRS/J.P. Richards ACC607)*

6400 Class tank engines

Nos 6400–39 built 1932–7.

7400 Class tank engines

Nos 7400–29 built 1936 and 1937.

5700 Class tank engines

Nos 3600–99 built 1936–8.
Nos 4600–99 built 1941–5.
Nos 5700–99 built 1929 and 1930.
Nos 6700–49 built 1930 and 1931.
Nos 6750–7 built 1947, with another twenty built after nationalisation.
Nos 7700–99 built 1930 and 1931.
Nos 8700–99 built 1931–4.
Nos 9600–82 built 1945 and 1946.
Nos 9700–99 built 1931–6.

9400 Class tank engines

0–6–0 pannier tank, built using the same boiler as the 2251 Class tender locomotive.
Nos 9400–9 built before nationalisation, with another 175 built after nationalisation by three different firms of locomotive builders.

0–6–2T

5600 Class tank engines

This unusual configuration had been favoured by
many of the companies operating in South Wales,
including the Taff Vale, Rhymney and Barry
railways, and when the GWR decided on new
engines, it was found that this configuration was
the most suitable for the replacements.
Nos 5600–99 built 1924–7.
Nos 6600–49 built 1927 and 1928.
Nos 6650–99 built 1928.

2–4–2T

3600 Class 'Birdcage' tank class

Gained the 'Birdcage' nickname as vertical bars
were placed to protect the back windows from
damage when coaling.
Nos 3600–30, built 1900 (prototype) and 1902–3.

2–6–0 Mogul

4300 Class Tender Locomotives

Built as a mixed-traffic locomotive capable of
handling goods, local trains or short main-line
expresses. Many of these were renumbered in the
mid-1940s.
Nos 4301–20 built 1911.
Nos 4300, 4321–99, 5300–99*, 6300–41, 6370–99,
7300–19 built 1913–22.
Nos 6342–69, 7320/1 built 1923–5.
Nos 9300–19 built 1932.
* Eleven locomotives from this batch were sent to
France during the First World War and operated by
the British Army.

Top: End of the line. Awaiting the breakers at Swindon in
1938 was 0–4–0ST No. 45, looking very sorry for itself.
(HMRS/J.E. Cull AEP521)

Centre: No. 2202 of the so-called 'Baby' 'Castle' class for
less heavy work. *(Kevin Robertson)*

Bottom: A 2–6–0 class 43XX, believed to be No. 5336, with
a long mixed goods near Bilston, *c.* 1930. *(HMRS/D.H.
Haines AEV411)*

2600 Class or 'Aberdare'

2–6–0 tender locomotives whose main duty was hauling coal from Aberdare to Swindon, hence the nickname.
Nos 2600–80 built 1900–7.

2–6–2T Prairie

5101 Class tank locomotives

No 3100 built in 1903 and ran for two years as a prototype.
Nos 3111–49 built 1905–6.
Nos 3150–90 built 1906–8.
Nos 5150–89 built 1929.
Nos 5150–89 built 1930–1.
Nos 6100–59 built 1931–3.
Nos 5190–9 built 1934.
Nos 6160–9 built 1935.

Nos 4100–39 built 1935–9.
Nos 3100–4, 8100–9, built 1938–9.
Nos 4140–79 built 1946–9.

4400 and 4500 Class tank locomotives

The 4400 Class were smaller versions of the original 5101 Class Prairie tank engines introduced in 1903, with smaller driving wheels to enable them to cope with the steeply graded lines of the West Country and Wales. The class was successful, but when further locomotives were needed, larger driving wheels were fitted which increased both speed and range, as the 4500 Class.
Nos 4400–10 built 1904–6.
Nos 4500–29 built 1906–10.
Nos 4530–54 built 1913–15.
Nos 4555–74 built 1924.
Nos 4575–99, 5500–74 built 1927–9.

A 2–8–0 ROD, No. 3017, on a mixed-goods working near Twyford, with a 'Mink D' van leading. (*HMRS/J. Scott-Morgan AAC223*)

2–8–0

2800 Class tender locomotives

Designed to haul heavy goods trains over long distances, the prototype was the first locomotive of this wheel configuration to operate in the United Kingdom.

No. 2800 built in 1903 and operated as a prototype for two years, initially numbered 97.
Nos 2801–20 built 1905.
Nos 2821–30 built 1907.
Nos 2831–55 built 1911–13.
Nos 2856–83 built 1918–19.
Nos 2884–99, 3800–66 built 1938–42.

4700 Class tender locomotives

Originally intended as the ultimate in heavy goods engines, the power of these locomotives was such that they were also to be found on heavy summer holiday expresses. Their heavy axle loading limited their route availability, hence the small number built.

No. 4700 built in 1919 as a prototype.
Nos 4701–8 built 1922–3.

2–8–0T

4200 Class tank engines

Intended as heavy freight locomotives. Originally a 2–8–2T configuration was considered, but rejected at the time because of the tight curves on many of the lines in South Wales.

No. 4201 built in 1910 as a prototype, somewhat unusually leaving No. 4200 to appear some years later.
Nos 4202–41 built 1912–14.
Nos 4242–61 built 1916–17.
Nos 4262–99, 4200, 5200–54 built 1919–25.
Nos 5255–64 built 1940.

2–8–2T

7200 Class tank engines

Many rebuilt from the 4200 and 5205 classes as the new wheel configuration allowed for larger bunkers and a longer range.
Nos 7200–53 built 1934–9.

4–4–0

The disappearance of the broad gauge in 1892 seemed to coincide with a renaissance in GWR locomotive and carriage design. While in the early days of the broad gauge greater speed had been promised as one of the advantages, in later years this was never fulfilled and many would claim that the GWR never exploited the broad gauge's full potential. Possibly it was inhibited from doing so by the controversy it had aroused. Within a few years of the final conversion the GWR had the distinction of running the first steam locomotive, the 4–4–0 No. 3440 *City of Truro*, at more than 100mph, albeit an unofficial record.

The 4–4–0 wheel arrangement came after some years of building 4–2–2 locomotives, starting with the 3031 Class of 1894, although these were followed closely by the first four 4–4–0s, and by 1899 the 4–4–0 wheel arrangement had shown that it offered better adhesion. Other changes were also in hand, with Churchward redesigning boilers and adopting new designs of firebox, while there were experiments with different sizes of driving wheel looking for the ideal combination of adhesion and speed. Even so, at a time when much less was known about non-destructive testing and metal fatigue than today, there were some early problems with underframes, especially on the early 'Bulldog' class. The 'Atbara' class and the 'Flower' and 'Bird' classes that followed reflected these improvements.

4–4–0 Class 4120 'Atbara' class express locomotives

Despite being in the Sudan, the name 'Atbara' was chosen because these locomotives were designed during the Boer War and an increasingly publicity-conscious GWR thought it a good idea to use names in the public eye during Britain's colonial wars. The class was relegated to non-express duties from 1922 onwards and all were withdrawn by 1931.

Nos 3373–3412, but later renumbered 4120–48, built 1900–1, although 3382 had to be scrapped after an accident and was never renumbered. Ten, Nos 3401–10, were rebuilt as 'City' class locomotives between 1902 and 1909.

Locomotives and names:
4120 *Atbara* built 1900 as No. 3373. Withdrawn 1929.
4121 *Baden Powell* built 1900 as No. 3374. Withdrawn 1928.
4122 *Colonel Edgcumbe* built 1900 as No. 3375. Withdrawn 1928.
4123 *Herschell* built 1900 as No. 3376. Withdrawn 1928.
4124 *Kitchener* built 1900 as No. 3377. Withdrawn 1930.
4125 *Khartoum* built 1900 as No. 3378. Withdrawn 1927.

4126 *Kimberley* built 1900 as No. 3379. Withdrawn 1927.

4127 *Ladysmith* built 1900 as No. 3380. Withdrawn 1929.

4128 *Maine* built 1900 as No. 3381. Withdrawn 1927.

4129 *Kekewich* built 1900 as No. 3383. Withdrawn 1928.

4130 *Omdurman* built 1900 as No. 3384. Withdrawn 1930.

4131 *Powerful* built 1900 as No. 3385. Withdrawn 1929.

4132 *Pembroke* built 1900 as No. 3386. Withdrawn 1931.

4133 *Roberts* built 1900 as No. 3387. Withdrawn 1927.

4134 *Sir Redvers* built 1900 as No. 3388. Withdrawn 1927.

4135 *Pretoria* built 1900 as No. 3389. Withdrawn 1927.

4136 *Terrible* built 1900 as No. 3390. Withdrawn 1927.

4137 *Wolseley* built 1900 as No. 3391. Withdrawn 1928.

4138 *White* built 1900 as No. 3392. Withdrawn 1929.

4139 *Auckland* built 1901 as No. 3393. Withdrawn 1928

4140 *Adelaide* built 1901 as No. 3394. Withdrawn 1929.

4141 *Aden* built 1901 as No. 3395. Withdrawn 1930.

4142 *Brisbane* built 1901 as No. 3396. Withdrawn 1928.

4143 *Cape Town* built 1901 as No. 3397. Withdrawn 1929.

4144 *Colombo* built 1901 as No. 3398. Withdrawn 1927

4145 *Dunedin* built 1901 as No. 3399. Withdrawn 1930.

4146 *Sydney* built 1901 as No. 3410. Withdrawn 1927.

4147 *St Johns* built 1901 as No. 3411. Withdrawn 1927

4148 *Singapore* built 1901 as No. 3412. Withdrawn 1931.

4–4–0 Class 3441 'Bird' class express passenger locomotives

The locomotives of the 'Bird' class showed the 'Bulldog' series in its final form, retaining the same size driving wheels but having deeper and stiffer frames for greater durability.
Nos 3441–55 built 1909–10.

Locomotives and names:

3441 *Blackbird* built 1909 as No. 3731. Withdrawn 1949.

3442 *Bullfinch* built 1909 as No. 3732. Withdrawn 1948.

3443 *Chaffinch* built 1909 as No. 3733. Withdrawn 1949.

3444 *Cormorant* built 1909 as No. 3734. Withdrawn 1951.

3445 *Flamingo* built 1909 as No. 3735. Withdrawn 1948.

3446 *Goldfinch* built 1909 as No. 3736. Withdrawn 1948.

3447 *Jackdaw* built 1909 as No. 3737. Withdrawn 1951.

A study in 4–4–0 design. This is class 3252 No. 3287 *Mercury* in 1936, with the neat and still relatively new logo on the tender. Note the curved frame. (*HMRS/J.P. Richards ACC810*)

By comparison, class 32XX No. 3202 *Earl of Dudley*, seen here at Old Oak Common in 1935, has a straight frame. (*HMRS/Dr N.R. Ferguson AEP108*)

3448 *Kingfisher* built 1909 as No. 3738. Withdrawn 1949.

3449 *Nightingale* built 1909 as No. 3739. Withdrawn 1951.

3450 *Peacock* built 1909 as No. 3740. Withdrawn 1949.

3451 *Pelican* built 1910 as No. 3741. Withdrawn 1951.

3452 *Penguin* built 1910 as No. 3742. Withdrawn 1948.

3453 *Seagull* built 1910 as No. 3743. Withdrawn 1951.

3454 *Skylark* built 1910 as No. 3744. Withdrawn 1951.

3455 *Starling* built 1910 as No. 3745. Withdrawn 1950.

4–4–0 Class 3300 'Bulldog' class express passenger locomotives

Nos 3320–60 built 1899–1900.

Nos 3300–19 rebuilt from 'Duke' class locomotives 1902–9.

Nos 3361–3440 built 1902–9.

Of these, 3300–40 used a curved frame as on the 'Duke' class, while 3341–3440 used a straight frame. Strangely, although known as the 'Bulldog' class, *Bulldog* was not No. 3300 but No. 3311.

Locomotives and names:

3300 *Pendennis Castle* rebuilt from 'Duke' class No. 3253, 1908. Name removed 1923 to avoid confusion with the 'Castle' class. Withdrawn 1936.

3301 *Powderham* rebuilt from 'Duke' class No. 3362, 1906. Name removed 1923. Withdrawn 1931.

3302 *Sir Lancelot* rebuilt from 'Duke' class No. 3263, 1907. Withdrawn 1932.

3303 *St Anthony* rebuilt from 'Duke' class No. 3264, 1907. Withdrawn 1932.

3304 *River Tamar* rebuilt from 'Duke' class No. 3268, 1907. Withdrawn 1934.

3305 *Tintagel* rebuilt from 'Duke' class No. 3269, 1907. Withdrawn 1936.

3306 *Amorel* rebuilt from 'Duke' class No. 3273, 1902. Withdrawn 1939.

3307 *Exmoor* rebuilt from 'Duke' class No. 3279, 1907. Withdrawn 1934.

3308 *Falmouth* rebuilt from 'Duke' class No. 3280, 1909. Withdrawn 1938.

3309 *Maristow* rebuilt from 'Duke' class No. 3282, 1907. Withdrawn 1934.

3310 *St Just* rebuilt from 'Duke' class No. 3286, 1908. Withdrawn 1932.

3311 rebuilt from 'Duke' class No. 3312, 1906. Withdrawn 1932.

3312 *Isle of Guernsey* rebuilt from 'Duke' class No. 3316, 1908. Withdrawn 1931.

3313 *Jupiter* rebuilt from 'Duke' class No. 3318, 1908. Withdrawn 1946.

3314 *Mersey* rebuilt from 'Duke' class No. 3322, 1907. Withdrawn 1934.

3315 *Quantock* rebuilt from 'Duke' class No. 3324, 1908. Withdrawn 1931.

3316 *St Columb* rebuilt from 'Duke' class No. 3325, 1908. Named removed 1930 to avoid confusion with destination. Withdrawn 1938.

3317 *Somerset* rebuilt from 'Duke' class No. 3327, 1908. Withdrawn 1931.

3318 *Vulcan* rebuilt from 'Duke' class No. 3330, 1908. Withdrawn 1934.

3319 *Weymouth* rebuilt from 'Duke' class No. 3331, 1907. Withdrawn 1934.

3320 *Avalon* built as No. 3332, 1899. Withdrawn 1929.

3321 *Brasenose* built as No. 3333, 1899. Withdrawn 1935.

3322 *Eclipse* built as No. 3334, 1899. Withdrawn 1935.

3323 *Etona* built as No. 3335, 1899. Withdrawn 1935.

3324 *Glastonbury* built as No. 3336, 1899. Withdrawn 1935.

3325 *Kenilworth* built as No. 3337, 1899. Withdrawn 1935.

3326 *Laira* built as No. 3338, 1900. Withdrawn 1933.

3327 *Marco Polo* built as No. 3339, 1900. Withdrawn 1936.

3328 *Marazion* built as No. 3340, 1900. Name removed 1931 to avoid confusion with destination. Withdrawn 1934.

3329 *Mars* built as No. 3341, 1900. Withdrawn 1932.

3330 *Orion* built as No. 3342, 1900. Withdrawn 1938.

3331 *Pegasus* built as No. 3343, 1900. Withdrawn 1934.

3332 *Pluto* built as No. 3344, 1900. Withdrawn 1931.

3333 *Perseus* built as No. 3345, 1900. Withdrawn 1932

3334 *Tavy* built as No. 3346, 1900. Withdrawn 1930.

3335 *Tregothan* built as No. 3347, 1900. Name removed 1930 to avoid confusion with destination. Withdrawn 1948.

3336 *Titan* built as No. 3348, 1900. Withdrawn 1936.

3337 *The Wolf* built as No. 3349, 1900. Withdrawn 1934.

3338 *Swift* built as No. 3350, 1900. Withdrawn 1933.

3339 *Sedgemoor* built as No. 3351, 1900. Withdrawn 1936.

3340 *Camel* built as No. 3352, 1900. Withdrawn 1934.

3341 *Blasius* built as No. 3353, 1900. Withdrawn 1949.

3342 *Bonaventura* built as No. 3354, 1900. Withdrawn 1938.

3343 *Camelot* built as No. 3355, 1900. Withdrawn 1934.

3344 *Dartmouth* built as No. 3356, 1900. Name

Steam locomotive operation involved considerable work over and above rostered duties, such as clearing out ash from the firebox, as is being done with 4–4–0 class 32XX No. 3283 *Comet* in 1923. *(HMRS/D.A. Bayliss AEP516)*

The most famous 4–4–0 of them all, another class 32XX, No. 3717 *City of Truro* was the first locomotive to exceed 100mph, and was already in preservation at York in 1938. *(HMRS/N. Wilkinson ACW234)*

removed 1930 to avoid confusion with destination. Withdrawn 1934.

3345 *Smeaton* built as No. 3357, 1900. Withdrawn 1936.

3346 *Godolphin* built as No. 3358, 1900. Withdrawn 1934.

3347 *Kingsbridge* built as No. 3359, 1900. Name removed 1930 to avoid confusion with destination. Withdrawn 1936.

3348 *Launceston* built as No. 3360, 1900. Name removed 1930 to avoid confusion with destination. Withdrawn 1934.

3349 *Lyonesse* built as No. 3361, 1900. Withdrawn 1934.

3350 *Newlyn* built as No. 3362, 1900. Name removed 1930 to avoid confusion with destination. Withdrawn 1935.

3351 *One and All* built as No. 3363, 1900. Withdrawn 1931.

3352 *Pendragon* built as No. 3364, 1900. Withdrawn 1933.

3353 *Plymouth* built as No. 3365, 1900. Name removed 1927 to avoid confusion with destination. Withdrawn 1946.

3354 *Restormel* built as No. 3366, 1900. Name removed 1930 to avoid confusion with the 'Castle' class. Withdrawn 1934.

3355 *St Aubyn* built as No. 3367, 1900. Name removed 1930 to avoid confusion with destination. Withdrawn 1934.

3356 *Sir Stafford* built as No. 3368, 1900. Withdrawn 1936.

3357 *Trelawney* built as No. 3369, 1900. Withdrawn 1934.

3358 *Tremayne* built as No. 3370, 1900. Withdrawn 1945.

3359 *Tregeagle* built as No. 3371, 1900. Withdrawn 1936.

3360 *Torquay* built as No. 3372, 1902. Name removed 1930 to avoid confusion with destination. Withdrawn 1934.

3361 *Edward VII* built as No. 3413, 1902. Withdrawn 1947.

3362 *Albert Brassey* built as No. 3414, 1902. Withdrawn 1937.

3363 *Alfred Baldwin* built as No. 3415, 1903. Withdrawn 1949.

3364 *Frank Bibby* built as No. 3416, 1903. Withdrawn 1949.

3365 *Charles Grey Mott* built as No. 3417, 1903. Withdrawn 1930.

3366 *Earl of Cork* built as No. 3418, 1903. Name removed May 1936 to avoid confusion with 'Earl' class. Withdrawn 1948.

3367 *Evan Llewllyn* built as No. 3419, 1903. Withdrawn 1935.

3368 *Sir Ernest Palmer* built as No. 3420, 1903. Withdrawn 1935.

3369 *David MacIver* built as No. 3421, 1903. Withdrawn 1936.

3370 *Sir John Llewelyn* built as No. 3422, 1903. Withdrawn 1939.

3371 *Sir Massey Lopes* built as No. 3423, 1903. Withdrawn 1944.

3372 *Sir N Kingscote* built as No. 3424, 1903. Withdrawn 1936.

3373 *Sir William Henry* built as No. 3425, 1903. Withdrawn 1939.

3374 *Walter Long* built as No. 3426, 1903. Withdrawn 1937.

3375 *Sir Watkin Wynn* built as No. 3427, 1903. Withdrawn 1947.

3376 *River Plym* built as No. 3428, 1903. Withdrawn 1948.

3377 *Penzance* built as No. 3429, 1903. Name removed 1930 to avoid confusion with destination. Withdrawn 1951.

3378 *River Taw* built as No. 3430, 1903. Withdrawn 1945.

3379 *River Fal* built as No. 3431, 1903. Withdrawn 1948.

3380 *River Yealm* built as No. 3432, 1903. Withdrawn 1938.

3381 *Birkenhead* built as No. 3443, 1903. Name removed 1930 to avoid confusion with destination. Withdrawn 1935.

3382 *Cardiff* built as No. 3444, 1903. Name removed 1930 to avoid confusion with destination. Withdrawn 1949.

3383 *Ilfracombe* built as No. 3445, 1903. Name removed 1930 to avoid confusion with destination. Withdrawn 1949.

3384 *Swindon* built as No. 3446 *Liverpool*, 1903. Renamed *Swindon* 1903. Name removed 1930 to avoid confusion with destination. Withdrawn 1936.

3385 *Newport* built as No. 3447, 1903. Name removed 1927 to avoid confusion with destination. Withdrawn 1934.

3386 *Paddington* built as No. 3448, 1903. Name removed 1927 to avoid confusion with destination. Withdrawn 1949.

3387 *Reading* built as No. 3449, 1903. Name removed 1927 to avoid confusion with destination. Withdrawn 1934.

3388 *Swansea* built as No. 3450, 1903. Name removed 1927 to avoid confusion with destination. Withdrawn 1935.

3389 *Taunton* built as No. 3451, 1903. Name removed 1927 to avoid confusion with destination. Withdrawn 1945.

3390 *Wolverhampton* built as No. 3452, 1903. Name removed 1927 to avoid confusion with destination. Withdrawn 1939.

3391 *Dominion of Canada* built as No. 3453, 1903. Withdrawn 1948.

3392 *New Zealand* built as No. 3454, 1903. Withdrawn 1937.

3393 *Australia* built as No. 3455, 1903. Withdrawn 1949.

3394 *Albany* built as No. 3456, 1904. Withdrawn 1934.

3395 *Tasmania* built as No. 3457, 1904. Withdrawn 1948.

3396 *Natal Colony* built as No. 3458, 1904. Withdrawn 1948.

3397 *Toronto* built as No. 3459, 1904. Withdrawn 1934.

3398 *Montreal* built as No. 3460, 1904. Withdrawn 1935.

3399 *Ottawa* built as No. 3461, 1904. Withdrawn 1947.

3400 *Winnipeg* built as No. 3462, 1904. Withdrawn 1947.

3401 *Vancouver* built as No. 3463, 1904. Withdrawn 1949.

3402 *Jamaica* built as No. 3464, 1904. Withdrawn 1937.

3403 *Trinidad* built as No. 3465, 1904. Withdrawn 1937.

A curved frame again. This is 4–4–0 class 32XX No. 3302 *Sir Lancelot* with its safety valve dismantled. *(HMRS AAD119)*

3404 *Barbados* built as No. 3466, 1904. Withdrawn 1937.

3405 *Empire of India* built as No. 3467, 1904. Withdrawn 1937.

3406 *Calcutta* built as No. 3468, 1904. Withdrawn 1951.

3407 *Madras* built as No. 3469, 1904. Withdrawn 1949.

3408 *Bombay* built as No. 3470, 1904. Withdrawn 1948.

3409 *Queensland* built as No. 3471, 1904. Withdrawn 1939.

3410 *Columbia* built as No. 3472, 1904. Withdrawn 1936.

3411 *Stanley Baldwin* built as No. 3701, 1906, named 1909. Withdrawn 1938.

3412 *John G Griffiths* built as No. 3702, 1906, named 1914. Withdrawn 1936.

3413 *James Mason* built as No. 3703, 1906, named 1914. Withdrawn 1936.

3414 *Sir Edward Elgar* built as No. 3704, 1906, named *A H Mills* 1914, renamed 1932. Withdrawn 1938.

3415 *George A Wills* built as No. 3705, 1906, named 1914. Withdrawn 1937.

3416 *John W Wilson* built as No. 3706, 1906, named 1914. Withdrawn 1936.

3417 *Lord Mildmay of Fleet* built as No. 3707, 1906, named 1916. Withdrawn 1948.

3418 *Sir Arthur Yorke* built as No. 3708, 1906, named 1916. Withdrawn 1949.

3419 built as No. 3709, 1906 unnamed, withdrawn 1949.

3420 built as No. 3710, 1906 unnamed, withdrawn 1937.

3421 built as No. 3711, 1906 unnamed, withdrawn 1948.

3422 *Aberystwyth* built as No. 3712, 1906, named 1916. Withdrawn 1936.

3423 built as No. 3713, 1906 unnamed, withdrawn 1939.

3424 built as No. 3714, 1906 unnamed, withdrawn 1936.

3425 built as No. 3715, 1906 unnamed, withdrawn 1938.

3426 built as No. 3716, 1906 unnamed, withdrawn 1949.

3427 built as No. 3717, 1906 unnamed, withdrawn 1938.

3428 built as No. 3718, 1906 unnamed, withdrawn 1936.

3429 built as No. 3719, 1906 unnamed, withdrawn 1939.

3430 *Inchcape* built as No. 3720, 1906, named 1921.

Withdrawn 1948.

3431 built as No. 3721, 1906 unnamed, withdrawn 1948.

3432 built as No. 3722, 1906 unnamed, withdrawn 1949.

3433 built as No. 3723, 1906 unnamed, withdrawn 1939.

3434 *Joseph Shaw* built as No. 3724, 1906, named 1917. Withdrawn 1948.

3435 built as No. 3725, 1906 unnamed, withdrawn 1945.

3436 built as No. 3726, 1906 unnamed, withdrawn 1938.

3437 built as No. 3727, 1906 unnamed, withdrawn 1939.

3438 built as No. 3724, 1906 unnamed, withdrawn 1948.

3439 *Weston-super-Mare* built as No. 3729, 1906, named 1913, but name removed 1930 to avoid confusion with destination. Withdrawn 1936.

3440 built as No. 3730, 1906, unnamed, withdrawn 1948.

Class 3700 'City' class express locomotives

After using 'Atbara' class No. 3705 *Mauritius* as a prototype with a larger boiler in 1902, ten new locomotives were built as the 'City' class, followed by further 'Atbara' class rebuilds. Fame for the class was won by No. 3717 *City of Truro*, which set an unofficial record of 102.3mph at Whiteball in 1904. Despite this sparkling performance, and the introduction of superheating on the locomotives of the class, after the First World War the 'City' class was soon displaced by the new generation of 4–6–0 locomotives.

Nos 3700–19 built 1902–3, 1907–9.

Named locomotives:

3700 *Durban* rebuilt from 'Atbara' class 3400, 1907. Withdrawn 1929.

3701 *Gibraltar* rebuilt from 'Atbara' class 3401, 1907. Withdrawn 1928.

3702 *Halifax* rebuilt from 'Atbara' class 3402, 1908. Withdrawn 1929.

3703 *Hobart* rebuilt from 'Atbara' class 3403, 1909. Withdrawn 1929.

3704 *Lyttelton* rebuilt from 'Atbara' class 3404, 1907. Withdrawn 1928.

3705 *Mauritius* rebuilt from 'Atbara' class 3405, 1902. Used as prototype for the class. Withdrawn 1928.

3706 *Melbourne* rebuilt from 'Atbara' class 3406, 1908. Withdrawn 1929.

3707 *Malta* rebuilt from 'Atbara' class 3407, 1908. Withdrawn 1929.

3708 *Killarney* rebuilt from 'Atbara' class 3408, 1907, as *Orphir*. Name changed later in 1907. Withdrawn 1929.

3709 *Quebec* rebuilt from 'Atbara' class 3409, 1907. Withdrawn 1929.

3710 *City of Bath* built as No. 3433, 1903. Involved in a serious accident at Yeovil, 1913, when it ran into the back of an excursion train, killing three passengers. Withdrawn 1928.

3711 *City of Birmingham* built as No. 3434, 1903. Withdrawn 1930.

3712 *City of Bristol* built as No. 3435, 1903. Withdrawn 1931.

3713 *City of Chester* built as No. 3436, 1903. Withdrawn 1929.

3714 *City of Gloucester* built as No. 3437, 1903. Withdrawn 1929.

3715 *City of Hereford* built as No. 3438, 1903. Withdrawn 1929.

3716 *City of London* built as No. 3439, 1903. Withdrawn 1929.

3717 *City of Truro* built as No. 3440, 1903. Established unofficial world speed record of 102.3mph in 1904. Withdrawn 1931.

3718 *City of Winchester* built as No. 3441, 1903. Withdrawn 1927.

3719 *City of Exeter* built as No. 3442, 1903. Withdrawn 1929.

Class 3800 'County' class express locomotives

These were designed to run on the cross-country Shrewsbury to Hereford line owned jointly by the GWR and the London & North Western. The latter refused to allow 4–6–0 locomotives on the route, so the GWR had to design a locomotive that could work this line, but that also had sufficient power to be used elsewhere. In the end, the locomotives were so powerful for their wheelbase that they were relatively unstable and thus became known to their crews as 'Churchward's Rough Riders'. Attempts to dampen the ride included experiments with locomotives using the large eight-wheel tender built for *The Great Bear*.
Nos 3800, 3831–9 built 1904.
Nos 3801–20 built 1906.
Nos 3821–30 built 1911–12.

Named locomotives:
3800 *County of Middlesex*, built 1904, withdrawn 1931.
3801 *County Carlow*, built 1906, withdrawn 1931.
3802 *County Clare*, built 1906, withdrawn 1931.
3803 *County Cork*, built 1906, withdrawn 1932.
3804 *County Dublin*, built 1906, withdrawn 1931.
3805 *County Kerry*, built 1906, withdrawn 1933.
3806 *County Kildare*, built 1906, withdrawn 1931.
3807 *County Kilkenny*, built 1906, withdrawn 1930.
3808 *County Limerick*, built 1906, withdrawn 1931.
3809 *County Wexford*, built 1906, withdrawn 1931.
3810 *County Wicklow*, built 1906, withdrawn 1931.
3811 *County of Bucks*, built 1906, withdrawn 1931.
3812 *County of Cardigan*, built 1906, withdrawn 1932.
3813 *County of Carmarthen*, built 1906, withdrawn 1931.
3814 *County of Chester*, built 1906, withdrawn 1933.
3815 *County of Hants*, built 1906, withdrawn 1932.
3816 *County of Leicester*, built 1906, withdrawn 1931.
3817 *County of Monmouth*, built 1906, withdrawn 1931.
3818 *County of Radnor*, built 1906, withdrawn 1931.
3819 *County of Salop*, built 1906, withdrawn 1931.
3820 *County of Worcester*, built 1906, withdrawn 1931.
3821 *County of Bedford*, built 1911, withdrawn 1931.
3822 *County of Brecon*, built 1911, withdrawn 1933.
3823 *County of Carnarvon*, built 1911, withdrawn 1931.
3824 *County of Cornwall*, built 1911, withdrawn 1931.
3825 *County of Denbigh*, built 1911, withdrawn 1931.
3826 *County of Flint*, built 1912, withdrawn 1931.
3827 *County of Gloucester*, built 1912, withdrawn 1931.
3828 *County of Hereford*, built 1912, withdrawn 1933.
3829 *County of Merioneth*, built 1912, withdrawn 1931.
3830 *County of Oxford*, built 1912, withdrawn 1931.
3831 *County of Berks*, built 1904, withdrawn 1930.
3832 *County of Wilts*, built 1904, withdrawn 1930.
3833 *County of Dorset*, built 1904, withdrawn 1930.
3834 *County of Somerset*, built 1904, withdrawn 1933.
3835 *County of Devon*, built 1904, withdrawn 1931.
3836 *County of Warwick*, built 1904, withdrawn 1931.
3837 *County of Stafford*, built 1904, withdrawn 1931.
3838 *County of Glamorgan*, built 1904, withdrawn 1930.
3839 *County of Pembroke*, built 1904, withdrawn 1930.

Class 3252 'Duke' class express locomotives

While Dean's 'Singles' with their large driving wheel were capable of excellent performances on level track, something with better adhesion was required for the steeply graded lines of the south-west. A side view of one of these locomotives is just enough to convince one that there is a link with the

Double-heading a Penzance express, 4–6–0 No. 4092 pilots another locomotive near Ponsandane in 1938, while a Hall-class locomotive can be seen on the right. *(HMRS/E.S. Russell AEU427)*

single driving wheel locomotives, while the frames were curved around the driving wheels. The first locomotive was No. 3252 *Duke of Cornwall*. Initially the class was named after the second locomotive, *Pendennis Castle*, but the 'Duke' class title was adopted well before the advent of the 'Castle' class. To many GWR railwaymen, however, the class was nicknamed 'The Devons', because of their main operating area. In later years many of the 'Dukes' found their way to the main line of the former Cambrian Railway, whose 4–4–0 locomotives were found to be underpowered.

Nos 3252–61 built 1895.

Nos 3262–91 built 1896–7.

Nos 3312–31 built 1898–9.

Named locomotives

(NOTE: Duplicate and missing numbers relate to renumbering during the service lives of these locomotives, including a number taken for conversion to the 'Bulldog' class, while a further renumbering scheme was introduced for surviving locomotives of the 'Duke' class in 1946, but to avoid confusion is not covered here as it was of short duration until nationalisation.

3252 *Duke of Cornwall*, built 1895, withdrawn 1937.

3253 *Pendennis Castle*, built 1895, rebuilt 1908 as Bulldog-class 3300.

3253 *Boscawen*, built 1895 as 3254, withdrawn 1939.

3254 *Cornubia*, built 1895 as 3255, withdrawn 1950.

3255 *Excalibur*, built 1895 as 3256, withdrawn 1936.

3256 *Guinevere*, built 1895 as 3257, withdrawn 1939.

3257 *King Arthur*, built 1895 as 3258. Name dropped 1927 to avoid confusion with 'King' class. Withdrawn 1937.

3258 *The Lizard*, built 1895 as 3259, withdrawn 1938.

3259 *Merlin*, built 1895 as 3260, withdrawn 1938.

3260 *Mount Edgcumbe*, built 1895 as 3261, withdrawn 1938.

3261 *St Germans*, built 1896 as 3265, withdrawn 1937.

3262 *St Ives*, built 1896 as 3266, withdrawn 1937.

3262 *Powderham*, built 1896, rebuilt 1906 as 'Bulldog' class 3301.

3263 *St Michael*, built 1896 as 3267, withdrawn 1936.

3263 *Sir Lancelot*, built 1896, rebuilt 1907 as 'Bulldog' class 3302.

3264 *Trevithick*, built 1896 as 3270, withdrawn 1949.

3264 *St Anthony*, built 1896, rebuilt 1907 as 'Bulldog' class 3303.

3265 *Tre Pol and Pen*, built 1896 as 3271, withdrawn 1949.

3266 *Amyas*, built 1896 as 3271, withdrawn 1938.

3267 *Cornishman*, built 1896 as 3274, withdrawn 1936.

3268 *Chough*, built 1896 as 3275, withdrawn 1939.

3268 *River Tamar*, built 1896, rebuilt 1907 as

'Bulldog' class 3304.

3269 *Dartmoor*, built 1896 as 3276, withdrawn 1937.

3269 *Tintagel*, built 1896, rebuilt 1907 as 'Bulldog' class 3305.

3270 *Earl of Devon*, built 1897 as 3277. Name dropped when 'Dukedog' class introduced. Withdrawn 1939.

3271 *Eddystone*, built 1897 as 3278, withdrawn 1936.

3272 *Fowey*, built 1897 as 3281, withdrawn 1949.

3273 *Mounts Bay*, built 1897 as 3283, withdrawn 1949.

3273 *Armorel*, built 1896, rebuilt 1907 as 'Bulldog' class 3306.

3274 *Newquay*, built 1897 as 3284. Name removed 1930 to avoid confusion with destination. Withdrawn 1936.

3275 *St Erth*, built 1897 as 3285. Name removed 1930 to avoid confusion with destination. Withdrawn 1936.

3276 *St Agnes*, built 1897 as 3287. Name removed 1930 to avoid confusion with destination. Withdrawn 1949.

3277 *Isle of Tresco*, built 1897 as 3288, withdrawn 1937.

3278 *Trefusis*, built 1897 as 3289, withdrawn 1938.

3279 *Tor Bay* (sic), built 1897 as 3290, withdrawn 1938.

3279 *Exmoor*, built 1897, rebuilt 1907 as 'Bulldog' class 3307.

3280 *Tregenna*, built 1897 as 3291. Name dropped 1930 to avoid confusion with 'Castle' class. Withdrawn 1939.

3280 *Falmouth*, built 1897, rebuilt 1909 as 'Bulldog' class 3308.

3281 *Cotswold*, built 1899 as 3313, withdrawn 1937.

3282 *Chepstow Castle*, built 1899 as 3314. Name dropped 1930 to avoid confusion with 'Castle' class. Withdrawn 1937.

3282 *Maristowe* (sic), built 1897, rebuilt 1907 as 'Bulldog' class 3309

3283 *Comet*, built 1899 as 3315, withdrawn 1950.

3284 *Isle of Jersey*, built 1899 as 3317, withdrawn 1951.

3285 *Katerfelto*, built 1899 as 3319, withdrawn 1936.

3286 *Meteor*, built 1899 as 3320, withdrawn 1936.

3286 *St Just*, built 1897, rebuilt 1908 as 'Bulldog' class 3310.

3287 *Mercury*, built 1899 as 3321, withdrawn 1949.

3288 *Mendip*, built 1899 as 3323, withdrawn 1936.

3290 *Severn*, built 1899 as 3328, withdrawn 1939.

3291 *Thames*, built 1899 as 3329, withdrawn 1949.

3312 *Bulldog*, built 1899, rebuilt 1906 as 'Bulldog' class 3311.

3316 *Isle of Guernsey*, built 1899, rebuilt 1908 as 'Bulldog' class 3312.

3318 *Jupiter*, built 1899, rebuilt 1908 as 'Bulldog' class 3313.

3322 *Mersey*, built 1899, rebuilt 1907 as 'Bulldog' class 3314.

3324 *Quantock*, built 1899, rebuilt 1908 as 'Bulldog' class 3315.

3325 *St Columb*, built 1899, rebuilt 1908 as 'Bulldog' class 3316.

3326 *St Austell*, built 1899 as 3326. Name removed 1930 to avoid confusion with destination. Withdrawn 1951.

3327 *Somerset*, built 1899, rebuilt 1908 as 'Bulldog' class 3317.

Left: Piloted by 0–6–0 class 788 No. 1094, an unidentified 'Bulldog' handles a mixed goods near Bilston in 1929. *(HMRS/D.H. Haines AEV310)*

Opposite: Yet more varied rolling stock behind this unidentified 'Duke' class locomotive with a siphon vehicle and four carriages on an Aberystwyth to Oswestry working in 1936. *(HMRS/J. Tatchell ADC501)*

3330 *Vulcan*, built 1895, rebuilt 1908 as 'Bulldog' class 3318.

3331 *Weymouth*, built 1899, rebuilt 1907 as 'Bulldog' class 3319.

Class 3200 'Earl' class, also known as the 'Dukedog', express passenger locomotives

The first of this class was created using parts from No. 3265 *Tre Pol and Pen* when it was withdrawn in 1929, with a spare 'Duke' class boiler and the straight 'Bulldog' class frame of No. 3365, withdrawn at the beginning of 1930. The class was renumbered in 1946 in the 9000 series, with each locomotive remaining at the same position in the series which ran from 9000 to 9028.
Nos 3200–28 built 1936–9.

Named locomotives:

3200 *Earl of Mount Edgcumbe*, built 1936 using the frame of 3422 and the boiler of 3288. Name removed 1937. Withdrawn 1955.

3201 *Earl of Dunraven*, built 1936 using the frame of 3412 and the boiler of 3263. Name removed 1936. Withdrawn 1954.

3202 *Earl of Dudley*, built 1936 using the frame of 3416 and the boiler of 3286. Name removed 1937. Withdrawn 1954.

3203 *Earl Cawdor*, built 1936 using the frame of 3424

and the boiler of 3275. Name removed 1937. Withdrawn 1955.

3204 *Earl of Dartmouth*, built 1936 using the frame of 3439 and the boiler of 3271. Name removed 1937. Withdrawn 1960.

3205 *Earl of Devon*, built 1936 using the frame of 3413 and the boiler of 3255. Name removed 1937. Withdrawn 1959.

3206 *Earl of Plymouth*, built 1936 using the frame of 3428 and the boiler of 3267. Name removed 1937. Withdrawn 1948.

3207 *Earl of St Germans*, built 1936 using the frame of 3410 and the boiler of 3274. Name removed 1937. Withdrawn 1948.

3208 *Earl Bathurst*, built 1937 using the frame of 3403 and the boiler of 3285. Name removed 1937. Withdrawn 1957.

3209 *Earl of Radnor*, built 1937 using the frame of 3392 and the boiler of 3277. Name removed 1937. Withdrawn 1957.

3210 *Earl Cairns*, built 1937 using the frame of 3402 and the boiler of 3269. Name removed 1937. Withdrawn 1957.

3211 *Earl of Ducie*, built 1937 using the frame of 3415 and the boiler of 3281. Name removed 1937. Withdrawn 1957.

3212 *Earl of Eldon*, built 1937 using the frame of 3405 and the boiler of 3261. Name removed 1937. Withdrawn 1957.

3213 Allocated name *Earl of Powis*, but never

carried. Built 1937 using the frame of 3374 and the boiler of 3257. Withdrawn 1958.

3214 Allocated name *Earl Waldegrave*, but never carried. Built 1937 using the frame of 3434 and the boiler of 3252. Withdrawn 1960.

3215 Allocated name *Earl of Clancarty*, but never carried. Built 1937 using the frame of 3420 and the boiler of 3262. Withdrawn 1958.

3216 Allocated name *Earl St Aldwyn*, but never carried. Built 1938 using the frame of 3404 and the boiler of 3282. Withdrawn 1957.

3217 Allocated name *Earl of Berkeley*, but never carried. Built 1938 using the frame of 3425 and the boiler of 3258. Withdrawn 1960.

3218 Allocated name *Earl of Birkenhead*, but never carried. Built 1938 using the frame of 3380 and the boiler of 3266. Withdrawn 1960.

3219 Allocated name *Earl of Shaftesbury*, but never carried. Built 1938 using the frame of 3327 and the boiler of 3260. Withdrawn 1948.

3220 Built unnamed in 1938 using the frame of 3414 and the boiler of 3279. Withdrawn 1957.

3221 Built unnamed in 1938 using the frame of 3411 and the boiler of 3259. Withdrawn 1958.

3222 Built unnamed in 1938 using the frame of 3436 and the boiler of 3278. Withdrawn 1957.

3223 Built unnamed in 1938 using the frame of 3423 and the boiler of 3253. Withdrawn 1957.

3224 Built unnamed in 1939 using the frame of 3409 and the boiler of 3290. Withdrawn 1957.

3225 Built unnamed in 1939 using the frame of 3437 and the boiler of 3268. Withdrawn 1957.

3226 Built unnamed in 1939 using the frame of 3390 and the boiler of 3270. Withdrawn 1957.

3227 Built unnamed in 1939 using the frame of 3433 and the boiler of 3280. Withdrawn 1957.

3228 Built unnamed in 1939 using the frame of 3429 and the boiler of 3256. Withdrawn 1957.

Class 4101 'Flower' class express passenger locomotives

A development of the 'Atbara' class but with a deep straight frame.
Nos 4149–68 (originally 4101–20) built 1908.

Named locomotives:

4149 *Auricula*, built 1908 as No. 4101. Withdrawn 1929.

4150 *Begonia*, built 1908 as No. 4102. Withdrawn 1931.

4151 *Calceolaria*, built 1908 as No. 4103. Withdrawn 1927.

4152 *Calendula*, built 1908 as No. 4104. Withdrawn 1928.

4153 *Camellia*, built 1908 as No. 4105. Withdrawn 1927.

4154 *Campanula*, built 1908 as No. 4106. Withdrawn 1930.

4155 *Cineraria*, built 1908 as No. 4107. Withdrawn 1927.

4156 *Gardenia*, built 1908 as No. 4108. Withdrawn 1929.

4157 *Lobelia*, built 1908 as No. 4109. Withdrawn 1928.

4158 *Petunia*, built 1908 as No. 4110. Withdrawn 1927.

4159 *Anemone*, built 1908 as No. 4111. Withdrawn 1929.

4160 *Carnation*, built 1908 as No. 4112. Withdrawn 1927.

4161 *Hyacinth*, built 1908 as No. 4113. Withdrawn 1929.

4162 *Margerite*, built 1908 as No. 4114. Withdrawn 1929.

4163 *Marigold*, built 1908 as No. 4115. Withdrawn 1929.

4164 *Mignonette*, built 1908 as No. 4116. Withdrawn 1930.

4165 *Narcissus*, built 1908 as No. 4117. Withdrawn 1927.

4166 *Polyanthus*, built 1908 as No. 4118. Withdrawn 1927.

4167 *Primrose*, built 1908 as No. 4119. Withdrawn 1929.

4168 *Stephanotis*, built 1908 as No. 4120. Withdrawn 1930.

4–4–2T
Class 2221 'County Tank' class mixed traffic tank engines

Intended to replace the Class 3600 'Birdcage' 2–4–2T, these were a tank version of the 'County' class tender locomotive, and despite the tender and trailing bogie, shared the poor riding characteristics of that class, which no doubt contributed to the fact that all but three were withdrawn by 1934.
Nos 2221–40 built 1905–9.
Nos 2241–50 built 1912.

4–6–0
Class 4073 'Castle' class express passenger locomotives

A development of the earlier 'Star' class, the 'Castle' class was the most economical express locomotive of its size and power when first introduced in 1919. The enduring quality of the design can be judged by the long period in production, although, of course, later locomotives incorporated many improvements and these were added to earlier locomotives whenever they underwent a major overhaul. Inevitably, the 'Castle' class was a heavy locomotive, although not so heavy as the 'King' class that followed, and was limited to main lines. However, it offered the GWR much greater flexibility than *The Great Bear*, Churchward's and the GWR's sole excursion into the Pacific 4–6–2 wheel arrangement, which proved too heavy and was indeed to suffer the fate of being rebuilt as a 'Castle' in 1922. Many of the 'Castle' class were in fact rebuilt members of the earlier 'Star' class, an economical way of maintaining an up-to-date stud of locomotives. One of the 'Castle' class, No. 5005 *Manorbier Castle*, was fitted with partial streamlining in March 1935, with a bullet nose to the front of the smokebox and coverings over the external cylinders, and air-smoothing of a number of other items.

It says much for the 'Castle' class that a fourteen-year-old locomotive, No. 4086 *Builth Castle*, managed to run at 100mph for 4½ miles on 31 July 1939, while in normal passenger service.

Nos 100, 111, 4000, 4016, 4032, 4037, 4073–7007 built 1919–46.

100 *100 A1 Lloyds*. Originally rebuilt as No. 4009 *Shooting Star*, 1925. Renamed and numbered 1936.

111 *Viscount Churchill*. Built using parts of No. 111 *The Great Bear*, September 1924.

4000 *North Star*. Rebuilt from the 'Star' class locomotive, November 1929.

4016 *The Somerset Light Infantry (Prince Albert's)*. Rebuilt as *Knight of the Golden Fleece*, from the 'Star' class locomotive, 1925. Renamed 1938.

4032 *Queen Alexandra*. Rebuilt from the 'Star' class locomotive, 1926.

4037 *South Wales Borderers*. Rebuilt as *Queen Philippa* from the 'Star' class locomotive, 1926. Renamed 1937.

4073 *Caerphilly Castle*. Built 1923.

4074 *Caldicot Castle*. Built 1923. Used in the GWR–LNER locomotive trials of 1925 against Gresley Class A1 Pacific No. 4474 *Victor Wild* running between Paddington and Plymouth.

4075 *Cardiff Castle*. Built 1924.

4076 *Carmarthen Castle*. Built 1924.

4077 *Chepstow Castle*. Built 1924.

4078 *Pembroke Castle*. Built February 1924.

4079 *Pendennis Castle*. Built 1924.

4080 *Powderham Castle*. Built 1924.

4081 *Warwick Castle*. Built 1924

4082 *Windsor Castle*. Built 1924. Renamed and numbered 7013 *Bristol Castle* post-nationalisation.

4083 *Abbotsbury Castle*. Built 1925.

4084 *Aberystwyth Castle*. Built 1925.

4085 *Berkeley Castle*. Built 1925.

4086 *Builth Castle*. Built 1925. Ran at 100mph for 4½ miles on 31 July 1939 with a Paddington to Worcester express.

4087 *Cardigan Castle*. Built 1925.

4088 *Dartmouth Castle*. Built 1925. Incident with No. 2975 *Lord Palmer*, 13 November 1942 at Appleford Crossing.

4089 *Donnington Castle*. Built 1925.

4090 *Dorchester Castle*. Built 1925.

4091 *Dudley Castle*. Built 1925.

4092 *Dunraven Castle*. Built 1925.

4093 *Dunster Castle*. Built 1926.

4094 *Dynevor Castle*. Built 1926.

4095 *Harlech Castle*. Built 1926.

4096 *Highclere Castle*. Built 1926.

4097 *Kenilworth Castle*. Built 1926.

4098 *Kidwelly Castle*. Built 1926.

4099 *Kilgerran Castle*. Built 1926.

5000 *Launceston Castle*. Built 1926.

5001 *Llandovery Castle*. Built 1926.

5002 *Ludlow Castle*. Built 1926.

5003 *Lulworth Castle*. Built 1927.

5004 *Llanstephan Castle*. Built 1927.

5005 *Manorbier Castle*. Built 1927. In March 1935, fitted with partial streamlining.

5006 *Tregenna Castle*. Built 1927.

5007 *Rougemont Castle*. Built 1927.

5008 *Raglan Castle*. Built 1927.

5009 *Shrewsbury Castle*. Built 1927.

5010 *Restormel Castle*. Built 1927.

5011 *Tintagel Castle*. Built 1927.

5012 *Berry Pomeroy Castle*. Built 1927.

5013 *Abergavenny Castle*. Built 1932.

5014 *Goodrich Castle*. Built 1932.

5015 *Kingswear Castle*. Built 1932.

5016 *Montgomery Castle*. Built 1932.

5017 *The Gloucester Regiment 28th, 61st*. Built as *St Donat's Castle*, 1932. Renamed post-nationalisation.

5018 *St Mawes Castle*. Built 1932.

5019 *Treago Castle*. Built 1932.

5020 *Trematon Castle*. Built 1932.

5021 *Whittington Castle*. Built 1932.

5022 *Wigmore Castle*. Built 1932.

5023 *Brecon Castle*. Built 1932.

5024 *Carew Castle*. Built 1934.

5025 *Chirk Castle*. Built 1934.

5026 *Criccieth Castle*. Built 1934.

5027 *Farleigh Castle*. Built 1934.

5028 *Llantilio Castle*. Built 1934.

5029 *Nunney Castle*. Built 1934.

5030 *Shirburn Castle*. Built 1934.

5031 *Totnes Castle*. Built 1934.

5032 *Usk Castle*. Built 1934.

5033 *Broughton Castle*. Built 1935.

5034 *Corfe Castle*. Built 1935.

5035 *Coity Castle*. Built 1935.

5036 *Lyonshall Castle*. Built 1935.

5037 *Monmouth Castle*. Built 1935.

5038 *Morlais Castle*. Built 1935.

5039 *Rhuddlan Castle*. Built 1935.

5040 *Stokesay Castle*. Built 1935.

5041 *Tiverton Castle*. Built 1935.

5042 *Winchester Castle*. Built 1935.

5043 *Earl of Mount Edgcumbe*. Originally built as *Banbury Castle*, 1936. Renamed 1937.

5044 *Earl of Dunraven*. Originally built as *Beverston Castle*, 1936. Renamed 1937.

5045 *Earl of Dudley*. Originally built as *Bridgwater Castle*, 1936. Renamed 1937.

5046 *Earl of Cawdor*. Originally built as *Clifford Castle*, 1936. Renamed 1937.

5047 *Earl of Dartmouth*. Originally built as *Compton Castle*, 1936. Renamed 1937.

5048 *Earl of Devon*. Originally built as *Cranbrook Castle*, 1936. Renamed August 1937.

5049 *Earl of Plymouth*. Originally built as *Denbigh Castle*, 1936. Renamed August 1937.

5050 *Earl of St Germans*. Originally built as *Devizes Castle*, 1936. Renamed August 1937.

5051 *Earl Bathurst*. Originally built as *Drysllwyn Castle*, 1936. Renamed 1937.

5052 *Earl of Radnor*. Originally built as *Eastnor Castle*, 1936. Renamed 1937.

5053 *Earl Cairns*. Originally built as *Bishop's Castle*, 1936. Renamed 1937.

5054 *Earl of Ducie*. Originally built as *Lamphey Castle*, 1936. Renamed 1937.

5055 *Earl of Eldon*. Originally built as *Lydford Castle*, 1936. Renamed 1937.

5056 *Earl of Powis*. Originally built as *Ogmore Castle*, 1936. Renamed 1937.

5057 *Earl Waldegrave*. Originally built as *Penrice Castle*, 1936. Renamed 1937.

5058 *Earl of Clancarty*. Originally built as *Newport Castle*, 1937. Renamed 1937.

5059 *Earl of St Aldwyn*. Originally built as *Powis Castle*, 1937. Renamed 1937.

5060 *Earl of Berkeley*. Originally built as *Sarum Castle*, 1937. Renamed 1937.

5061 *Earl of Birkenhead*. Originally built as *Sudeley Castle*, 1937. Renamed 1937.

5062 *Earl of Shaftesbury*. Originally built as *Tenby Castle*, 1937. Renamed 1937.

5063 *Earl Baldwin*. Originally built as *Thornbury Castle*, 1937. Renamed 1937.

5064 *Bishop's Castle*. Originally built as *Tretower Castle*, June 1937. Renamed 1937.

5065 *Newport Castle*. Originally built as *Upton Castle*, 1937. Renamed 1937.

5066 *Sir Felix Pole*. Originally built as *Wardour Castle*, 1937. Renamed post-nationalisation.

5067 *St Fagans Castle*. Built 1937.

5068 *Beverston Castle*. Built 1938.

5069 *Isambard Kingdom Brunel*. Built 1938.

5070 *Sir Daniel Gooch*. Built 1938.

5071 *Spitfire*. Originally built as *Clifford Castle*, 1938. Renamed 1940.

5072 *Hurricane*. Originally built as *Compton Castle*, 1938. Renamed 1940.

5073 *Blenheim*. Originally built as *Cranbrook Castle*, 1938. Renamed 1941.

5074 *Hampden*. Originally built as *Denbigh Castle*, 1938. Renamed 1941.

5075 *Wellington*. Originally built as *Devizes Castle*, 1938. Renamed 1940.

5076 *Gladiator*. Originally built as *Drysllwyn Castle*, 1938.

5077 *Fairey Battle*. Originally built as *Eastnor Castle*, 1938. Renamed 1940.

5078 *Beaufort*. Originally built as *Lamphey Castle*, 1939. Renamed 1941.

5079 *Lysander*. Originally built as *Lydford Castle*, 1939. Renamed 1940.

5080 *Defiant*. Originally built as *Ogmore Castle*, 1939. Renamed 1941.

5081 *Lockheed Hudson*. Originally built as *Penrice Castle*, 1939. Renamed 1941.

5082 *Swordfish*. Originally built as *Powis Castle*, 1939. Renamed 1941.

5083 *Bath Abbey*. Rebuilt from 'Star' class No. 4063 *Bath Abbey*, 1937.

5084 *Reading Abbey*. Rebuilt from 'Star' class No. 4064 *Reading Abbey*, 1937.

5085 *Evesham Abbey*. Rebuilt from 'Star' class No. 4065 *Evesham Abbey*, 1939.

5086 *Viscount Horne*. Rebuilt from 'Star' class No. 4066 *Viscount Horne*, 1937.

5087 *Tintern Abbey*. Rebuilt from 'Star' class No. 4067 *Tintern Abbey*, 1940.

5088 *Llanthony Abbey*. Rebuilt from 'Star' class No. 4068 *Llanthony Abbey*, 1939.

5089 *Westminster Abbey*. Rebuilt from 'Star' class No. 4069 *Westminster Abbey*, 1939.

5090 *Neath Abbey*. Rebuilt from 'Star' class No. 4070

Neath Abbey, 1939.

5091 *Cleeve Abbey*. Rebuilt from 'Star' class No. 4071 *Cleeve Abbey*, 1938.

5092 *Tresco Abbey*. Rebuilt from 'Star' class No. 4072 *Tresco Abbey*, 1938.

5093 *Upton Castle*. Built 1939.

5094 *Tretower Castle*. Built 1939.

5095 *Barbury Castle*. Built 1939.

5096 *Bridgwater Castle*. Built 1939.

5097 *Sarum Castle*. Built 1939.

5098 *Clifford Castle*. Built 1946.

5099 *Compton Castle*. Built 1946.

7000 *Viscount Portal*. Built 1946.

7001 *Sir James Milne*. Originally built as *Denbigh Castle*, 1946. Renamed 1948.

7002 *Devizes Castle*. Built 1946.

7003 *Elmley Castle*. Built 1946.

7004 *Eastnor Castle*. Built 1946.

7005 *Sir Edward Elgar*. Originally built as *Lamphey Castle*, 1946. Renamed post-nationalisation.

7006 *Lydford Castle*. Built 1946.

7007 *Great Western*. Originally built as *Ogmore Castle*, 1946. Last passenger express engine built at Swindon. Renamed 1948.

Class 6000 'King' class 4–6–0 express passenger locomotives

Nos 6000–29 built 1927–30 and in 1936.

The 'King' class was the ultimate expression of the GWR's 4–6–0 concept and the heaviest of any of the company's classes with this wheel arrangement, which probably explains the relatively small number of locomotives in the class, since they were too heavy to work west of Plymouth and north of Shrewsbury, or between Oxford and Worcester. It was to the company's credit that these locomotives were commissioned at a time when traffic was less than healthy and dividends for the shareholders were dwindling, while employees had taken a 2.5 per cent cut in gross pay. These locomotives had the highest tractive power of any in service in the British Isles at the time, and were capable of handling what was then the longest non-stop run in the country, between Paddington and Plymouth. In fact, the GWR had dogmatically given the power of a 4–6–2 to a 4–6–0. Performance might have been even better had not the GWR provided such modest superheating, although in the company's favour, it used the best coal from South Wales and superheating became more important as coal quality declined.

So proud and certain of these locomotives was the GWR that the first of them, No. 6000 *King George V*, was shipped to the United States in 1927 to take part in the Fair of the Iron Horse promoted by the Baltimore & Ohio Railway to celebrate its centenary, and gave impressive performances on the American company's tracks. The locomotive had to conform to US railway regulations, so acquired all of the necessary accoutrements of any self-respecting (not to say legal) American locomotive, and on its return to the GWR retained the American-style bell and plaques commemorating its visit: 'The Bell' immediately became its nickname among railwaymen.

One of the 'King' class, No. 6014 *King Henry VII*, was fitted with partial streamlining during 1935, with a bullet nose to the front of the smokebox and coverings over the external cylinders, and air-smoothing of a number of other items.

This was what a 'King', or class 60XX, really looked like. No. 6012 *King Edward VI* stands at a coaling stage in 1930. The wagons with the coal can be seen on the upper-level track on the right. *(HMRS/ J. Scott-Morgan ABX120)*

Along with the 'Castles', the 'Kings' epitomised the Great Western for many. This is No. 6023, *King Edward II*. (*Kevin Robertson*)

Two of the 'Kings' were involved in accidents. No. 6007 *King William III* was involved at Shrivenham, covered in Chapter Fifteen, and as a result of the severe damage had to be scrapped and a replacement built, while No. 6028 *King George VI* was involved at Norton Fitzwarren and suffered heavy damage.

Locomotives and names:
6000 King George V, built 1927 and almost immediately visited the United States, as mentioned above.
6001 *King Edward VII*, built 1927.
6002 *King William IV*, built 1927.
6003 *King George IV*, built 1927.
6004 *King George III*, built 1927.
6005 *King George II*, built 1927.
6006 *King George I*, built 1928.
6007 *King William III*, built 1928. After being 'written-off' in the Shrivenham accident, a replacement was built using many of the parts from the original, entering service in 1936 and carrying the same number and name.
6008 *King James II*, built 1928.
6009 *King Charles II*, built 1928.
6010 *King Charles I*, built 1928.
6011 *King James I*, built 1928.
6012 *King Edward VI*, built 1928.
6013 *King Henry VIII*, built 1928.
6014 *King Henry VII*, built 1928. In 1935 this locomotive was fitted with partial streamlining.
6015 *King Richard III*, built 1928.

6016 *King Edward V*, built 1928.
6017 *King Edward IV*, built 1928.
6018 *King Henry VI*, built 1928.
6019 *King Henry V*, built 1928.
6020 *King Henry IV*, built 1930.
6021 *King Richard II*, built 1930.
6022 *King Edward III*, built 1930.
6023 *King Edward II*, built 1930.
6024 *King Edward I*, built 1930.
6025 *King Henry III*, built 1930.
6026 *King John*, built 1930.
6027 *King Richard I*, built 1930.
6028 *King George VI*, built as *King Henry II*, 1930. Renamed 1937.
6029 *King Edward VIII*, built as *King Stephen*, 1930. Renamed 1936.

Class 1000 'County' class

A development of the 'Saint' class to keep a 4–6–0 express locomotive within the 20-ton axle weight limit necessary for many of the GWR's main lines, this was the main work of F.W. Hawksworth, the GWR's last chief mechanical engineer. The locomotives incorporated a new design of boiler, while still retaining the GWR tapered style. One change from the earlier Class 3800 'County' class was that no Irish counties were included this time round, most of Ireland having become independent in 1922 and, bearing in mind the attitudes of the day, the Irish Republic had been neutral throughout the Second World War.

Locomotives and names:

1000 *County of Middlesex* built unnamed 1945, named 1946. Withdrawn 1964.

1001 *County of Bucks* built unnamed 1945, named 1947. Withdrawn 1963.

1002 *County of Berks* built unnamed 1945, named 1946. Withdrawn 1963.

1003 *County of Wilts* built unnamed 1945, named 1947. Withdrawn 1962.

1004 *County of Somerset* built unnamed 1945, named 1946. Withdrawn 1962.

1005 *County of Devon* built unnamed 1945, named 1946. Withdrawn 1963.

1006 *County of Cornwall* built unnamed 1945, named 1948. Withdrawn 1963.

1007 *County of Brecknock* built unnamed 1945, named 1948. Withdrawn 1962.

1008 *County of Cardigan* built unnamed 1945, named 1947. Withdrawn 1963.

1009 *County of Carmarthen* built unnamed 1945, named 1948. Withdrawn 1963.

1010 *County of Caernarvon* built unnamed 1945, named 1947. Withdrawn 1964.

1011 *County of Chester* built unnamed 1946, named 1947. Withdrawn 1964.

1012 *County of Denbigh* built unnamed 1946, named 1946. Withdrawn 1964.

1013 *County of Dorset* built unnamed 1946, named 1947. Withdrawn 1964.

1014 *County of Glamorgan* built unnamed 1946, named 1948. Withdrawn 1964.

1015 *County of Gloucester* built unnamed 1946, named 1947. Withdrawn 1964.

1016 *County of Hants* built unnamed 1946, named 1946. Withdrawn 1963.

1017 *County of Hereford* built unnamed 1946, named 1946. Withdrawn 1962.

1018 *County of Leicester* built unnamed 1946, named 1946. Withdrawn 1962.

1019 *County of Merioneth* built 1946. Withdrawn 1963.

1020 *County of Monmouth* built 1946. Withdrawn 1964.

1021 *County of Montgomery* built 1946. Withdrawn 1963.

1022 *County of Northampton* built 1946. Withdrawn 1962.

1023 *County of Oxford* built 1947. Withdrawn 1963.

1024 *County of Pembroke* built 1947. Withdrawn 1964.

1025 *County of Radnor* built 1947. Withdrawn 1963.

1026 *County of Salop* built 1947. Withdrawn 1962.

1027 *County of Stafford* built 1947. Withdrawn 1963.

1028 *County of Warwick* built 1947. Withdrawn 1963.

1029 *County of Worcester* built 1947. Withdrawn 1962.

Class 6800 'Grange' class

Nos 6800–79 built 1936–7, and in 1939.
Basically a variation on the 'Hall' class with smaller wheels, the locomotives of this class were intended to replace the 43XX class 2–6–0 locomotives, but reusing their wheels and motion under new boilers and frames. Although there were 300 locomotives in the 43XX class, only eighty 'Grange' class locomotives had been completed on the outbreak of war in 1939, and work was discontinued and never revived, possibly because of the existence of the 'Hall' class, revived with improved superheating.

Locomotives and names:

6800 *Arlington Grange*, built 1936.
6801 *Aylburton Grange*, built 1936.
6802 *Bampton Grange*, built 1936.
6803 *Bucklebury Grange*, built 1936.
6804 *Brockington Grange*, built 1936.
6805 *Broughton Grange*, built 1936.
6806 *Blackwell Grange*, built 1936.
6807 *Birchwood Grange*, built 1936.
6808 *Beenham Grange*, built 1936.
6809 *Burghclere Grange*, built 1936.
6810 *Blakemere Grange*, built 1936.
6811 *Cranbourne Grange*, built 1936.
6812 *Chesford Grange*, built 1936.
6813 *Eastbury Grange*, built 1936.
6814 *Enborne Grange*, built 1936.
6815 *Frilford Grange*, built 1936.
6816 *Frankton Grange*, built 1936.
6817 *Gwenddwr Grange*, built 1936.
6818 *Hardwick Grange*, built 1936.
6819 *Highnam Grange*, built 1936.
6820 *Kingstone Grange*, built 1937.
6821 *Leaton Grange*, built 1937.
6822 *Manton Grange*, built 1937.
6823 *Oakley Grange*, built 1937.
6824 *Ashley Grange*, built 1937.
6825 *Llanvair Grange*, built 1937.
6826 *Nannerth Grange*, built 1937.
6827 *Llanfrechfa Grange*, built 1937.
6828 *Trellech Grange*, built 1937.
6829 *Burmington Grange*, built 1937.
6830 *Buckenhill Grange*, built 1937.
6831 *Bearley Grange*, built 1937.
6832 *Brockton Grange*, built 1937.
6833 *Calcot Grange*, built 1937.
6834 *Dummer Grange*, built 1937.
6835 *Eastham Grange*, built 1937.
6836 *Estevarney Grange*, built 1937.

Another 4–6–0 class was the 'Grange' class. No. 6802 *Bampton Grange* looks smartly turned out in this 1930 shot. *(HMRS/J. Scott-Morgan ABX119)*

6837 *Forthhampton Grange*, built 1937.
6838 *Goodmoor Grange*, built 1937.
6839 *Hewell Grange*, built 1937.
6840 *Hazeley Grange*, built 1937.
6841 *Marlas Grange*, built 1937.
6842 *Nunhold Grange*, built 1937.
6843 *Poulton Grange*, built 1937.
6844 *Penhydd Grange*, built 1937.
6845 *Paviland Grange*, built 1937.
6846 *Ruckley Grange*, built 1937.
6847 *Tidmarch Grange*, built 1937.
6848 *Toddington Grange*, built 1937.
6849 *Walton Grange*, built 1937.
6850 *Cleeve Grange*, built 1937.
6851 *Hurst Grange*, built 1937.
6852 *Headbourne Grange*, built 1937.
6853 *Morehampton Grange*, built 1937.
6854 *Roundhill Grange*, built 1937.
6855 *Saighton Grange*, built 1937.
6856 *Stowe Grange*, built 1937.
6857 *Tudor Grange*, built 1937.
6858 *Woolston Grange*, built 1937.
6859 *Yiewsley Grange*, built 1937.
6860 *Aberporth Grange*, built 1939.
6861 *Crynant Grange*, built 1939.
6862 *Derwent Grange*, built 1939.
6863 *Dolhywel Grange*, built 1939.
6864 *Dymock Grange*, built 1939.
6865 *Hopton Grange*, built 1939.
6866 *Morfa Grange*, built 1939.
6867 *Peterston Grange*, built 1939.
6868 *Penrhos Grange*, built 1939.
6869 *Resolven Grange*, built 1939.

6870 *Bodicote Grange*, built 1939.
6871 *Bourton Grange*, built 1939.
6872 *Crawley Grange*, built 1939.
6873 *Caradoc Grange*, built 1939.
6874 *Haughton Grange*, built 1939.
6875 *Hindford Grange*, built 1939.
6876 *Kingsland Grange*, built 1939.
6877 *Llanfair Grange*, built 1939.
6878 *Longford Grange*, built 1939.
6879 *Overton Grange*, built 1939.

Class 4900 'Hall' class

Nos 4900–6980, built 1928–47.
While the GWR received good service from its 2–6–0 Mogul locomotives, the shorter wheelbase gave problems when matched with a powerful locomotive, and there was a tendency towards poor riding and 'nosing'. Many felt that a 4–6–0 locomotive would be the ideal for mixed traffic and for working over most of the GWR network. Churchward in his programme to standardise the GWR locomotive stock inclined to the view that a ten-wheel locomotive would indeed be ideal, but his own preference was for a 2–8–0 configuration which he felt would provide a better tractive effort, and this led him to design the 28XX class. When Collett took over as chief mechanical engineer in 1922, one of his first duties was to design a 4–6–0 that would replace the 43XX class. The solution chosen was to reduce the size of the driving wheels on one of the 'Saint' class, No. 2925 *Saint Martin*, and use this locomotive as a prototype for trials

The 4–6–0 'Hall' class was a handy mixed-traffic locomotive, but capable of handling expresses, as in this case with *Fairleigh Hall* at the head of an express near Penzance in 1934. One of the vehicles is a twelve-wheel carriage, while even more than ten years after the grouping, several are still in the lake colour scheme. *(HMRS/D.H. Haines AEV031)*

from 1924. The design must have been successful, since in 1928 an order was given for an initial batch of eighty locomotives, and subsequent batches followed, with the basic design remaining in production until 1947, although later batches incorporated modifications, including a number designed by Hawksworth during the war years. A number of the later locomotives were not named at first, but this omission was remedied later.

Locomotives and names:

4900 *Saint Martin* rebuilt from No. 2925 *Saint Martin* in 1924.
4901 *Adderley Hall*, built 1928.
4902 *Aldenham Hall*, built 1928.
4903 *Astley Hall*, built 1928.
4904 *Binnegar Hall*, built 1928.
4905 *Barton Hall*, built 1928.
4906 *Bradfield Hall*, built 1928.
4907 *Broughton Hall*, built 1929.
4908 *Broome Hall*, built 1929.
4909 *Blakesley Hall*, built 1929.
4910 *Blaisdon Hall*, built 1929.
4911 *Bowden Hall*, built 1929. Hit by German bomb on 2 April 1941, and scrapped.
4912 *Bennington Hall*, built 1929.
4913 *Baglan Hall*, built 1929.
4914 *Cranmore Hall*, built 1929.
4915 *Candover Hall*, built 1929.
4916 *Crumlin Hall*, built 1929.
4917 *Crosswood Hall*, built 1929.
4918 *Dartington Hall*, built 1929.
4919 *Donnington Hall*, built 1929.

4920 *Dumbleton Hall*, built 1929.
4921 *Eaton Hall*, built 1929.
4922 *Enville Hall*, built 1929.
4923 *Evenley Hall*, built 1929.
4924 *Evdon Hall*, built 1929.
4925 *Eynsham Hall*, built 1929.
4926 *Fairleigh Hall*, built 1929.
4927 *Farnborough Hall*, built 1929.
4928 *Gatacre Hall*, built 1929.
4929 *Goytrey Hall*, built 1929.
4930 *Hagley Hall*, built 1929.
4931 *Hanbury Hall*, built 1929.
4932 *Hatherton Hall*, built 1929.
4933 *Himley Hall*, built 1929.
4934 *Hindlip Hall*, built 1929.
4935 *Ketley Hall*, built 1929.
4936 *Kinlet Hall*, built 1929.
4937 *Lanelay Hall*, built 1929.
4938 *Liddington Hall*, built 1929.
4939 *Littleton Hall*, built 1929.
4940 *Ludford Hall*, built 1929.
4941 *Llangedwyn Hall*, built 1929.
4942 *Maindy Hall*, built 1929.
4943 *Marrington Hall*, built 1929.
4944 *Middleton Hall*, built 1929.
4945 *Milligan Hall*, built 1929.
4946 *Moseley Hall*, built 1929. Had the doubtful distinction of being the first locomotive to carry the British Railways logo after nationalisation.
4947 *Nanhoran Hall*, built 1929.
4948 *Northwick Hall*, built 1929.
4949 *Packwood Hall*, built 1929.
4950 *Patshull Hall*, built 1929.

A useful mixed-traffic locomotive was the 'Hall' class, otherwise known as class 49XX. This is No. 4972 *St Bride's Hall* with a larger tender outside Swindon Works. *(HMRS/J.P. Gill ABL007)*

4951 *Pendeford Hall*, built 1929.
4952 *Peplow Hall*, built 1929.
4953 *Pitchford Hall*, built 1929.
4954 *Plaish Hall*, built 1929.
4955 *Plaspower Hall*, built 1929.
4956 *Plowden Hall*, built 1929.
4957 *Postlip Hall*, built 1929.
4958 *Priory Hall*, built 1929.
4959 *Purley Hall*, built 1929.
4960 *Pyle Hall*, built 1929.
4961 *Pyrland Hall*, built 1929.
4962 *Ragley Hall*, built 1929.
4963 *Rignall Hall*, built 1929.
4964 *Rodwell Hall*, built 1929.
4965 *Rood Ashton Hall*, built 1929.
4966 *Shakenhurst Hall*, built 1929.
4967 *Shirenewton Hall*, built 1929.
4968 *Shotton Hall*, built 1929.
4969 *Shrugborough Hall*, built 1929.
4970 *Sketty Hall*, built 1929.
4971 *Stanway Hall*, built 1930.
4972 *Saint Brides Hall*, built 1930. Converted to oil-firing, 1947, but reconverted the following year.
4973 *Sweeney Hall*, built 1930.
4974 *Talgarth Hall*, built 1930.
4975 *Umberslade Hall*, built 1930.
4976 *Warfield Hall*, built 1930.
4977 *Watcombe Hall*, built 1930.
4978 *Westwood Hall*, built 1930.
4979 *Wootton Hall*, built 1930.
4980 *Wrottesley Hall*, built 1930.

4981 *Abberley Hall*, built 1930.
4982 *Acton Hall*, built 1931.
4983 *Albert Hall*, built 1931.
4984 *Albrighton Hall*, built 1931.
4985 *Allesley Hall*, built 1931.
4986 *Aston Hall*, built 1931.
4987 *Brockley Hall*, built 1931.
4988 *Bulwell Hall*, built 1931.
4989 *Cherwell Hall*, built 1931.
4990 *Clifton Hall*, built 1931.
4991 *Cobham Hall*, built 1931.
4992 *Crosby Hall*, built 1931.
4993 *Dalton Hall*, built 1931.
4994 *Downton Hall*, built 1931.
4995 *Easton Hall*, built 1931.
4996 *Eden Hall*, built 1931.
4997 *Elton Hall*, built 1931.
4998 *Eyton Hall*, built 1931.
4999 *Gopsal Hall*, built 1931.
5900 *Hinderton Hall*, built 1931.
5901 *Hazel Hall*, built 1931.
5902 *Howick Hall*, built 1931.
5903 *Keele Hall*, built 1931.
5904 *Kelham Hall*, built 1931.
5905 *Knowsley Hall*, built 1931.
5906 *Lawton Hall*, built 1931.
5907 *Marble Hall*, built 1931.
5908 *Moreton Hall*, built 1931.
5909 *Newton Hall*, built 1931.
5910 *Park Hall*, built 1931.
5911 *Preston Hall*, built 1931.

5912 *Queen's Hall*, built 1931.
5913 *Rushton Hall*, built 1931.
5914 *Ripon Hall*, built 1931.
5915 *Trentham Hall*, built 1931.
5916 *Trinity Hall*, built 1931.
5917 *Westminster Hall*, built 1931.
5918 *Walton Hall*, built 1931.
5919 *Worsley Hall*, built 1931.
5920 *Wycliffe Hall*, built 1931.
5921 *Bingley Hall*, built 1933.
5922 *Caxton Hall*, built 1933.
5923 *Colston Hall*, built 1933.
5924 *Dinton Hall*, built 1933.
5925 *Eastcote Hall*, built 1933.
5926 *Grotian Hall*, built 1933.
5927 *Guild Hall*, built 1933.
5928 *Haddon Hall*, built 1933.
5929 *Hanham Hall*, built 1933.
5930 *Hannington Hall*, built 1933.
5931 *Hatherley Hall*, built 1933.
5932 *Haydon Hall*, built 1933.
5933 *Kingsway Hall*, built 1933.
5934 *Kneller Hall*, built 1933.
5935 *Norton Hall*, built 1933.
5936 *Oakley Hall*, built 1933.
5937 *Stanford Hall*, built 1933.
5938 *Stanley Hall*, built 1933.
5939 *Tangley Hall*, built 1933.
5940 *Whitbourne Hall*, built 1933.
5941 *Campion Hall*, built 1933.
5942 *Doldowlod Hall*, built 1935.
5943 *Elmdon Hall*, built 1935.
5944 *Ickenham Hall*, built 1935.
5945 *Leckhampton Hall*, built 1935.
5946 *Marwell Hall*, built 1935.
5947 *Saint Benet's Hall*, built 1935.
5948 *Siddington Hall*, built 1935.
5949 *Trematon Hall*, built 1935.
5950 *Wardley Hall*, built 1935.
5951 *Clyffe Hall*, built 1935.
5952 *Cogan Hall*, built 1935.
5953 *Dunley Hall*, built 1935.
5954 *Faendra Hall*, built 1935.
5955 *Garth Hall*, built 1935.
5956 *Horsley Hall*, built 1935.
5957 *Hutton Hall*, built 1935.
5958 *Knolton Hall*, built 1936.
5959 *Mawley Hall*, built 1936.
5960 *Saint Edmund Hall*, built 1936.
5961 *Toynbee Hall*, built 1936.
5962 *Wantage Hall*, built 1936.
5963 *Wimpole Hall*, built 1936.
5964 *Wolseley Hall*, built 1936.
5965 *Woollas Hall*, built 1936.

5966 *Ashford Hall*, built 1937.
5967 *Bickmarsh Hall*, built 1937.
5968 *Cory Hall*, built 1937.
5969 *Honington Hall*, built 1937.
5970 *Hengrave Hall*, built 1937.
5971 *Merevale Hall*, built 1937.
5972 *Olton Hall*, built 1937.
5973 *Rolleston Hall*, built 1937.
5974 *Wallsworth Hall*, built 1937.
5975 *Winslow Hall*, built 1937.
5976 *Ashwicke Hall*, built 1938.
5977 *Beckford Hall*, built 1938.
5978 *Bodinnick Hall*, built 1938.
5979 *Cruckton Hall*, built 1938.
5980 *Dingley Hall*, built 1938.
5981 *Frensham Hall*, built 1938.
5982 *Harrington Hall*, built 1938.
5983 *Henley Hall*, built 1938.
5984 *Linden Hall*, built 1938.
5985 *Mostyn Hall*, built 1938.
5986 *Arbury Hall*, built 1939.
5987 *Brocket Hall*, built 1939.
5988 *Bostock Hall*, built 1939.
5989 *Cransley Hall*, built 1939.
5990 *Dorford Hall*, built 1939.
5991 *Gresham Hall*, built 1939.
5992 *Horton Hall*, built 1939.
5993 *Kirby Hall*, built 1939.
5994 *Roydon Hall*, built 1939.
5995 *Wick Hall*, built 1940.
5996 *Mytton Hall*, built 1940.
5997 *Sparkford Hall*, built 1940.
5998 *Trevor Hall*, built 1940.
5999 *Wollaton Hall*, built 1940.
6900 *Abney Hall*, built 1940.
6901 *Arley Hall*, built 1940.
6902 *Butlers Hall*, built 1940.
6903 *Belmont Hall*, built 1940.
6904 *Charfield Hall*, built 1940.
6905 *Claughton Hall*, built 1940.
6906 *Chichley Hall*, built 1940.
6907 *Davenham Hall*, built 1940.
6908 *Downham Hall*, built 1940.
6909 *Frewin Hall*, built 1940.
6910 *Gossington Hall*, built 1940.
6911 *Holker Hall*, built 1941.
6912 *Helmster Hall*, built 1941.
6913 *Levens Hall*, built 1941.
6914 *Langton Hall*, built 1941.
6915 *Mursley Hall*, built 1941.
6916 *Misterton Hall*, built 1941.
6917 *Oldlands Hall**, built 1941.
6918 *Sandon Hall**, built 1941.
6919 *Tylney Hall**, built 1941.

6920 *Barningham Hall**, built 1941.
6921 *Borwick Hall**, built 1941.
6922 *Burton Hall**, built 1941.
6923 *Croxteth Hall**, built 1941.
6924 *Grantley Hall**, built 1941.
6925 *Hackness Hall**, built 1941.
6926 *Holkham Hall**, built 1941.
6927 *Lilford Hall**, built 1941.
6928 *Underley Hall**, built 1941.
6929 *Whorlton Hall**, built 1941.
6930 *Aldersley Hall**, built 1941.
6931 *Aldborough Hall**, built 1941.
6932 *Burwarton Hall**, built 1941.
6933 *Birtles Hall**, built 1941.
6934 *Beachamwell Hall**, built 1941.
6935 *Browshome Hall**, built 1941.
6936 *Breccles Hall**, built 1942.
6937 *Conyngham Hall**, built 1942.
6938 *Corndean Hall**, built 1942.
6939 *Calveley Hall**, built 1942.
6940 *Didlington Hall**, built 1942.
6941 *Fillongley Hall**, built 1942.
6942 *Eshton Hall**, built 1942.
6943 *Farnley Hall**, built 1942.
6944 *Fledborough Hall**, built 1942.
6945 *Glasfryn Hall**, built 1942.
6946 *Heatherden Hall**, built 1942.
6947 *Helmingham Hall**, built 1942.
6948 *Holbrooke Hall**, built 1942.
6949 *Haberfield Hall**, built 1942. Converted to oil-
   firing 1947, but reconverted in 1949.
6950 *Kingsthorpe Hall**, built 1942.
6951 *Impney Hall**, built 1943.
6952 *Kimberley Hall**, built 1943.
6953 *Leighton Hall**, built 1943.
6954 *Lotherton Hall**, built 1943.
6955 *Lydcott Hall**, built 1943.
6956 *Mottram Hall**, built 1943.
6957 *Norcliffe Hall**, built 1943. Converted to oil-
   firing 1947, but reconverted in 1950.
6958 *Oxburgh Hall**, built 1943.
6959 *Peatling Hall*†, built 1944.
6960 *Raveningham* Hall†, built 1944.
6961 *Stedham Hall*†, built 1944.
6962 *Soughton Hall*†, built 1944.
6963 *Throwley Hall*†, built 1944.
6964 *Thornbridge Hall*†, built 1944.
6965 *Thirlestaine Hall*†, built 1944.
6966 *Witchingham Hall*†, built 1944.
6967 *Willesley Hall*†, built 1944.
6968 *Woodcock Hall*†, built 1944.
6969 *Wraysbury Hall*†, built 1944.
6970 *Whaddon Hall*†, built 1944.
6971 *Athelhampton Hall***, built 1947.

6972 *Beningbrough Hall***, built 1947.
6973 *Bricklehampton Hall***, built 1947.
6974 *Bryngwyn Hall***, built 1947.
6975 *Capesthorne Hall***, built 1947.
6976 *Graythwaite Hall***, built 1947.
6977 *Grundisburgh Hall***, built 1947.
6978 *Haroldstone Hall***, built 1947.
6979 *Helperly Hall***, built 1947.
6980 *Llanrumney Hall***, built 1947.

*   Built unnamed
†   Modified 'Hall' class, built unnamed
** Modified 'Hall' class

Class 7800 'Manor' class

Nos 7800–19, built 1938–9, with a further ten
locomotives built in 1950.

   The 'Manor' class was intended to be a lighter-
weight variant of the 'Grange' class, and like
'Granges' and first twenty used reconditioned parts
from the 43XX class, although the last ten used new
components.

Locomotives and names:
7800 *Torquay Manor*. Originally *Ashley Manor* but
changed before completion. Built January 1938.
7801 *Anthony Manor*. Built January 1938.
7802 *Bradley Manor*. Built January 1938.
7803 *Barcote Manor*. Built January 1938.
7804 *Baydon Manor* Built February 1938.
7805 *Broome Manor*. Built March 1938.
7806 *Cockington Manor*. Built March 1938.
7807 *Compton Manor*. Built March 1938.
7808 *Cookham Manor*. Built March 1938.
7809 *Childrey Manor*. Built April 1938.
7810 *Draycott Manor*. Built December 1938.
7811 *Dunley Manor*. Built December 1938.
7812 *Erlestoke Manor*. Built January 1939.
7813 *Freshford Manor*. Built January 1939.
7814 *Fringford Manor*. Built January 1939.
7815 *Fritwell Manor*. Built January 1939.
7816 *Frilsham Manor*. Built January 1939.
7817 *Garsington Manor*. Built January 1939.
7818 *Granville Manor*. Built January 1939.
7819 *Hinton Manor*. Built February 1939.
7820 *Dinmore Manor* to 7829 built post-
nationalisation.

Class 2900 'Saint' class

Nos 2900–88, prototypes built 1902–3, remainder
1905–13.

The 'Saint' class was something of a revelation when
it first appeared in 1902, marking a break with what

With substantial numbers of locomotives in many classes, names sometimes became a problem, which is probably why 'Saint' No. 2950 is called *Taplow Court*. (*Kevin Robertson*)

had been until then the GWR tradition, and it was not surprising that no fewer than three prototypes were built and operated. The new chief mechanical engineer, George Churchward, was anxious to standardise design, and while some maintained that the new locomotives had a slight 'American' look, and he had been studying American boiler design, the motion owed much to French influence, with a 4–4–2 locomotive ordered from the Société Alsacienne. The first locomotive, No. 100, appeared initially with a parallel boiler in 1902, replaced by a half-cone boiler the following year, and then with a superheated half-cone in 1910. The second prototype, No. 98, appeared with a half-cone boiler in 1903, and with differences to the motion. The third prototype, No. 171, was initially built as a 4–6–0, but was soon converted to a 4–4–2 to make comparison with the French-built locomotive more straightforward. The GWR did not wait for the outcome of this extensive trial programme, but went ahead and ordered nineteen production locomotives, hedging its bets on the most suitable wheel arrangement by having thirteen built as 4–4–2 locomotives and the remaining six as 4–6–0s. The depth of development and research with the 'Saint' class was to pay dividends for the rest of the GWR's existence, as the subsequent 4–6–0 classes all owed much to these early examples, most of which were built with the hallmark tapered boiler. It was to the credit of Churchward and to his superiors that such extensive and costly trialling, and the purchase of a foreign locomotive, was allowed. Not for the last time the GWR showed itself receptive to ideas from outside

and concerned to discover what would today be described as 'best practice'.

Locomotives and names:

2900 *William Dean*, first prototype, built 1902 unnamed and originally numbered 100, named late 1902. Withdrawn 1932.

2901 *Lady Superior*, built 1906, initially unnamed, withdrawn 1933.

2902 *Lady of the Lake*, built 1906, initially unnamed, withdrawn 1949.

2903 *Lady of Lyons*, built 1906, initially unnamed, withdrawn 1949.

2904 *Lady Godiva*, built 1906, named 1907, withdrawn 1932.

2905 *Lady Macbeth*, built 1906, named 1907, withdrawn 1948.

2906 *Lady of Lynn*, built 1906, named 1907, withdrawn 1952.

2907 *Lady Disdain*, built 1906, named 1907, withdrawn 1933.

2908 *Lady of Quality*, built 1906, named 1907, withdrawn 1950.

2909 *Lady of Provence*, built 1906, named 1907, withdrawn 1931.

2910 *Lady of Shalott*, built 1906, named 1907, withdrawn 1931.

2911 *Saint Agatha*, built 1907, withdrawn 1935.

2912 *Saint Ambrose*, built 1907, withdrawn 1951.

2913 *Saint Andrew*, built 1907, withdrawn 1951.

2914 *Saint Augustine*, built 1907, withdrawn 1946.

2915 *Saint Bartholomew*, built 1907, withdrawn 1950.

2916 *Saint Benedict*, built 1907, withdrawn 1948.

2917 *Saint Bernard*, built 1907, withdrawn 1934.

2918 *Saint Catherine*, built 1907, withdrawn 1935.

2919 *Saint Cuthbert*, built 1907 as *Saint Cecelia*, renamed 1907, withdrawn 1932.

2920 *Saint David*, built 1907, withdrawn 1953.

2921 *Saint Dunstan*, built 1907, withdrawn 1945.

2922 *Saint Gabriel*, built 1907, withdrawn 1944.

2923 *Saint George*, built 1907, withdrawn 1934.

2924 *Saint Helena*, built 1907, withdrawn 1950.

2925 *Saint Martin*, built 1907, became prototype for the 'Hall' class, renumbered 4900.

2926 *Saint Nicholas*, built 1907, withdrawn 1951.

2927 *Saint Patrick*, built 1907, withdrawn 1951.

2928 *Saint Sebastian*, built 1907, withdrawn 1948.

2929 *Saint Stephen*, built 1907, withdrawn 1948.

2930 *Saint Vincent*, built 1907, withdrawn 1949.

2931 *Arlington Court*, built 1911, withdrawn 1951.

2932 *Ashton Court*, built 1911, withdrawn 1951.

2933 *Bibury Court*, built 1911, withdrawn 1953.

2934 *Butleigh Court*, built 1911, withdrawn 1952.

2935 *Caynham Court*, built 1911, withdrawn 1948.

2936 *Cefntilla Court*, built 1911, withdrawn 1951.

2937 *Clevedon Court*, built 1911, withdrawn 1953.

2938 *Corsham Court*, built 1911, withdrawn 1951.

2939 *Croome Court*, built 1911, withdrawn 1950.

2940 *Domey Court*, built 1911, withdrawn 1952.

2941 *Easton Court*, built 1911, withdrawn 1952.

2942 *Fawley Court*, built 1912, withdrawn 1949.

2943 *Hampton Court*, built 1912, withdrawn 1951.

2944 *Highnam Court*, built 1912, withdrawn 1951.

2945 *Hillingdon Court*, built 1912, withdrawn 1953.

2946 *Langford Court*, built 1912, withdrawn 1949.

2947 *Madresfield Court*, built 1912, withdrawn 1951.

2948 *Stackpole Court*, built 1912, withdrawn 1951.

2949 *Stanford Court*, built 1912, withdrawn 1952.

2950 *Taplow Court*, built 1912, withdrawn 1952.

2951 *Tawstock Court*, built 1913, withdrawn 1952.

2952 *Twineham Court*, built 1913, withdrawn 1951.

2953 *Titley Court*, built 1913, withdrawn 1952.

2954 *Tockenham Court*, built 1913, withdrawn 1952.

2955 *Tortworth Court*, built 1913, withdrawn 1950.

2971 *Albion*, built 1903 as third prototype and numbered 171. Converted to 4–4–2 1904 and named *Albion*, renamed *The Pirate*, 1907, converted to 4–6–0 1907 and resumed name of *Albion*, renumbered 1913. Withdrawn 1946.

2972 *The Abbot*, built 1905 as 4–4–2 No. 172 *Quicksilver*, renamed 1907 and rebuilt to 4–6–0 1912. Withdrawn 1935.

2973 *Robins Bolitho*, built 1905 as No. 173, *Robins Bolitho*. Withdrawn 1933.

2974 *Lord Barrymore*, built 1905 as No. 174 *Barrymore*, renamed 1905. Withdrawn 1933.

2975 *Lord Palmer*, built 1905 as No. 175, but named *Viscount Churchill* 1907, and renamed *Sir Ernest Palmer* 1924, then *Lord Palmer* 1933. Involved in Appleford Crossing accident 1942. Withdrawn 1944.

2976 *Winterstoke*, built 1905 as No. 176, named 1907. Withdrawn 1934.

2977 *Robertson*, built 1905 as No. 177, named 1907. Withdrawn 1935.

2978 *Charles J Hambro*, built 1905 as No. 178 *Kirkland*, renamed 1935. Withdrawn 1946.

2979 *Quentin Durward*, built 1905 as 4–4–2 No. 179 *Magnet*, renamed 1907. Rebuilt 1912, withdrawn 1951.

2980 *Coeur de Lion*, built 1905 as 4–4–2 No. 180, named 1907. Rebuilt 1913, withdrawn 1948.

2981 *Ivanhoe*, built 1905 as 4–4–2 No. 181. Rebuilt 1912, withdrawn 1951.

2982 *Lalla Rookh*, built 1905 as 4–4–2 No. 182, named 1906. Rebuilt 1912, withdrawn 1946.

2983 *Redgauntlet*, built 1905 as 4–4–2 No. 183. Rebuilt 1912, withdrawn 1946.

2984 *Guy Mannering*, built 1905 as 4–4–2 No. 184 *Churchill*, renamed *Viscount Churchill* 1906 and renamed 1907. Rebuilt 1912, withdrawn 1933.

2985 *Peveril of the Peak*, built 1905 as 4–4–2 No. 185, named *Winterstoke* 1906, renamed 1907. Rebuilt 1912, withdrawn 1931.

2986 *Robin Hood*, built 1905 as 4–4–2 No. 186, named 1906. Rebuilt 1912, withdrawn 1932.

2987 *Bride of Lammermoor*, built 1905 as 4–4–2 No. 187, named 1906. Rebuilt 1912, withdrawn 1949.

2988 *Rob Roy*, built 1905 as 4–4–2 No. 188, named 1907. Rebuilt 1912, withdrawn 1948.

2989 *Talisman*, built 1905 as 4–4–2 No. 189, named 1906. Rebuilt 1912, withdrawn 1948.

2990 *Waverley*, built 1905 as 4–4–2 No. 190, named 1906. Rebuilt 1912, withdrawn 1939.

2998 *Ernest Cunard*, built as second prototype 1903 as No. 98. Named *Persimmon* 1906, renamed *Vanguard* 1907, renamed again 1907. Withdrawn 1933.

Class 4000 'Star' class

Nos 4000–72, built 1906–14 and 1922–3.

The 'Star' class was the first fruit of the work carried out in developing the 'Saint' class. The first locomotive, No. 40, was initially completed as a 4–4–2 and once again owed much to French experience, before being converted to 4–6–0 configuration, renumbered No. 4000 and given the name *North Star*. The initial batch of production locomotives had straight framing while the second batch had curved framing, which the prototype also received when converted to 4–6–0 in 1909. During their lives, many of the 'Star' class received larger cylinder bores to enhance performance, while many of them, including No. 4000, but also many of the later 'Star' or so-called 'Abbey' class, were rebuilt as members of the 'Castle' class.

Locomotives and names:
4000 *North Star*, built 1906 as the prototype as 4–4–2 No. 40, and rebuilt as 4–6–0, renamed and renumbered 1909. Later rebuilt as a 'Castle' class locomotive.
4001 *Dog Star*, built 1907, withdrawn 1934.
4002 *Evening Star*, built 1907, withdrawn 1933.
4003 *Lode Star*, built 1907, withdrawn 1951.
4004 *Morning Star*, built 1907, withdrawn 1948.
4005 *Polar Star*, built 1907, withdrawn 1934.
4006 *Red Star*, built 1907, withdrawn 1932.
4007 *Swallowfield Park*, built 1907 as *Rising Star*, withdrawn 1934.
4008 *Royal Star*, built 1907, withdrawn 1935.
4009 *Shooting Star*, built 1907, rebuilt as 'Castle' class 1925.
4010 *Western Star*, built 1907, withdrawn 1934.
4011 *Knight of the Garter*, built 1908, withdrawn 1932.
4012 *Knight of the Thistle*, built 1908, withdrawn 1949.
4013 *Knight of St Patrick*, built 1908, withdrawn 1950.
4014 *Knight of the Bath*, built 1908, withdrawn 1946. Nicknamed 'Friday Night' by railwaymen.
4015 *Knight of St John*, built 1908, withdrawn 1951.
4016 *Knight of the Golden Fleece*, built 1908, rebuilt as 'Castle' class 1925.
4017 *Knight of the Liege*, built 1908 as *Knight of the Black Eagle*, withdrawn 1949.
4018 *Knight of the Grand Cross*, built 1908, withdrawn 1951.
4019 *Knight Templar*, built 1908, withdrawn 1949.
4020 *Knight Commander*, built 1908, withdrawn 1951.
4021 *British Monarch*, built 1909 as *King Edward*, renamed 1927, withdrawn 1952.
4022, built 1909 as *King William*, renamed *Belgian Monarch* 1927, but name removed 1940 and withdrawn 1952.
4023, built 1909 as *King George*, renamed *Danish Monarch* 1927, but name removed 1940 and withdrawn 1952.
4024, built 1909 as *King James*, renamed *Dutch Monarch* 1927, withdrawn 1935.
4025, built 1909 as *King Charles*, renamed *Italian Monarch* 1927, but name removed 1940 and withdrawn 1950.

4026, built 1909 as *King Richard*, renamed *Japanese Monarch* 1927, but name removed 1941 and withdrawn 1950.
4027, built 1909 as *King Henry*, renamed *Norwegian Monarch* 1927, withdrawn 1934.
4028, built 1909 as *King John*, renamed *Roumanian Monarch* 1927, but name removed 1940 and withdrawn 1951.
4029, built 1909 as *King Stephen*, renamed *Spanish Monarch* 1927, withdrawn 1934.
4030, built 1909 as *King Harold*, renamed *Swedish Monarch* 1927, but name removed 1940 and withdrawn 1950.
4031 *Queen Mary*, built 1910, withdrawn 1951.
4032 *Queen Alexandria*, built 1910, rebuilt as 'Castle' class 1926.
4033 *Queen Victoria*, built 1910, withdrawn 1951.
4034 *Queen Adelaide*, built 1910, withdrawn 1952.
4035 *Queen Charlotte*, built 1910, withdrawn 1951.
4036 *Queen Elizabeth*, built 1910, withdrawn 1952.
4037 *Queen Philippa*, built 1910, rebuilt as 'Castle' class 1926.
4038 *Queen Berengaria*, built 1911, withdrawn 1952.
4039 *Queen Matilda*, built 1911, withdrawn 1950.
4040 *Queen Boadicea*, built 1911, withdrawn 1951.
4041 *Prince of Wales*, built 1913, withdrawn 1951.
4042 *Prince Albert*, built 1913, withdrawn 1951.
4043 *Prince Henry*, built 1913, withdrawn 1952.
4044 *Prince George*, built 1913, withdrawn 1953.
4045 *Prince John*, built 1913, withdrawn 1950.
4046 *Princess Mary*, built 1914, withdrawn 1951.
4047 *Princess Louise*, built 1914, withdrawn 1951.
4048 *Princess Victoria*, built 1914, withdrawn 1953.
4049 *Princess Maud*, built 1914, withdrawn 1953.
4050 *Princess Alice*, built 1914, withdrawn 1952.
4051 *Princess Helena*, built 1914, withdrawn 1950.
4052 *Princess Beatrice*, built 1914, withdrawn 1953.
4053 *Princess Alexandra*, built 1914, withdrawn 1950.
4054 *Princess Charlotte*, built 1914, withdrawn 1952.
4055 *Princess Sophia*, built 1914, withdrawn 1957.
4056 *Princess Margaret*, built 1914, withdrawn 1957.
4057 *Princess Elizabeth*, built 1914, withdrawn 1952.
4058 *Princess Augusta*, built 1914, withdrawn 1951.
4059 *Princess Patricia*, built 1914, withdrawn 1952.
4060 *Princess Eugenie*, built 1914, withdrawn 1952.
4061 *Glastonbury Abbey*, built 1922, withdrawn 1957.
4062 *Malmesbury Abbey*, built 1922, withdrawn 1956.
4063 *Bath Abbey*, built 1922, rebuilt as 'Castle' class No. 5083, 1937.
4064, *Reading Abbey*, built 1922, rebuilt as 'Castle' class No. 5084, 1937.

4065 *Evesham Abbey*, built 1922, rebuilt as 'Castle' class No. 5085, 1937.
4066 *Viscount Horne*, built 1922 as *Malvern Abbey*, renamed *Sir Robert Horne* 1935, then *Viscount Horne* 1937, rebuilt as 'Castle' class No. 5086, 1937.
4067 *Tintern Abbey*, built 1923, rebuilt as 'Castle' class No. 5087, 1940.
4068 *Llanthony Abbey*, built 1923, rebuilt as 'Castle' class No. 5088, 1939.

4069 *Westminster Abbey*, built 1923 as *Margam Abbey*, renamed 1923 and rebuilt as 'Castle' class No. 5089, 1939.
4070 *Neath Abbey*, built 1923, rebuilt as 'Castle' class No. 5090, 1939.
4071 *Cleeve Abbey*, built 1923, rebuilt as 'Castle' class No. 5091, 1938.
4072 *Tresco Abbey*, built 1923, rebuilt as 'Castle' class No. 5092, 1938.

Appendix V

Diesel Railcars and Shunters

Diesel Railcars

No. 1: Powered by AEC 8.85 litre diesel, bodywork by Park Royal, 2+3 seating for sixty-nine passengers. Entered service December 1933.

Nos 2–4: As above, but fitted with a buffet bar capable of serving hot and cold drinks as well as snacks, and 2+2 seating with removable tables for forty-four passengers. Entered service July 1934.

Nos 5–7: Bodywork by Gloucester Railway Carriage & Wagon Company and reverted to 2+3 with a total of seventy seats. In this form, these remaining three railcars of the 1933 order entered service in July and August 1935.

Nos 8, 9, 13–16: Similar to 5–7.

Nos 10–12: Seating reduced to sixty-three as a result of installing a lavatory.

No. 17: Express parcels van with sliding doors.

No. 18: Seating reduced to forty-nine, with baggage compartment. Two 13-litre diesel engines, and able to haul a load of up to 60 tons. Bodywork by GWR, Swindon.

Nos 19–33: GWR bodywork. Designed for branch lines, 2+2 seats, forty-eight passengers, derated diesel engines, less streamlining. Entered service 1940. No. 33 modified to take place of No. 37, 1947.

No. 34: Express parcels van with hinged doors.

Nos 35–8: Single-ended and operated in pairs as two-car diesel multiple units with buffets and toilets for the Birmingham–Cardiff business express and 2+2 seating arrangement. Could operate with corridor coach between the two cars. Entered service 1941/2. No. 37 damaged by fire 1947.

Shunters

While a Sentinel 0–4–0 petrol shunter was put to work at an industrial estate at Park Royal, in West London, in 1926, it was not until some time later that the GWR introduced diesel shunters.

GWR No. 1: Diesel-electric, delivered 1933 from John Fowler of Leeds. Used at Swindon Works.

GWR No. 2: Diesel-electric, delivered 1935 from Hawthorn Leslie. Used at Acton marshalling yard.

Absorbed Locomotives at the Grouping

In 1923 the Great Western Railway found itself overnight with an additional 700 steam locomotives from its constituent and subsidiary companies, as the wording of the Railways Act 1921 would described them. Their arrival was no great surprise, as the legislation had been known for some time, and the railway companies were given a clear twelve months to get themselves in order. Given such diversity, which might be a delight to the enthusiast, the railway had the nightmare of a wide variety of motive power with differing boilers and motion as well as varied wheel arrangements, of different ages and coming from owners with differing standards. There were only two solutions: either scrap the lot and build new locomotives, which would be costly; or convert as many as were worth keeping to Great

An inherited locomotive was this 0–6–0ST, seen sandwiched between two pannier tanks in 1935, originally numbered 1381 by the GWR but changed to No. 1331 after rebuilding in 1927. *(HMRS/Dr N.R. Ferguson AEP110)*

Western standards and technology to ease maintenance and ensure that locomotives could be transferred to wherever they were needed, giving operational flexibility. The latter was the solution, but even so a considerable volume of new construction was also started, and the 0–6–2 tank engines built for the lines into the South Wales valleys were a case in point.

The railway companies are listed in alphabetical order.

Alexandra (Newport & South Wales) Docks and Railway

This company ran an assortment of fifty-six steam locomotives and two rail motors, but of these just thirty-nine passed into Great Western ownership. The locomotives had been numbered 1 to 37, plus two named locomotives *Alexandra* and *Trojan*.

0–4–0T

Alexandra and *Trojan*, built Avonside, GWR Nos 1341, 1340, withdrawn 1946, 1932.

0–4–2T

No. 14, GWR No. 1426, built GWR, withdrawn 1930.

0–6–0T

Nos 1–5, 15, 20/1, GWR Nos 674–8, 688, 669/70, built R. Stephenson, withdrawn 1925–9.

Nos 12–13, GWR Nos 664/5, built R.W. Hawthorn, withdrawn 1930 and 1926.

Nos 16/17, GWR Nos 671/2, built Hawthorn Leslie, withdrawn 1937 and 1924.

Nos 18/19, GWR Nos 669/70, built Peckett, withdrawn 1929 and 1948.

Nos 27/8, 33, GWR Nos 1679, 1683, 993, built GWR, withdrawn 1926 and 1930.

No. 32, GWR No. 1356, built Fletcher Jennings, withdrawn 1923.

Nos 34/5, GWR Nos 666/7, built Kerr Stuart, withdrawn 1955 and 1954.

0–6–2T

No. 26, GWR No. 663, built Kitson, withdrawn 1926.

Nos 29–31, GWR Nos 190–2, built Andrew Barclay, withdrawn 1948, 1934, 1946.

0–6–4T

Nos 22–4, GWR Nos 1344–6, built Beyer-Peacock, withdrawn 1923–7.

2–6–2T

Nos 6–11, GWR Nos 1207–9, 1211, 1201, 1204, built Beyer-Peacock, withdrawn 1929.

No. 25, GWR No. 1199, built Kitson, withdrawn 1931.

Nos 36/7, GWR Nos 1205/6, built Hawthorn Leslie, withdrawn 1956 and 1951.

Barry Railway Company

0–4–4T

Nos 66–9, GWR Nos 2–4, 9, built Vulcan Foundry, withdrawn 1925–9.

2–4–2T

Nos 21/2, 94–8, GWR Nos 1322/3, 1317–21, built Sharp-Stewart, withdrawn 1926 and 1928.

Nos 86–91, GWR Nos 1311–16, built Hudswell-Clarke, withdrawn 1926–30.

0–6–0T

Nos 1–5, 37, 47–9, 70–2, 99–104, GWR Nos 699/700/702, 703, 706, 708, 710–12, 716–24, built Sharp-Stewart, withdrawn 1926–36.

Nos 33/4, 50–3, GWR Nos 781–4, 713, 785, built Hudswell-Clarke, withdrawn 1932 and 1939.

Nos 127–38, GWR Nos 725/6, 807, 729, 742, 747, 754, 776–80, built North British and Hudswell-Clarke, withdrawn 1922–37.

Nos 64/5, GWR Nos 714/15, built Vulcan Foundry, withdrawn 1932 and 1934.

0–6–2T

Nos 6–20, 23–32, 38–46, 73–8, 105–26, GWR Nos 223–35, 238, 240–4, 255–72, 193–7, 273–7, built Sharp-Stewart, withdrawn 1932–51.

Nos 54–63, GWR Nos 245–54, built Vulcan Foundry, withdrawn 1932–49.

0–6–4T

Nos 139–48, GWR Nos 1347–55, 1357, built Hudswell-Clarke, withdrawn 1926.

0–8–0

Nos 35/6, 92/3, GWR Nos 1387–90, built Sharp-Stewart, withdrawn 1927/8.

0–8–2T

Nos 79–85, GWR Nos 1380–6, built Sharp-Stewart, withdrawn 1925–30.

Brecon & Merthyr Tydfil Junction Railway

2–4–0T

Nos 9–12, 25, GWR Nos 1402, 1452, 1460, 1458, built Stephenson.

4–4–2T

No. 44, GWR No. 1391, built Beyer Peacock.

0–6–0T

Nos 1–8, 13–18, 22, 24, 27–35. GWR Nos 2177–91, 2169–73, 1685, 1693, 1694, 2161; 1–4, 13/14, built Fowler, 5–8, 15/16, built Stephenson, 17/18, built Sharp Stewart, 22, 24, built Kitson, 27–9, built Nasmyth Wilson, 32–4, built GWR, 35, built Kerr Stuart.

0–6–2T

Nos 19/20, 23, 26, 36–43, 45–50, GWR Nos 1674, 1677, 1692, 1833, 11, 21, 332, 504, 698, 888, 1084, 1113; 19–26, built Vulcan, 36–50, built Stephenson.

Burry Port & Gwendraeth Valley Railway

0–6–0T

Nos 1–15, GWR Nos 2192, 2162, 2193–6, 2176, 2197, 2163, 2198, 2164, 2168; 1, 3, built Chapman, 2, 8–15, built Hudswell Clarke, 4–7, built Avonside.

Cambrian Railways

2–4–0

Nos 1, 10, GWR Nos 1329, 1328, built GWR.

Nos 41, 43, 53, 55, GWR No. 1330–3, built Sharp-Stewart.

2–4–0T

No. 44, 56–9, GWR Nos 1190–2, 1196/7, built Sharp-Stewart.

0–4–4T

Nos 3, 5–9, 23, GWR Nos 10, 11, 15, 19, 20/1, built Nasmyth-Wilson.

4–4–0

Nos 11, 19, GWR Nos 1068, 1082, built Cambrian Railway.

Nos 16/17, 20/1, 50, 60–72, 81, 83/4, GWR Nos 1115–18, 1110, 1112, 1088, 1090–3, 1096/7, 1100–5, 1084, 1106/7, built Sharp-Stewart.

Nos 32, 47, 85/86, 94–8, GWR Nos 1085/6, 1108/9, 1014, 3546, 1029, 1035, 1043, built R. Stephenson.

Nos 34, 36, GWR Nos 1113/14, built Beyer-Peacock.

No. 82, GWR No. 3521, built GWR.

4–4–0T

Nos 2, 12, 33, 37, GWR Nos 1129–32, built Beyer-Peacock.

0–6–0

Nos 4, 14, 40, 45/6, 48/9, 51/2, GWR Nos 897–901, 908–11, built Sharp-Stewart.

Nos 15, 29, 31, 38, 42, 54, 99–102, GWR Nos 844, 849, 855, 864, 873/4, 893–6, built Beyer-Peacock.

Nos 73–7, 87/8, GWR Nos 875–80, 884/5, built Neilson.

Nos 78–80, GWR Nos 881–3, built Vulcan.

Nos 89–93, GWR No. 887–92, built R. Stephenson.

0–6–0T

No. 23, GWR No. 819, built Hunslet.

Nos 26, 35, GWR Nos 820/1, built Chapman.

No. 30, GWR No. 824, built Manning Wardle.

Cardiff Railway

0–4–0T

Nos 5/6, GWR Nos 1338/9.

2–4–2T

No. 1327, GWR No. 1327.

0–6–0T

Nos 2–4, 7/8, 12–19, 23–5, 29–32, GWR Nos 693, 686/7, 685, 688, 694, 690, 682/3, 695, 696/7, 1676, 698, 1689, 692, 691, 1667.

0–6–2T

Nos 1, 9–11, 20–2, 26–8, 33–5, GWR Nos 156–60, 151, 161, 152, 163, 162, 159, 153–4.

The Taff Vale Railway brought the largest number of locomotives to the grouping, and had the highest proportion retained by the GWR of any of the constituent and subsidiary companies, partly because of their condition and partly because many had been built by the Great Western itself. This appears to be a posed photograph of 0–6–0ST, ex-TVR No. 265, renumbered No. 796, on the turntable at Cardiff Docks. *(HMRS/J. Tatchell ADH332)*

Cleobury Mortimer & Ditton Priors Light Railway

0–6–0ST

Cleobury and *Burwarton* became GWR Nos 28 and 29 respectively, both built Manning Wardle, survived nationalisation.

Corris Railway

0–4–0T

Nos 3–7, 11/12, 14, and unnumbered *Dorothy*, GWR Nos 696, 779, 795, 921, 925, 927, 935, 928, *Dorothy* became 942; 3/4, 11/12, built Peckett, withdrawn 1952, 1961, 1928, 1961, 5/6, built Brush, 7, built Avonside, withdrawn 1929, 14, built Barclay, withdrawn 1927, *Dorothy*, built Hawthorn Lesley, withdrawn 1955.

Llanelly & Mynydd Mawr Railway

All locomotives were 0–6–0T and named, without numbers.

George Waddell, built by A. Barclay, became GWR No. 312, withdrawn 1934.

Tardndune, Hilda, Ravelston, Merkland, built by Hudswell Clarke, became GWR Nos 339, 359, 803, 937, withdrawn 1943, 1954, 1951, 1923.

Victory, built by Manning Wardle, became GWR No. 704, withdrawn 1943.

Great Mountain, built by Avonside, became GWR No. 944, withdrawn 1928.

Seymour Clarke, built by Fox Walker, became GWR No. 969, withdrawn 1925.

Hardly the most modern-looking locomotive, even in 1924, was 2–4–0T 517 class No. 1448. *(HMRS/D.A. Bayliss AEP505)*

Midland & South Western Junction Railway

0–4–4T

No. 15, GWR No. 23, built Beyer Peacock.

2–4–0

Nos 15–17, GWR Nos 1334–6, built Dubs.

4–4–0

Nos 10–12, GWR Nos 1119–27; 1–8, built North British, 9 built Dubs.

0–6–0

Nos 19–28, GWR Nos 1003–11, 1013, built Beyer Peacock.

0–6–0T

Nos 13/14, GWR Nos 825, 843, built Dubs.

2–6–0

No. 16, GWR No. 24, built Beyer Peacock.

Neath & Brecon Railway

2–4–0T

No. 6, GWR No. 1400, built Sharp-Stewart, withdrawn 1926.

4–4–0T

No. 5, GWR No. 1392, built Yorkshire, withdrawn 1926.

0–6–0T

Nos 1–3, 7/8, 14–16, GWR Nos 2189, 2199, 1882, 2174/5, 1563, 1591, 1715; 1/2, built Avonside, withdrawn 1931, 3, 14–16, built GWR, withdrawn 1946, 1931, 1922, 1949, 7/8, built Nasmyth Wilson, withdrawn 1927, 1933.

0–6–2T

Nos 9–13, GWR Nos 1327, 1371, 1114, 1117, 1277, built Stephenson, withdrawn 1929–30.

Port Talbot Railway & Docks

2–4–0T

No. 37, GWR No. 1189, built Sharp-Stewart.

2–4–2T

No. 36, GWR No. 1326, built Sharp-Stewart.

0–6–0T

Nos 3, 15, 22–7, GWR Nos 815/16, 808/9, 811–14; 3, 15 built Stephenson, 22–7, built Hudswell Clarke.

0–6–2T

Nos 8–14, GWR Nos 183–9, built Stephenson.

0–8–2T

Nos 17–21, GWR Nos 1358–60, 1378/9; 17–19 built Sharp-Stewart, 20/1 built Cooke.

Rhondda & Swansea Bay Railway

2–4–2T

Nos 17–19, GWR Nos 1207/1309, 1310, built Kitson.

0–6–0T

Nos 1–3, 5–7, 29–37, GWR Nos 799, 1660, 801, 802, 805/6, 637, 1834, 1652, 728, 2756, 1167, 1756, 1710, 1825; 1, 3, 5–7, built Beyer Peacock, 2, 29–37, built GWR.

0–6–2T

Nos 4, 8–16, 20–28, GWR Nos 181, 168–80, 182, 164–7; 4–22, 25–8, built Kitson, 23/24, built Stephenson.

Rhymney Railway

2–4–2T

Nos 65/6, GWR Nos 1324/5.

0–6–0T

Nos 32–4, 48–56, 111–14, 120/1, 33, 36, GWR Nos 604–6, 612, 614, 618/19, 622, 625, 629, 631, 657, 608–11, 661/2, 659/60.

0–6–2T

Nos 1–31, 35–47, 57–64, 67–119, GWR Nos 30–2, 82, 76, 83–6, 52–7, 33/4, 58–77, 78–81, 35–43, 87–91, 44, 149/50, 97–101, 105–10, 112–15, 117–19, 122, 127, 129–31, 133–9, 46, 140–5, 147/8, 47–51, 71–5.

Swansea Harbour Trust

Although locomotives 3, 7–10 and 17 were all withdrawn by 1929, most of the remainder stayed in service until 1959 or 1960.

0–4–0T

Nos 3, 5, 7–14, 18, GWR Nos 150, 701, 886, 926, 930, 933, 929, 968, 974, 943, 1098; 3, 14, built Hudswell Clarke, 5 built A. Barclay, 7–12, 18, built Peckett, 3, built Hawthorn Leslie.

0–6–0T

Nos 15–17, GWR Nos 1085/6, 937, built Peckett.

Taff Vale Railway

0–4–0T

Nos 266/7, GWR Nos 1343, 1342.

4–4–0T

Nos 285–7, GWR Nos 1133, 1184, 999.

0–6–0

Nos 210, 217, 219, 220, 235/6, 239, 242, 245, 252/3, 259, 261, 281, 283/4, 288, 297/8, 301/2, 304, 313/14, 316, 320, 322, 325, 327/8, 335–7, 339/40, 354–60, GWR Nos 921/2, 912, 923–8, 929, 913–16, 930, 917, 918, 931, 919, 932/3, 935/6, 938/9, 941–4, 946, 948, 968, 920, 969/70, 974, 978, 1000–2.

0–6–0T

Nos 99/100, 250, 264/5, 270, 275, 280, 290/1, GWR Nos 786/7, 797, 795/6, 798, 788/91.

0–6–2T

Nos 1–98, 101–98, 344, 349, 362, 364, 365, 400–16, GWR Nos 278/9, 438, 442/3, 280, 335, 281/2, 337, 343/4, 409, 444/5, 503, 283, 410/11, 345, 446, 505, 587, 506, 447–51, 602, 412/13, 452/3, 284, 414, 454, 285/6, 588, 455, 439, 287, 415, 346, 288, 416, 289/90, 507, 462, 440, 508, 466, 417, 291, 418, 292/3, 471–6, 419, 294/5, 420, 477/8, 589, 479, 511, 347, 590/1, 480, 592, 348, 421–6, 481–4, 349, 351, 427/8, 296/7, 429, 298/9, 300/1, 430, 302, 236, 485/6, 310/11, 313–15, 317–20, 431, 321, 324, 441, 333, 352, 356/7, 360, 432, 489–502, 581, 593, 596–9, 603, 600, 582–6, 386–91, 393/4, 397–404, 406, 408.

Vale of Rheidol Light Railway

2–4–0T

Cambrian Railway No. 3 *Rheidol*, GWR No. 1198, built Bagnall, withdrawn 1924.

2–6–2T

Cambrian Railway No. 1 *Edward VIII*, No. 2 *Prince of Wales*, GWR Nos 1212, 1213, built Davies & Metcalf.

Welshpool & Llanfair Light Railway

0–6–0T

No. 1, *The Earl*, No. 2, *The Countess*, GWR Nos 822/3, built Beyer-Peacock.

Weston, Clevedon & Portishead Light Railway

0–6–0ST

Nos 1/2, GWR Nos 5/6, built LBSC and sold 1926 and 1937; No. 6 withdrawn 1948, No. 5 withdrawn 1950.

Ex-War Department

The Great Western acquired a number of ex-War Department Robinson-designed 2–8–0 goods locomotives after the First World War. The first twenty were almost new and numbered 3000–19. A further eighty-four were hired, but these had seen extensive service in France and were much neglected, so they were returned, no doubt with a sigh of relief at not having purchased them. Later, eighty locomotives were bought for just £1,500 each, little more than their scrap value, and put into service with the numbers 3020–99. After a short period of service they were withdrawn and it seemed that they would be scrapped. Nevertheless, thirty of the best were given a complete overhaul and acquired GWR features at Swindon before returning to service as 3020–49. The remainder were also put back into service as 3050–99, worked until they failed and then were scrapped immediately. Nos 3000–49 were kept working for many years and most survived nationalisation.

Great Western in Preservation

No steam railway has been treated as well by enthusiasts as the Great Western, for apart from its representation at the National Railway Museum in York, there are also the museums at Didcot, Birmingham and Swindon and both the Severn Valley and South Devon railways. Many other preserved railways and museums have locomotives and carriages of Great Western origin. Collections do change from time to time, as new items are added or as locomotives or rolling stock undergo attention in the workshops.

Some of the leading museums and preserved railways are:

Birmingham Railway Museum, Tyseley Depot, Warwick. Tel: 0121 707 4696. This has 2 miles of track.

Didcot Railway Centre. Tel: 01235 817200. This has 1,000yd of track.

Festiniog Railway, Portmadog. Tel: 01766 512340. This is a scenic 13½-mile ride.

National Railway Museum, Leeman Road, York. Tel: 01904 621261.

Paignton & Dartmouth Railway, Paignton, Devon. Tel: 01803 555872. This has 7 miles of track.

Severn Valley Railway, Bewdley, Worcs. Tel: 01299 401001. This has 16½ miles of track.

South Devon Railway, Buckfastleigh, Devon. Tel: 01364 642338. This has 7 miles of track.

Bibliography

To give an exhaustive list of books on the Great Western Railway would require almost a book in itself. These are some of the more useful, while at the same time those interested in further research could also use the internet – simply putting 'Great Western Railway' into a search engine will present many pages of information on the company and on preserved rolling stock.

Allen, Cecil J., *Titled Trains of Great Britain*, Ian Allan, London, 1946–67

Barman, Christian, *The Great Western Railway's Last Look Forward*, David & Charles, Newton Abbot, 1972

Hamilton Ellis, C., *The Trains We Loved*, Allen & Unwin, London, 1947

Haswell, E.G.F., *Great Western Shed Designs*, Ian Allan, London, 1969

Jackson, Alan, *London's Termini*, David & Charles, Newton Abbot, 1969

Jones, Richard Bagnold, *British Narrow Gauge Railways*, Adam & Charles Black, London, 1958

Maggs, Colin G., *The GWR Swindon to Bath Line*, Sutton, Stroud, 2003

Nock, O.S., *The Great Western Railway in the Twentieth Century*, Ian Allan, London, 1971

——, *Britain's Railways at War 1939–1945*, Ian Allan, London, 1971

——, *Sixty Years of Western Express Running*, Ian Allan, London, 1973

Robertson, Kevin, *The Great Western Railway Gas Turbines*, Sutton, Stroud, 1989

——, *Odd Corners of the GWR from the Days of Steam*, Sutton, Stroud, 1999

——, *More Odd Corners of the GWR*, Sutton, Stroud, 2003

Russell, J.H., *A Pictorial Record of Great Western Coaches, Part II (1903–1948)*, Oxford Publishing Company, Oxford, 1973

——, *A Pictorial Record of Great Western Absorbed Engines*, Oxford Publishing Company, Oxford, 1978

Simmons, Jack and Biddle, Gordon, *The Oxford Companion to British Railway History*, Oxford University Press, Oxford, 2000

Thomas, David St John, *A Regional History of the Railways of Great Britain: Volume 1 – The West Country*, David & Charles, Newton Abbot, 1960

Tomkins, N.S. and Sheldon, P., *Swindon & the GWR*, Sutton, Stroud, 1990

Vinter, J., *Railway Walks GWR & SR*, Sutton, Stroud, 1990

Wilson, Roger Burdett, *Go Great Western – A History of GWR Publicity*, David & Charles, Newton Abbot, 1970

Index

Locomotives are covered in the appendices, and listings of locomotives, listed as 'locomotive classes' and 'locomotives' below refer to mentions in the text and to photographs, which are in italics. Named trains are grouped together and entered as such, as are ships.